Secondary Curriculum for a Changing World

Frank L. Steeves
Marquette University

Fenwick W. English
*American Association of
School Administrators*

CHARLES E. MERRILL PUBLISHING COMPANY
A Bell & Howell Company
Columbus   Toronto   London   Sydney

TO OUR MOTHERS:

A. Gladys Steeves and Phyllis Bradford English,
who long before such phrases as *performance
objectives* and *educational accountability*
became popular, applied performance expectations
to their children and taught that rising to
responsibility is a matter of pride. We are
grateful for the lessons.

Published by
Charles E. Merrill Publishing Company
A Bell & Howell Company
Columbus, Ohio 43216

This book was set in Times Roman.
The Production Editor was Cynthia Donaldson.
The cover was prepared by Will Chenoweth.

Cover photographs courtesy of William J. Stoll.

Photo Credits: p. 0, University of Maryland; p. 6, E. Bernstein; p. 74, Editorial
Photocolor Archives (Daniel S. Brody); p. 80, W. Stoll; p. 102, L. Hamill; p. 118,
W. Stoll; p. 134, E. Bernstein; p. 160, 184, and 190, University of Maryland; p. 214,
L. Hamill; p. 262, W. Stoll; p. 268, Copyright © 1975, *The Courier-Journal and
Louisville Times Co.;* p. 294, Copyright © 1976, *The Courier-Journal.*

International Standard Book Number:
0-675-08424-5

Library of Congress Catalog Card Number:
77-087773

1 2 3 4 5 6 7 8 -- 83 82 81 80 79 78

Printed in the United States of America

Preface

This book is about curriculum planning in a constantly changing world. Shifting social and political emphases must be considered in curriculum development. Change in the technological environment influences the selection and organization of content. A decreasing pool of natural resources results in increased attention to all aspects of the natural environment. Changing perceptions about human development and learning affect decisions about what content should be offered, to whom, when, and why. Considerations derived from analysis of these factors is the basis for the content of this volume. From fundamental factors in curriculum change set forth in chapter one, through a process for charting the course for curriculum change presented in chapter fourteen, the text illustrates environmental influences on the process of curriculum improvement and also suggests that revision of content without understanding the nature and needs of learners is a waste of time.

Part I introduces fundamental factors in curriculum planning, a focus brought into sharper clarity in Part IV where accountability for decision-making, curriculum evaluation, and planning for curriculum change are treated. Parts II and III discuss issues, problems, reform, and trends in each of the major subject fields and school services. Throughout the book we included factual accounts illustrating historical development in the belief that understanding how programs evolve is basic to program improvement.

Also, we freely expressed our judgments and opinions about contemporary problems of the secondary school. We included recommendations and suggestions for improvement wherever it seemed appropriate to do so. Not everyone will agree with all of the opinions and recommendations, but that is not important. What is important is that at a time when almost every critic seems to be writing and talking about a crisis in secondary education, someone propose concrete ideas for improvement. Our purpose in writing this volume was to do exactly that.

The book is intended as a basic text in curriculum courses for teachers and administrators where the emphasis is upon secondary education. It is also presented as a guide for in-service efforts by local schools and school systems as they organize for curriculum assessment.

We believe that the task of the secondary school is to prepare for a world in which its graduates will live and not for a world which lives only in the memories of old men and women. This has always been the job of schools set up for the instruction of developing adults. The schools of any age grow upon hopes, dreams, and plans for the future. They decline in influence and pass away when they look exclusively to the past as a source of strength and information. This is the way it was and this is the way it is. One adapts or one perishes.

The paradox for the school is that it cannot teach what is not known. The school cannot reach into the future for its curriculum. Yet, it must prepare students to live in a future, the conditions of which are only dimly perceived. To meet the challenge we draw upon past experience as a guide. We adapt content to the needs of students in the current environment. We emphasize the unsolved problems of humanity. And, in the end, we can only trust that the process produces citizens with the adaptability and problem-solving ability to shape the future with which they must cope.

FLS
FWE

Acknowledgments

No single writer or pair of writers could prepare a comprehensive work on the secondary-school curriculum without relying heavily upon the ideas, prior publications, and constructive criticisms of others. We appreciate the cooperation of those whose published writings, researches, and private documents are quoted in this volume. We are equally grateful to all those whose writings are cited as references.

However, a general statement of gratitude is not sufficient recognition for the contributions of a number of colleagues and friends who worked with specific parts of the manuscript.

Dr. Floyd Boschee, Sioux Falls College, Sioux Falls, South Dakota, was instrumental in developing the initial outline for the book. Dr. Boschee also contributed the organization and much of the writing for chapter ten, "Interscholastic Athletics." We appreciate his willingness to donate his expertise and experience in this field to the volume.

For the same reasons we acknowledge the contributions of two others. Dr. William F. Stier, Jr., Cardinal Stritch College, Milwaukee, Wisconsin, wrote the original manuscript from which chapter five, "Physical Education and Health," was adapted. Mr. Albert J. Shannon, Milwaukee Public Schools, research, organized, and prepared original material for the section on "Reading in the Secondary School" which appears in chapter eight.

The section on Academic Study about Religion" which appears in chapter eight was read and criticized by Dr. Nicholas Piediscalzi, Public Education Religion Studies Center, Wright State University, Dayton, Ohio. We are deeply grateful to Dr. Piediscalzi, not only for his constructive criticisms, but also for permission to quote from PERSC sources. We readily admit that most of our commentary in this sensitive area is derived from work done by others and disseminated by PERSC.

During the preparation of portions of the manuscript, we relied upon library searches conducted by two dedicated assistants. Miss R. Christine Gibson, librarian and secretary in the Teaching Resources Center, Marquette University, applied superb library skills as information was gathered for the many topics discussed in Part III. She also prepared requests for permission to quote and assisted with correspondence pertaining the the manuscript. An equally conscientious researcher worked with her at a critical point during the calendar set for completing the work. Mr. Walter Lewke II, Research Assistant, Marquette University Graduate School, located, read, and classified hundreds of articles in professional journals. He also double-checked each source finally used as a reference. Without the help of Miss Gibson and Mr. Lewke, the task could not have been completed as scheduled.

Finally, we owe much to the patience of our wives, Lolita K. English and Louise P. Steeves, who listened as we thought out loud for many months, and who read the manuscript with critical skill.

Although acknowledging the contributions and assistance of others, we reserve to ourselves whatever errors or shortcomings may have found their way into these pages. In this regard it should be noted that the contributions of Dr. English were written in his private capacity and are not necessarily expressions of the policy or viewpoints of the American Association of School Administrators.

FLS
FWE

Contents

I Fundamental Considerations in Curriculum Planning

Following the launching of Sputnik I by the USSR in 1957, the United States expended more than a billion dollars in federal money to upgrade teaching in science, mathematics, and foreign languages and to improve guidance services. No sooner were these academic programs well launched when the nation discovered that such programs did not meet the needs of millions of disadvantaged youth.

Advanced work in physics is appropriate for some but has no meaning for the sixteen-year-old who does not yet have command of fundamental processes in arithmetic. The study of a foreign language is futile for the adolescent whose progress in English stopped at the fourth grade level. Educational guidance is irrelevant for young people who remain in school only because the law compels their attendance, and who leave school as soon as the requisite chronological age is reached. Career guidance is equally meaningless if the curriculum of the school does not reflect a philosophy of commitment to preparation for careers. Hence, during the early 1960s the schools struggled simultaneously to retrain teachers to work with advanced, reorganized course content in some areas while other teachers concentrated on programs geared to mastery of fundamental skills.

Concurrently, during the 1950s and 1960s, strictly educational proposals such as team teaching, modular scheduling, programmed learning, computer-assisted instruction, and differentiated staffing gained degrees of acceptance, albeit what is practiced today under these names in one school may bear little resemblance to practice in another.

Today, the secondary schools, especially central city schools, are confronted by massive problems of disorder and crime and steadily diminishing academic quality. To a degree the problems within the schools merely reflect societal conditions in general. For example, twenty years of using schools as the focal point for achieving racial balance may be perceived as a contributing factor. It is hardly reasonable to expect young people of varying ethnic backgrounds to immediately establish harmonious in-school relationships when the factors that bring them together result from bitterly contested public issues, court rulings rejected by large numbers of citizens, and, all too frequently, violence in the streets and neighborhoods. Under the circumstances, it is a tribute to administrative leadership and the dedication of teachers that many urban high schools continue to function as well as they do.

To these general factors of educational innovation, federal influence, and social legislation, add the occasional local flareup centering on some specific issue of curricular content and the situation, at best, is one of unrest in secondary education.

The writers suggest that the time has come to call for a period of respite from untested innovation. Time is needed to evaluate hastily injected social programs. Opportunity is needed to think through the themes and aspirations of secondary education in this country, both as it is and as it would become. If such expectations are unreasonable, the writers of this volume see little future for the high school as an academic institution. In the effort, however noble, to find solutions for all the ills of society, the school can only lose sight of its major function which, after all, is the academic education of American youth. Such education at the secondary level takes on meaning only if it leads to careers, to further education, or to both. If the needs of secondary school youth for career preparation and further education are not met in the schools, it follows inevitably that alternate institutions will be devised to meet the challenge. In that event, one would be hard pressed to find reasons for the maintenance of an extensive system of postelementary schools for nonacademic purposes.

However, at the outset of this book, it should be emphasized that the outlook for the secondary school structure in America is not bleak. The high school has weathered all challenges during its hundred-year history. It has met the demands of each new generation as they were posed. For the most part, secondary school programs and services have developed in an orderly fashion, with periods of relative tranquility interposed between periods of rapid growth and/or shifts of emphasis. Perhaps it is not too much to call for the period of curricular evaluation and analysis that has been lacking during the past two decades. Indeed, if those responsible for the conduct of secondary education agree that this is the challenge all confront together, the power to bring about this desirable state is theirs.

To this end, it is well to reflect upon certain fundamental considerations in curriculum planning. What philosophical positions form the foundation for the secondary school, both as it is and as it would become? Have curriculum planners at the national level overlooked or ignored social forces which cannot be brushed aside at the local level? Have curriculum workers at all levels moved too far toward implementing a single psychological theory of learning? How has technological progress affected work in the schools? How will the development of strong teachers' and administrators' unions and associations influence curriculum planning? What is the work of the curriculum director or coordinator, and what facilities are needed for curriculum development and improvement? What are the goals of secondary education at the local, state, and national levels? How may such goals be made more acceptable and understandable? And, finally, what is happening at the classroom level, the only level where curricular ideas and theories really matter?

The four chapters which follow were designed to provide opportunity for reflection on some of these questions. The volume as a whole is concerned with all of them. Directions for curriculum change must be based ultimately upon the answers agreed to by teachers, administrators, and thoughtful citizens.

1 Basic Factors in Curriculum Change

Curriculum Meanings in This Book

Short definitions of the word *curriculum* offer certain advantages. They suggest what the person doing the defining has in mind, and they indicate a framework for discussion. At the same time, definitions of curriculum appearing in print reveal widely varying ideas concerning what the curriculum is all about.

One of the most sweeping definitions to be offered focused on the experiences of the child and suggested that the curriculum includes whatever happens to the child, no matter what it is or when it occurs. (1) Such a broad viewpoint appears to exclude much of the curriculum from school control, therefore permitting little chance for curriculum improvement, evaluation, or development. It also relieves the school of responsibility. Schools cannot be held accountable for what happens to children outside their auspices. Consequently, most definitions, even those that center on the experiences of the child, limit the experiences to those planned by the school (2) or scheduled under school direction. (3)

Curriculum definitions may also center on the content of instruction, the major fields of study, and the subjects organized within the fields. Other, more specialized meanings are given to curriculum and are used commonly in educational literature. The curriculum may be perceived as consisting of sequences of courses planned for particular purposes, such as college preparatory and commercial work. Or, the curriculum may be seen to include all the courses and experiences designed within a particular field of study, for instance, home economics. Curriculum has been used to identify various ways of organizing content for instruction; the subject curriculum, when the subjects are taught separately; the correlated curriculum, where relationships among subjects are taught deliberately; and various problem-solving approaches such as the core curriculum, in which problems cutting across subject divisions become the basis for instruction.

In theory, curriculum may be focused upon the learner or upon the subject to be learned. In practice, these distinctions merge and the curriculum becomes both what is planned and what is learned. Theoreticians tend to highlight distinctions; practitioners tend to modify differences.

The writers of the present volume suggest that no single short definition of curriculum is completely adequate. We look upon the curriculum in different ways at various places in this book, depending on the context within which it is approached. In the following chapter, we distinguish the curriculum from school organization and administration. The word *content* is used to identify the curriculum and to separate it, at least for discussion purposes, from school management. Both content and techniques and methods for dealing with content are influenced directly by the ways in which a school is organized and administered.

Content, however, as a single word, is an inadequate way to identify the curriculum when the concern becomes that of curriculum evaluation. Content must be evaluated both from the viewpoints of *accuracy* and *appropriateness.* Questions about the accuracy of content are answerable by reference to subject matter. Questions about the appropriateness of content must be answered in terms of learners. For example, concepts from such disciplines as anthropology, biology, and history planned for a sixth-grade program of studies may be entirely accurate according to sources and specialists in these areas, but entirely inappropriate for the age-grade-experience level of pupils. The readiness of students for learning in any particular subject is a consideration in curriculum planning that cannot be ignored.

Thus, in chapter thirteen, which discusses curriculum evaluation, the curriculum is defined as the selection and specification of content within some planned order of scope and sequence. These ideas suggest that unless experiences planned for students are presented sequentially and in some logical order, resulting in cumulative learning, teachers and students can go through the motions of teaching and learning without much of either taking place.

Content, as a focal point for curriculum improvement, is reaffirmed in chapter fourteen where planning for curriculum change is the consideration. However, the only evidence of real curriculum improvement rests with what happens to learners. The paper curriculum planned for students could be modified through eternity without being much more than an intellectual exercise for teachers and curriculum planners. Unless the results of planning are shown to result in achievement by students, the curriculum process is incomplete. A distinction is drawn in chapter fourteen between the curriculum planned for students and the real curriculum which, in the end, becomes what the student actually possesses.

In this volume, the curriculum is presented both in terms of *content,* that which is planned for students, and as *learning,* that which is achieved by students. And, because learning occurs through a variety of school experiences, the subject divisions, although central to teaching and learning in the secondary school, do not constitute the entire curriculum. The meaning of curriculum is expanded to include all that schools do in the name of their students. Finally, even though schools cannot be held accountable for learning which is not planned or sponsored by them, it is well to recognize that much is learned outside school doors and much is learned inside school buildings that school people hardly plan to happen. The effects of extraschool forces acting upon the planned programs of the school are treated in chapter nine. Consideration of these forces leads to the inevitable conclusion that there is only one curriculum and that it includes all that has been suggested here.

The Scope of Secondary Education

When the elementary school covered a common and basic program of studies for the first eight grades and the high school was a separate four-year institution, there was no talk of anything called secondary education. Books were written about the high school, the elementary or common school, and the university. The three levels of education were not considered to be overlapping. Each level prepared students for the one to follow.

Extension of the high school downward into grades seven and eight and the consequent development of the junior high school as grades seven to nine resulted in the phrase *secondary education* coming to mean the junior and senior high school years. Despite occasional argument that secondary education should also include the first two years of college, most of the profession and the public continued to look upon all grade levels beyond high school as part of higher education. Gradually, secondary education was applied to the junior and senior high school years; elementary education meant grades kindergarten through six.

Because the United States does not have a federal school system, all local school districts did not reorganize to reflect the junior high school movement. Many districts, especially in small town and rural areas, continued to operate schools on the 8-4 plan and, in these communities, secondary education simply became synonymous with the four-year high school.

Many modern sources continue to emphasize the high school years in their titles (4) and in their content when discussing secondary education. The report, *The Reform of Secondary Education,* is almost entirely concerned with the high school years, and the high school is mentioned over and over again as the focus of the report. (5) In fact, one of the recommendations of the commission which produced the report was that only the first eight grades beyond kindergarten continue to be required. (6) This is another way of saying that the high school should become a selective institution, a recommendation that the American people are unlikely to accept for their own children. The recommendation is repeated in another manner by saying that the compulsory age of school attendance should be dropped to age fourteen. (7)

The negative social consequences of implementing this recommendation without creating attractive alternatives for formal schooling are obvious. This is a simplistic solution for disciplinary and other problems of the high school, a "solution" that would cost society more in dollars and wasted lives than any of the costs of operating the present system. Of course, the high school should become a more effective institution, but within the comprehensive philosophy of opportunity for all that has shaped its history in the twentieth century.

Because of the failure of many junior high schools to perform the exploratory and transitional functions originally envisioned for these grade levels, a new type of intermediate unit emerged in the 1950s. Termed the *middle school* and organized as grades five through eight, six through eight, or seven through eight, the middle school seems almost certainly destined to be classified as part of secondary education. It is so treated in this book (see chapter two, *The Rise of the Middle School as Expansion of Secondary Education*) and so perceived by others who have examined the place of the middle school in school organization. (8)

Not all agree with this point of view. Those who see the middle school as a transitional unit set up to carry out the functions originally established for the junior high school define the middle school in terms of the personal and educational development of students beyond elementary education and prior to secondary education. (9)

Regardless of how the middle school is ultimately classified, it is fervently hoped that it does not follow the path of the junior high school and become an imitation high school, specializing in academic content too soon and, although populated by younger students, taking on the trappings of high schools and colleges. Some undesirable signs that this is already happening are evident. Departmental specialization is in effect in some middle schools and/or the upper elementary grades. Interscholastic athletic competition, complete with officials and cheerleaders, have moved down into grade six and lower. Teachers who specialize in disciplines as specific as physics have found their ways into these grades. These practices are characteristic of school work in the upper secondary grades.

The writers suggest that education for the emerging adolescent years should and can be planned regardless of the form of school organization. The needs of students do not change at each grade level just because the administrative organization changes from 8-4 to 6-3-3 or to some other plan. The curriculum needs of students are constant no matter how the school system is organized. Any organizational plan that permits flexibility can work. These ideas are explored more fully in the following chapter.

In any event, this volume is concerned with the education of emerging adolescents and young adults. No matter how the school system is organized administratively, the concern here is with that education planned for and attained by young people from the preteen years, approximately ages eleven-twelve, to young adulthood, ages seventeen-eighteen.

The Inevitability of Curriculum Change

The inevitability of change is understood by anyone who has lived for more than three or four years. The father is transferred or moves into a new job, and the family leaves the established neighborhood for a new address, a new school, and new relationships. Pets come and go, from the goldfish which may survive for a day to the dog or cat which may remain with the family for years. Older brothers and sisters finish or leave school and move on to their own careers. Marriages and births are announced. Aged neighbors, family friends, and relatives die. The earth goes on, but all of the people on it are touched by change from their earliest years.

Once change is perceived as a normal part of human existence, the child begins to grow up. Adjustment to change is evidence of maturity. As long as change results from an orderly progression of events which the person has a chance to understand, there is no problem. Even if he or she does not have a voice in making events happen, the child can and probably will adapt, with understanding.

Catastrophic change which shatters families, such as death, divorce, or disabling illness, is different. Even adults have difficulty adjusting to life after an experience with a natural calamity, such as fire, flood, tornado, or earthquake. Even the most mature, stable, and self-disciplined adults adjust slowly to the loss of loved ones or other major changes in life which may be classed as personal tragedy.

However, except in chapter nine, where catastrophic interruptions of school life are set forth as major influences on what is really learned, this volume does not deal with calamity. Rather, this book is concerned with change as the result of rational human thought and decision-making. Particularly applied to curriculum change, deliberate action preceded by reflection and reason is suggested as a more certain route to curriculum improvement than the road suggested by the too-typical compromise with external forces, either demanding change or resisting it.

Make no mistake; no curriculum is set in place for all time. Whether conceived as the content of a body of knowledge, or seen as a series of experiences for children, the curriculum is subject to continuous change. Nations that did not even exist a decade ago make their positions known in world organizations and announce decisions that have a profound effect on the affairs of other countries. These new nations, their policies, and their peoples become part of the changing content of the social studies. The United States moves from war to recession, from violent social upheaval to hope, from political chicanery to Constitutional law, in a range of shifting problems that must be understood by the citizens of a participatory republic.

Content revision in all the major fields of study merely sets the stage for further revision. The process never stops. Analysis of content is a lifelong task during the careers of professional teachers.

And, as must be understood, the process of curriculum improvement is not easy. Quick and apparently direct solutions for complex problems have been tried and have failed. State and local laws have been passed requiring specified subjects. In response, schools dutifully schedule the courses or assign the required topics to the content of existing courses. What happens in the classes to the content considered so important by lawmakers? Each teacher teaches the material in his or her own fashion. As long as the school can show that the paper expectations of legal curricular requirements have been met, no one worries much about the learning outcomes that legislators may have had in mind. Outcomes established by teachers take priority.

Extensive content revision has been undertaken, but content revision without attention to the needs and capabilities of learners can result in little more than transitory improvement. Always slated for further revision and all too often destined for ultimate abandonment, content manipulation is, at best, only a beginning step. A case in point was the massive effort to move modern foreign languages into the elementary schools. Launched with millions of dollars and accompanied by volumes of publicity and praise, most of the courses were abandoned within ten years. Taxpayers, unhappy because of what they considered to be failure to teach the fundamentals of the English language arts, were not made happy because elementary school pupils achieved a degree of illiteracy in a foreign language.

Entire programs, printed in prose, programed, filmed, and computerized, have been bought and adapted for local use in piecemeal fashion. Local staffs soon came to see that no course devised outside the local

school system can be applied in its entirety. A hundred-thousand pur-
chased behavioral objectives can do no more than provide a departure
point for the local staff in its effort to improve the curriculum.

The writers know of no assembly line methods for curriculum
improvement, no recipes, no ready-made answers. Recommendations
which appear in various chapters throughout the remainder of this book
are based on the assumption that curriculum improvement only results
when orderly, disciplined, systematic processes are applied in efforts to
measure the actual outcomes of learning against the objectives planned
for learners. When outcomes are not planned and when the achievement
of learners is not known, it is difficult to understand how the curriculum
can be evaluated or improved. Programs where goals are undefined and
where the results of instruction are unknown do not lend themselves to
known processes of improvement. Those who persist with such programs evade responsibility for the direction and improvement of schooling.

Influences upon the Curriculum

As long as the high school program consisted of specific subjects needed
for college entrance, and as long as those subjects were taught and
learned in the same way, curriculum improvement was an easy matter. It
was necessary only to employ teachers with the necessary academic
training and put them together with selected students whose intelligence,
motivation, and social and economic background permitted success.
Under these circumstances it was easy to pinpoint failure. Either the
student or the teacher was at fault. Teachers whose students failed to
learn could be replaced by others with better academic preparation.
Failure ascribed to students, either because of lack of ability or as a
result of insufficient study, was correctable in the most direct manner.
After a first or second chance, the student was dropped from the school.
Until well into the 1900s, only one out of every ten students who started
high school remained to graduate. In a society where unskilled labor was
in high demand and which was still largely agrarian, this concept of high
school education was acceptable.

However, as the century progressed, society voiced higher, different, and varied expectations for the high school. Programs were demanded for preparation for citizenship, for preparation leading to an
increasing variety of skilled jobs, for preparation as family members, for
physical education as well as for academic studies, for increased emphasis on science, on commercial studies, on the fine arts. Indeed, by mid-

century the high schools were called upon to devise programs to meet needs not even anticipated fifty years earlier. A high school diploma became essential for entrance to all except the most menial occupational fields. The American high school became a comprehensive, nonselective institution intended to provide the best education that could be planned for each child and one that the child was capable of acquiring. (10) Obviously, this is as yet, an unrealized goal. However, as an ideal, it is supported by the people who, have come to expect nothing less than education through the high school years for all or nearly all of the population. The comprehensive nature of the goals proposed for American education and secondary education are explored in detail in chapter three.

On other fronts, advancing technology rendered some studies obsolete and resulted in the development of others. Problem-solving was presented as the most fruitful way of human learning (11), and both methodology and content were adapted to this approach. With the development of the junior high school and increasingly since, considerable attention was given to the nature of humanity and the biological and psychological development of adolescents. (12)

Recent concerns have been expressed for the natural environment and for the conservation of steadily diminishing supplies of natural resources. New books continue to emphasize concern for people and for human values. (13)

The following chapters illustrate the concern of the writers that the secondary school curriculum continue to reflect these values and that school programs remain sensitive to the total environment within which schools operate. This includes the natural and technological environments and, above all, the social-political sphere.

The Subject Fields in General and in Specialized Education

Each of the major subject fields includes content that should be part of the general or basic education of all secondary school students. At the same time, each of these fields should offer opportunity for specialization by those students whose needs or talents encourage such a curriculum. Sometimes termed a "constants and variables" program (14), the constants are those courses that all students must take, while the variables are elective. As might be expected, only courses in English, social studies, science, mathematics, and physical education had attained a significant degree of constancy by the early 1960s, even in the nation's junior high schools. (15) Such fields as art, music, foreign languages, and commercial studies remained predominantly elective.

Certain recent trends are not encouraging for those who believe that the schools, especially during the early secondary years, should offer a balanced, comprehensive, introductory, or exploratory opportunity for learning in each of the major subject fields. In particular, the spread of elective minicourses in English and the social studies is a matter of concern whenever such short courses replace existing, broad-field requirements. Short electives do offer opportunity for exploration, but they are not a sound substitute for the core or common requirements of general education. This idea is treated more specifically in chapter four where current trends in the traditional academic areas are examined.

Assumptions Underlying This Volume

To this point, a number of assumptions fundamental to the remainder this book have been set forth. They are:

1. The curriculum includes the selection and specification of content within a planned order of scope and sequence. As such, it means that which is planned for students in their courses and other school experiences. It also includes whatever is learned by students through these courses and experiences.
2. Secondary education is that education planned for and achieved by preadolescents from ages eleven-twelve to young adulthood, ages seventeen-eighteen. The emerging middle school is becoming part of secondary education for the same reasons that caused the junior high school to be so classified.
3. Change in the human condition is inevitable and, except for catastrophic change, is accepted and understood as part of the maturing process. Curriculum change is equally certain and should not be left to happen by chance or by response to pressure and crisis. Rather, curriculum change should result from orderly, continuous, systematic effort to relate the achievement of learners to the objectives planned by teachers. The process of curriculum improvement is difficult, slow, and not subject to quick answers or solutions.
4. The present curriculum is a result of its history. The curriculum must be consistent with the social-political, technical, and natural environments within which schools function. The curriculum must also be concerned with the biological and psychological natures of learners and be sensitive to human values, whatever the subject under consideration.

5. All of the major subject fields have contributions to make to the general education of secondary school students, and each has a function in meeting specialized needs.
6. Secondary education should provide comprehensive opportunity for all American youth to develop their widely varying interests, needs, capacities, and talents.

In addition to the six assumptions noted above, the writers wish to list nine others which, although not articulated thus far, will be perceived as fundamental viewpoints or assumptions as the reader proceeds through the volume.

1. Curriculum cannot be improved without the active participation of teachers, students, and interested citizens. Administrators and curriculum experts cannot do the job alone and, even if they could, the task would hardly be worth accomplishing in the absence of implementation by informed teachers and support by a participating public.
2. To go somewhere we must know where we are now, how we got where we are, where we want to go, and why we want to go there.
3. Despite content revisions of the 1950s and 1960s, every major subject field needs further examination.
4. Teachers cannot assume that all pupils entering the secondary school have mastered the basic skills needed for success in school, in careers, or in life.
5. Curriculum improvement does not happen all at once or in exactly the same ways in every school.
6. Although teachers working alone can effect significant curriculum improvement, systematic improvement requires organization.
7. Efforts toward curriculum improvement should be consistent with goals established for the general educative process and focused on precise instructional objectives.
8. The early years of secondary education (grades five-eight) should require exploratory experience in each of the major subject fields combined with attention to the fundamental skills necessary for advanced work in each field. The high school years should permit further exploration and also should allow for specialized studies adapted to the needs, interests, personal goals, and talents of advanced students.
9. The school is a real place inhabited by real students, teachers, and administrators. The curriculum problems of the school are real prob-

lems that demand solution by realistic people. Concern of the curriculum is with immediate problems of human existence. Ontological discussion is not unimportant in educational theory but has little place in the day-to-day work of curriculum planning and improvement. One has to assume the reality of human life and human institutions.

Further, the assumption is made that if a process does not work it should be modified or abandoned. This does not say that merely because a procedure works it becomes "right." More properly, unless successful processes are devised for dealing with problems, there can be no starting point for improvement.

Thus, the philosophical bases for this book may be identified as both realistic and pragmatic, positions that surface from time to time in later chapters. (16)

It is now suggested that the reader peruse the introductory statements included at the beginning of each of the four parts of the book. This will complete the introduction and provide an overview of the concepts presented in the remainder of the volume.

CHAPTER REFERENCES

1. Roland C. Faunce and Nelson L. Bossing, *Developing the Core Curriculum* (Englewood Cliffs, N.J.: Prentice-Hall, 1951), p. 94.

2. For example, see Leonard H. Clark and Irving S. Starr, *Secondary School Teaching Methods,* 3rd ed. (New York: Macmillan, 1976), p. 33.

3. A viewpoint set forth more than two decades ago by Harl R. Douglass, ed., *The High School Curriculum* (New York: The Ronald Press Co., 1956), p. 11.

4. As an example, see Burton W. Gorman, *Secondary Education: The High School America Needs* (New York: Random House, 1971).

5. B. Frank Brown, Chairman, The National Commission of the Reform of Secondary Education, Charles F. Kettering Foundation, *The Reform of Secondary Education* (New York: McGraw-Hill, 1973).

6. Ibid., p. 21, Recommendation #29.

7. Ibid., p. 21, Recommendation #28.

8. See J. Lloyd Trump and Gordon F. Vars, "How Should Learning Be Organized?" Chapter 9 in William Van Til, ed., *Issues in Secondary Education,* 75th Yearbook of the National Society for the Study of Education, Part II (Chicago: NSSE, 1976).

9. For example, see Thomas E. Curtis and Wilma W. Bidwell, *Curriculum and Instruction for Emerging Adolescents* (Reading, Massachusetts: Addison-Wesley, 1977), Chapter 1, "Purposes of the Middle School."

10. For further reference, see James B. Conant, *The American High School Today* (New York: McGraw-Hill, 1959).

11. John Dewey, *How We Think* (Boston: D. C. Heath and Co., 1910).

12. For an up-to-date examination of theories of learning, see B. R. Hergenhahn, *An Introduction to Theories of Learning* (Englewood Cliffs, N.J.: Prentice-Hall, 1976).

13. For a recent text on curriculum theory which recommends programs sensitive to the problems of human existence, see Louise M. Berman and Jessie A. Roderick, *Curriculum: Teaching the What, Why, and How of Living* (Columbus, Ohio: Charles E. Merrill Publishing Co., 1977).

14. Roy O. Billett, *Improving the Secondary-School Curriculum: A Guide to Effective Curriculum Planning* (New York: Atherton Press, 1970), p. 9.

15. Ibid., pp. 16-17.

16. For a detailed examination of the multiplicity of academic philosophical positions, see Robert S. Zais, *Curriculum: Principles and Foundations* (New York: Thomas Y. Crowell Co., 1976). See Chapters 5 and 6, "Philosophy: Basic Considerations," and "Philosophy: The Nature of Knowledge."

●

FOR FURTHER READING

Beckner, Weldon, and Cornett, Joe D. *The Secondary School Curriculum.* Scranton, Pennsylvania: Intext Educational Publishers, 1972.

Bent, Rudyard K., and Unruh, Adolph. *Secondary School Curriculum.* Lexington, Massachusetts: D. C. Heath and Company, 1969.

Cawelti, Gordon. *Vitalizing the High School.* Washington, D.C.: Association for Supervision and Curriculum Development, 1974.

Cay, Donald F. *Curriculum: Design for Learning.* Indianapolis, Indiana: Bobbs-Merrill Co., 1966.

Clark, Leonard H., Klein, Raymond L., and Burks, John B. *The American Secondary School Curriculum,* 2nd ed. New York: Macmillan, 1972.

Cusick, Philip A. *Inside High School.* New York: Holt, Rinehart, and Winston, 1973.

Drews, Elizabeth Monroe, and Lipson, Leslie. *Values and Humanity.* New York: St. Martin's Press, 1971.

Eisner, Elliot W., and Vallance, Elizabeth. *Conflicting Conceptions of Curriculum.* Berkeley, California: McCutchan Publishing Corp., 1974.

Engle, Shirley H., and Longstreet, Wilma S. *A Design for Social Education in the Open Curriculum.* New York: Harper and Row, 1972.

Eurich, Alvin C., ed. *High School 1980: The Shape of Things of the Future in American Education.* New York: Pitman Publishing Corp., 1970.

Gorman, Burton W. *Secondary Education: The High School America Needs.* New York: Random House, 1971.

Gwynn, J. Minor, and Chase, John B., Jr. *Curriculum Principles and Social Trends,* 4th ed. New York: Macmillan, 1969.

McNeil, John D. *Curriculum: A Comprehensive Introduction.* Boston: Little, Brown and Co., 1977.

Oliver, Albert I. *Curriculum Improvement: A Guide to Problems, Principles, and Process, 2nd ed.* New York:Harper and Row, 1977

Porter, John W., Chairman. *The Adolescent, or Other Citizens, and Their High Schools,* Report of Task Force '74, The Charles F. Kettering Foundation. New York: McGraw-Hill, 1975.

Tanner, Daniel. *Secondary Education: Perspectives and Prospects.* New York: Macmillan, 1972.

Trump, J. Lloyd, and Miller, Delmas F. *Secondary School Curriculum Improvement,* 2nd ed. Boston: Allyn and Bacon, 1973.

Van Til, William, ed. *Curriculum: Quest for Relevance,* 2nd ed. Boston: Houghton Mifflin Co., 1974.

Vars, Gordon F., ed. *Common Learning: Core and Interdisciplinary Team Approaches.* Scranton, Pennsylvania: Intext Educational Publishers, 1969.

2 The Influence of Organization and Administration on Secondary Curriculum

If the curriculum represents the content of the secondary school, it seems apparent that the content is bounded by a structure or organizational pattern. The organization and administration of the secondary school exercises an important and perhaps pervasive influence upon the curriculum. If the school is graded, then the curriculum is graded, if not by design then by default. If the school is organized on a five or six period day of 45 or 50 minutes, and each subject or course is of the same length, then curriculum segments, units, lessons, and teaching methodology are affected by being forced to be fit into these time slots.

Perhaps the most obvious but overlooked fact about secondary education is that it is including younger students than before. Whereas the dominant pattern for school system organization in the United States was once the 8-4 plan, modified to the 6-3-3 with the advent of the junior high school, it is now moving towards the 4-4-4 or 5-3-4 plans. This means that whereas secondary education once included only the ninth through twelfth grades, it is now including grades five through twelve with the contemporary movement towards the middle school. The importance of this trend cannot be overemphasized.

It may be difficult for students of American secondary education to realize that the high school as the first component of universal secondary education was a controversial and debated concept. For example, in his penetrating analysis of nineteenth century school reform, Michael Katz reported that in 1860, by popular vote, the people of Beverly, Massachusetts abolished their high school. (1) Katz delved into the actual voting records of Beverly citizens (343 of 392) and separated each voter by geographical area and occupation. The results clearly indicated that the more prestigious and wealthy citizens of Beverly voted to retain the high school, while those in the working classes and those without children voted to abolish it. Katz' point is that from its very beginnings, the American high school has been a class dominated institution and despite the rhetoric of school reformers like Horace Mann, the reality of universal secondary education was that it was far from universal, and in some cases outright discriminatory against the poor. The relationship between socioeconomic wealth and school success was acknowledged some 62 years later when New York City Superintendent W. L. Ettinger concluded, in 1922, that the highest ratio of school failures would always be located in the poorest sections of that city. (2)

The evolution of the high school began with the Boston Latin School in 1635, the purpose of which was to prepare male students for entrance to Harvard. (3) But the educational needs of a rapidly growing nation could not be met with such schools alone. The establishment of academies during the period 1751 to 1860, (4) helped serve the interests of the middle and upper classes who could afford to pay the tuition. The first public high school was established in Boston in 1821 and was called the English Classical School. (5) Legislation in Massachusetts requiring each town of 500 families or more to provide such a school had a great impact on the development of the high school. The legislation further prescribed the curriculum: algebra, geometry, surveying, United States history and bookkeeping. If the town had over 4000 inhabitants, instruction also had to be provided in Greek, Latin, rhetoric, history and logic. A penality was attached to the law if towns failed to comply. (6)

The growth of the high school was slow because funds for such schools had to be raised by taxes. Several legal battles ensued as to whether taxes could be legitimately imposed for free secondary education. The famous 1874 Kalamazoo decision in Michigan provided a legal base for public support of the high school and thereafter was a rapid rise in the number of high schools, (7) growing from 321 in 1860 to 2526 by 1890. (8) Since 1910, with the exception of the decade of World War II, high school enrollments have gained by more than one million students every ten years. (9) While secondary school enrollment is expected to level off or begin a decline until the 1980s, a free, public secondary education has been firmly established as a general expectation for almost all of the population of young adults in the nation.

Organizational Patterns of Secondary Education

The four year high school constituted secondary education between 1850 and 1920, usually within a unified school system of 8-4. (10) After 1920 a variety of patterns began to prevail, sparked by the push for the junior high school. (11)

Organizational patterns influence curriculum in many important ways. First, such patterns form the boundaries of the age groups of learners to be included or excluded in a definition of secondary education. The trend towards the inclusion of younger students is important in deciding what shape secondary education should ultimately take in an organizational sense. Such organizational patterns usually reflect some overall philosophical purpose which then governs what is to be included or excluded in determining curricular content. The degree of curricular scope or breadth is also influenced not only from philosophical premises but from practical ones such as how large a school population might be to economically offer a comprehensive curriculum. In a small district a 6-6 plan might support a secondary school of 1200 students, thus enabling it economically to include advanced subjects in its curriculum. However, with only a four year high school the student body might only be 800 making such course offerings much more expensive and forcing a reduction in the scope of the program.

However, recent research has critically evaluated the outcomes of high school consolidation in rural areas and concluded that the rationale of reformers for reduced costs and increased quality education, undergirding the push to abandon small high schools, was only marginally correct at best, and flatly in error at the worst. "In short, there is no strong empirical base to support the assumptions and assertions of school and district consolidation advocates." (12) While it now seems that secondary curriculum was changed to fit the organizational scheme of a consolidated high school, the expected outcomes of that move have not materialized, largely because increased cost for transportation offset anticipated economies.

If the seventh and eighth grades are included in a 6-6 plan, they may be isolated by community desire to shield younger students from the influence of older ones. This may mean the continuation of an elementary school approach. On the other hand, the students may be integrated with the older students and take on a high school orientation to their studies. Because of a small student population it may be impossible to develop any special intermediate school for seventh and eighth graders in a 6-6 plan. On other occasions school facilities may play a larger role in defining the overall plan of a school system than educational philosophy.

The Impact of the Junior High School Movement

The major drawback of the dominant 8-4 pattern of school organization was that there was a significant loss of enrollment from the eighth to the ninth grade. One study by Leonard P. Ayers in 1909 revealed that only 40 percent of students in 59 school systems in the eighth grade actually went on to the ninth grade. (13) The movement towards the junior high school and the 6-3-3 organizational plan appeared to be twofold: move the ninth grade into an intermediate or middle school to introduce students more quickly into high school work thereby decreasing the loss of enrollment to the high school and increasing the retention power of the school system, and focus on the unique needs of the learners in age ranges twelve to thirteen. Junior high schools were introduced in Berkeley, California in 1910 significantly labeled introductory High Schools. (14)

Some secondary educators also believed that secondary education could become more socially relevant to a greater audience of learners if the secondary system could be freed from both the limitations of the elementary curriculum, and the strictures of the college and university expectations. (15) The intermediate school was to be a place where exploration and innovation could occur in "block of time" programs. Within these units learners had the advantages of greater curricular specialization without the necessity to select any particular one for college entrance. The rise of the junior high school reduced the number of school systems operating on the old 8-4 organizational pattern along with the strong push for consolidation of rural secondary schools. Whereas in 1920, 94 percent of the school districts functioned on the 8-4 plan, this was reduced to 24 percent by 1959, (16) The 6-3-3 plan appeared to be highly favored in urban areas and the 6-6 or junior-senior high school plan in rural or less populated areas. (17)

The Rise of the Middle School as Expansion of Secondary Education

Beginning in the 1950s there appeared a new type of intermediate unit, one which did not include the ninth grade but extended into the elementary school as far as the fifth grade. Called the "middle school" to differentiate its aim from that of the junior high school, this newer intermediate unit has experienced rapid growth. (18) As usual the movement contained a rationale which included serving the unique needs of its student population better than the junior high school. At the same time, the movement was a practical response to pressures to create integrated schools by busing students at an earlier age to a different neighborhood school site. (19)

The failures of the junior high school included abandoning its transition function between elementary and senior high schools by replicating high school education. The complete departmentalization of the junior high school with a full complement of extracurricular functions such as interscholastic athletics and clubs have merely extended high school education to the seventh grade level rather than the tenth.

The development of the middle school as a 5-8, 6-8, or 7-8 grade inclusion appropriately alters school district organization accordingly to a 4-4-4, 5-3-4, or 6-2-4. Which of the formerly elementary school grades should be included in the middle school appears to be dictated by factors other than philosophy or empirical evidence. The preponderance of middle schools nationwide appear to have adopted the 6-8 organizational plan. (20)

Research on the question of which grades to include in the middle school appears equivocal. Patrick Mooney studied the achievement and attendance of students in a middle school (5-8) with students in grades five and six of regular elementary schools, and grades seven and eight of regular junior high schools (7-9). Mooney found that the comparisons on school achievement and attendance favored the middle school. (21) Edward Trauschke performed an analysis of pupil self-concepts and attitudes towards school in a similar study of the same middle school included in Mooney's work and found that students in the middle school, when compared with students in conventional schools, achieved as well or better, held self-concepts at least equal, and had more favorable attitudes toward school. (22)

Jack Hillyer examined the maturity factors of elementary and middle school pupils in Missouri and found in his sample of 400 pupils that grades five, six, and seven should be included in a middle school. (23) On the other hand, Cameron Gateman studied fifth and sixth graders' academic achievement, self-concept, and school attitudes in New Jersey. His sample included 582 middle school pupils and 523 elementary school pupils and found that middle schools provided more appropriate programs for sixth grade pupils in terms of higher academic attainment in the basic skills and more positive self-concepts than the elementary school. Gateman also concluded that the ideal middle school program did consist of grades 6-8. (24)

The rise of the middle school movement has significantly expanded the secondary school population. It is the earnest hope of middle school advocates that the middle school will not become the same kind of victim to the high school as the junior high school did. Probably one of the critical factors in the failure of the junior high school idea was the inclusion of the ninth grade which, because it counted for college entrance based upon the old 8-4 plan, tended to extend departmentalization and specialization into both grades seven and eight. When the ninth grade is retained in the high school, this influence is gone. For this reason perhaps the middle school can develop more successfully the same ideals of the junior high school.

Nagging questions still remain with both the middle school and junior high school in terms of curriculum development and articulation with the elementary and high school. While the total departmentalization of the junior high school solved the articulation problem between the junior and senior high schools, the sharp break between the elementary school and the junior high school was as great for the 6-3-3 plan as for the 8-4. The 6-3-3 merely moved the break lower into the grades. There has to be a planned gradualism within school organization and the curriculum pattern to operationalize the concept of a transition between the elementary school and the totally departmentalized and graded high school. The amount and kind of gradualism contained in an organizational, staffing and curricular sense depends to some degree upon the kind of patterns employed at the elementary level and the high school.

The organizational pattern of secondary education establishes the "break" points for the school system between the elementary and secondary levels, and within the secondary level itself, i.e., between high school and the intermediate unit. The pattern also defines the secondary school population. Debates over the optimum school district organizational plan, whether 8-4, 6-3-3 or 4-4-4 or some other variation are largely unproductive. The choice of such plans is largely arbitrary and grounded in the dictates of local pragmatism. Research on such patterns has failed to demonstrate clearly that any one is superior to any other. Economic factors such as pupil-teacher ratios, degree of specialization required, and building utilization and conditions, or efforts to achieve a racially integrated district appear to be the most often considered factors in adopting or changing a school system organization pattern.

Curricular Patterns of Secondary Schools

Within the secondary schools there are a variety of curricular patterns present. The most traditional and dominant is the subject-centered curriculum complemented with the organizational component of departmentalization. The subject-centered curriculum traces its lineage to the classical liberal arts curriculum of antiquity which included geometry, drawing, music, grammar and rhetoric. (26) The subject-centered curriculum is arranged usually in order of difficulty, from simple to complex. The concept of prerequisites prevails from such inferences about order in the curriculum. Primary concerns of the subject-centered curriculum are scope or the degree of breadth of a subject and sequence, the manner of development or presentation.

While the subject-centered curriculum is without a doubt the predominant manner in which the secondary curriculum has been developed and is applied in the nation's secondary schools, it has not been without its critics. Smith, Stanley and Shores point out that the way a subject is taught is substantially different from the way it may be learned, i.e., presentation does not necessarily equal a given amount of learning. (27) The major teaching mode of the subject-centered curriculum has been the lecture and the major response by learners is memorization and recitation.

Despite efforts to develop curricular alternatives within the secondary schools, particularly the high school, the subject-centered curriculum will undoubtedly prevail for some time to come. The reasons are not difficult to pinpoint. First, teacher preparatory institutions train teachers within similar disciplines and secondly, states certify teachers as competent within the subjects. In many states it is contrary to law to assign a teacher outside of his or her area of certification. Interdisciplinary approaches to curriculum development in the secondary school consistently contradict the tenets of teacher training and licensing as developed in most of the states.

One of the major fallacies of the subject-centered curriculum is that of "coverage." Discussions about curricular alternatives often come down to the fact that so much information cannot be "covered" by the teacher within a given time period. As Hilda Taba pointed out with the subject-centered curriculum, without ranking or setting priorities within the curriculum areas, it is impossible to separate the important from the unimportant. If all subjects within the curriculum are of equal importance then coverage is a problem. If, however, curricular goals are ranked, a reasonable definition of coverage becomes possible. (28)

Most curriculum specialists agree that sequencing a curriculum is really a matter of arbitrarily determining what should come first, second, etc. There are few, if any, inviolate rules about developing a sequential curriculum. Even in such areas as mathematics, frequent violations in sequence are found in the presentation of concepts and skills. Studies of sequence show that none are necessarily better than others. Some educators have used the argument that if no sequence is really better than any other, sequence is not important. We would argue the opposite. If research indicates that no particular sequence is any better or worse than any other, then it is simply necessary to develop one which appears to be suitable to the school and school district. Sequence is important if a secondary school wants to improve learning based upon feedback showing that students are not learning what is deemed essential. Without having concrete information about where certain skills, knowledges and or attitudes should be acquired, it is impossible to bring about improvements in the instructional program.

Departmentalization

Departmentalization represents the process of defining the smallest administrative unit in the secondary school. As such, it is identified as part of the formal organization of the school or the division of labor. The division of labor in secondary schools is defined by separating teachers by subjects and chronological ages (grade levels) of the pupils to be taught. This division of labor serves as a basis for grouping teachers and for issuing instructions to various departments to coordinate a student's educational program. If one were to analyze the functional differences of teachers among departments, there would be few absolute differences. There are few, if any, functional differences in what teachers or department chairpersons are expected to perform within the various departments. Therefore secondary school departmentalization is not grounded on functional differences. Each department is expected to perform the same range of functions as every other department. For this reason secondary schools possess a very crude division of labor by departmentalization. (29)

If, however, there were differences such as teaching versus research or curriculum development by which one department specialized in handling various functions associated with each to the exclusion of others, a functional or process type of departmentalization would be present. Secondary school organization does not follow this way, rather it follows the delineation of subject matter specialization and reinforces administratively a subject-centered curriculum. Curriculum reformers of the secondary school who have attempted to move towards a thematic type of curricular delineation have often found themselves enmeshed in battles to retain administrative territory rather than involved in arguments pro or con over the merits of curricular consolidation. Departmentalization of the secondary school has therefore followed the delineation of curricular territory and reinforced whatever subject area demarcations were already present. Even with proposals to abandon age grading in the high school on the basis that this reform will increase the ability of pupils to progress at their own rates of learning, the division of labor by subject areas is not changed. Age grading refers to the way the secondary school divides the pupils. It does not imply any significant differences for teachers except perhaps for pacing or adjustments within subject disciplines. Such student delineations do not affect the functional differences among teachers.

Secondary school departmentalization has made it more difficult to achieve extensive horizontal integration of the subject areas in the curriculum. It has also served as a barrier to curricular innovation which attempts to conceptualize the school's curricular functions along some other line such as thematic, broad fields, or core. If, for example, the faculty wanted to deal instructionally with the idea of thinking critically on real life problems as a skill, it would be necessary to highlight this skill in each and every subject area of the curriculum. The alternative would be to select one topic which would involve all the subjects and have each department present a piece of everyday problem-solving, or include it in the broadest segment of the curriculum within a core class, as in English and social studies.

Departmentalization requires administrative coordination and negotiations among the administrative units about time, materials, budget, etc. Dealing with curricular "wholes" whether in the form of themes, ideas, or problems, is extremely difficult in a highly subject-centered and departmentalized secondary school.

Curriculum coordination is largely accomplished within each subject rather than among the subjects. This is the major reason why global school goals and/or objectives have not generally been translated into classroom practice. Goals are almost always interdisciplinary and do not fall within specific subject fields. Determining which curricular area is to have primacy of locating the responsibility within a subject area is more arbitrary than anything else. If materials and money are attached there is a tendency for all departments to claim priorities such as "all the departments teach reading," or "all teachers are responsible for guidance." If, however, accountability is to be established for what happens if learners do not learn reading, all the departments quickly point out they teach only those skills, knowledges and attitudes within their subject areas.

Recommendations on curricular reforms for secondary schools beginning with the Committee of Ten in 1893 and the Commission on the Reorganization of Secondary Education in 1918 created a consensus of what should be offered in the high school, at least what has been called the "standardized main-line subjects." (30)

Curricular innovations have fallen largely to the intermediate units of secondary education, i.e., the junior high school or middle school. If is at these levels that the core curriculum or broad fields type of curriculum is most commonly found. Such curricula attempt to create for the student more holistic learning and by organizing classroom teaching around interest areas or thematic units lays the groundwork for more meaningful integration of knowledge. The core curriculum is usually offered in block-of-time scheduling arrangements and involves two or more subjects ordinarily taught separately. It extends over two or more periods of the school's schedule. The use of block-of-time arrangements in the junior high school increased from 15.8 percent reporting such scheduling in 1949 to 40 percent in 1960. (31)

The Influence of School Scheduling Practices

The secondary school schedule establishes the frames of time into which the curriculum is fitted. It is the schedule that comprises the beginning and end of the daily sequence of learning activities. In many ways the building of the master schedule has dictated the impact or lack of impact of the school curriculum. The forty or fifty minute standard secondary schedule has become the egg crate of the subject-centered curriculum.

While many reformers of secondary education proposed changes to enable learners to pursue skill development and or individual interests which did not conform to the dictates of the standard schedule such ideas were often crushed under the realities of schedule building. Administrators and teachers who are close to scheduling acquire some idea of the complexity of even the simplest kinds of school schedules. The rise of reforms in the form of computerized schedules which allowed variations in the lengths of periods and activities was a response to the rigidities imposed by traditional secondary school schedules. The Stanford School Scheduling System(S^4) (32), the IndiFlex S of Indiana University, (33) GASP of Massachusetts Institute of Technology (34) and the daily demand schedule were some of the more popular computerized scheduling programs. The *flexible schedule,* as such programs came to be called, really allowed some of the ideas developed by J. Lloyd Trump to become a reality for the first time in the secondary schools. Some of these were:

1. The utilization of teaching assistants working under the supervision of, or in cooperation with, professionally certified, experienced, competent teachers;
2. The reorganization of administrative patterns;
3. The recognition of student responsibilities for learning;
4. Analysis of teacher roles and teacher competencies;
5. The utilization of material aids to instruction;
6. The utilization of physical plant in improving staff functioning;
7. Improved staff utilization through basic curriculum revision;
8. Utilization of effective techniques for interesting increased numbers of able young people in becoming teachers;
9. Analysis of contributions and relationships of various methods of staff utilization in a coordinated program. (35)

Trump's ideas called for variations in the length and frequency of class periods, varying class sizes in keeping with instructional purposes, utilizing more than teachers in the school in a variety of functions and utilizing school facilities more flexibly and efficiently.

The modular flexible schedule achieved a breakthrough in scheduling because on the basis of pupil demand, the computer built the master schedule. This reversed the usual order of building the master schedule first and then fitting pupil demands into the schedule. The computerized schedule allowed infinitely more variations than the traditional schedule, but it was far from flexible. Once the master schedule had been constructed via computer, the actual schedule was not much more malleable than its traditional predecessor.

Flexible scheduling continues to be a controversial innovation, largely because of its inclusion of pupil independent study and allowing choice of unscheduled time. (See chapter nine in this volume). While the computerized schedule enabled secondary school teachers to create more opportunities for students to learn at varying paces and thus individualize the curriculum, the staff often failed to utilize the new modes of instruction, causing a return to the more traditional type of scheduling and teaching.

Secondary School Staffing Innovations

The advancement of the modular flexible schedule also gave a practical method for differentiating or separating the teaching staff of the secondary school. The term *differentiated staffing* was developed to promote the idea of utilizing various teaching functions and skills in a way not possible within the rigidly egalitarian confines of the traditional secondary school schedule. When the school schedule permitted the development of large and small instructional groups and tutorial or independent study, it became possible to schedule teachers according to their strengths in these areas. Some teachers expert in giving an exciting lecture could specialize in large group instruction. Others who found the dynamics of small groups compatible with their professional interests and skills could likewise specialize. For the first time it became possible to conceptualize the curricular function within the secondary school as a bona fide full time responsibility without a teaching function. (36) When varying salary schedules were attached to these functions a method for separating the teaching cadre for further role specialization was instituted in the schools. Because it posed enormous threats to the internal security of teachers in collective bargaining it was stoutly opposed by the National Education Association and the American Federation of Teachers.

Differentiated staffing did not take hold in secondary education on a large scale for a variety of reasons. The opposition of the two large teaching groups was certainly a factor. The controversial salary differentiation broke the tradition of the single salary schedule and teachers were fearful of the impact it would have on certain segments of the group who were not at the upper levels of the hierarchy. In early models also there was not sufficient differentiation in some of the roles which were implemented to provide functional differences. (37) Although surveys of teachers revealed that the concepts of differentiated staffing were generally more popular at the secondary level than the elementary, (38) the concept is still not widely used in secondary education. A sort of miniature differentiation does exist with the department chairperson role.

Conceptualizing the Alternatives
for Secondary Schools

In order to help the reader examine the possible alternatives for secondary schools, some of them have been developed into mathematical possibilities. In this way it is easier to indicate how one type of change may lead to another and to examine what may be major or minor types of alternatives from the status quo. An example in simplified form is shown below. Suppose that the variables of secondary school organization were only three: scheduling, pupil grouping and curricular delineation. For purposes of analysis each is dichotomized into two possibilities.

Scheduling	*Pupil Grouping*	*Curricular* *Delinearion*
Schedule A	Grouping Plan A	Delineation A
Schedule B	Grouping Plan B	Delineation B

The possibilities of grouping these variables comprising secondary school organization are shown below:

A	A	A
A	B	B
A	A	B
B	A	A
B	A	B
B	B	A
B	B	B
A	B	A

There are eight possible variations of school organization. If A,A,A described the status quo it would become the most traditional or conventional of the types of organization. If B,B,B described the organization most unlike the conventional it would be termed the most radical of the possibilities.

Diagram 2-1 shows the major variables comprising a school staffing pattern for a secondary school. Each variable is assumed to be weighted equally. The total possible variations in staffing patterns would be thirty-two. If the same letter were employed for each variable as in the example, A would be the most conventional and B the most radical. The most conventional is also the most bureaucratized. A bureaucracy is characterized by role delineations arranged in a hierarchy, a division of labor, and routinized work which is largely repetitive. (39) The traditional secondary school staffing pattern conforms to these requirements for a bureaucracy. That secondary schools are bureaucracies should come as no great surprise. The invention of the graded school in 1848 was the last concept which cemented bureaucracy and the schools. Schedules, staffing, organization, and administration, reinforce and require processing students in "batches," i.e., grades. Curriculum is necessarily forced to also conform to these same requirements. While curriculum can be considered separately, without considering the impact of organization and administration it cannot be fully understood, nor can the possible alternatives be judged practically if educators desire to alter curriculum as it currently is defined in secondary schools. A utilization of Diagram 2-1 will show that curriculum which fosters breaking away from traditional scheduling or attempts to declassify students by grade and deal with them individually will be hard pressed to be successful without embracing organizational changes as well. Once organizational changes are proposed, the weight of the jobs and roles within the secondary school act as a barrier to such change. These are considerable obstacles to overcome as innovators have discovered.

A Look at Possible Alternatives

Organizational changes for secondary schools have been proposed and attempted in the form of schools within schools, alternative high schools, and magnet schools. A school within a school is an attempt in some cases to reduce the size of large secondary schools and create a curricular center for a suborganization within the larger school. Alternative schools within schools may be conceptualized around music and drama, Third World cultures and problems, and activity or field learning (schools without walls). Some of the alternative schools which have found acceptance are outlined next.

Fundamental Schools

These kinds of alternative schools stress basic skills, discipline and control and utilize dress and behavior codes.

Diagram 2-1

CRITICAL INDICES TO EXAMINE SCHOOL STAFFING PATTERNS

Index 1		Index 2		Index 3		Index 4		Index 5	
Type of Pupil Grouping (1)		Type of Curricular Grouping (2)		Type of Organizational Grouping		Type of Scheduling Organization		Type of Organizational Structure	
graded (chronological)	nongraded	subject and/or skill	nonsubject or skill based	self-contained	nonself-contained	time defined	nontime defined	bureaucratic (3)	nonbureaucratic
grades, i.e., fifth grade is largely ten year olds	interage nonage based grouping patterns	department skill areas viz. reading, typing	interdisciplinary thematic centered by problem or strand	permanent instructional grouping based on indices 1, 2, 4, & 5	nonpermanent & fluid groups, i.e., situational grouping	periods mods set blocks carnegie units	open blocks independent study skill based competency exams other non-time based definitions of learning	principals 5th grade teachers AV Coord. PE Coordinator Counselor etc. etc.	nonperm. roles situational authority matrix management

Notes
1. Some type of grouping is necessary for the economy of instruction to take place.
2. The question of sequence is generic to both types of curricular grouping.
3. The term *bureaucratic* is used in the sense it describes a pyramidal organization with set roles arranged in an hierarchical pattern with defined parameters of job authority.

Open Schools

These kinds of schools may be modeled along the lines of the British Summerhill (39) where students have a great deal of freedom to choose what they desire to learn and when they may learn it, including the option not to learn in formal academic ways until they see a purpose in such learning

Magnet or Specialized Schools

While the term *magnet school* usually has a special connotation of attracting students for purposes of achieving racial integration in large city systems, it is also typical of a move towards specialization, whereas an entire school focuses on a subject area of the curriculum such as math and science, vocational or performing arts.

Basically school organization follows curricular delineations in these alternatives. The curriculum may range from a narrow slice of the subject-centered approach, a thematic approach, or a school which begins with the concept that the curriculum is merely whatever any student may decide it is or is not. While the creation of special secondary schools represents an important trend, such alternatives only exist in a small fraction of school districts in the United States. (40) Pressures for their extension and expansion of such alternatives may be one or more of the following.

School Integration

Court ordered racial integration has been a spur towards creating alternative secondary schools in order to avoid mandatory busing in such cities as Houston, Cincinnati and others.

School Dropouts and Unemployment

The fact that high school dropouts and graduates lack employable skills on the job market has led to more emphasis being placed on vocational-technical education alternatives.

Student Militancy

While there has been some decrease in levels of secondary school student militancy, more active action oriented students have pressed for more curricular alternatives, if not directly then as a school response to tension and boredom.

Federal Legislation

Federal legislation on the handicapped and the availability of federal funds for gifted students have provided the impetus to consider further specialization in secondary school organization and curriculum.

Escalating Costs of Secondary Education

Certain areas of secondary education have brought increasing costs to maintaining a modern program. Perhaps the most dramatic increase has occurred within the vocational areas where the idea of replicating comprehensive shop equipment has become prohibitive for each junior or senior high school. This has forced a reconsideration of building one or two such well equipped vocational schools and busing students for part or all of the school day from within the entire school system.

The pressures for the creation of alternatives to the traditional high school have raised new issues within secondary education. The introduction of specialized alternatives directly challenge the viability of the comprehensive curriculum and the comprehensive high school as its major expression. Clearly, the increasing pluralism of American society is demanding not a "melting pot" in which various backgrounds and differences of students are lost, but a move towards increasing the differences and individualism of various groups. The creation of the melting pot concept was a pragmatic response to the urbanization of America and an attempt to ensure a modicum of cohesiveness of massive waves of immigration from abroad and from rural areas to urban areas. The response towards specialization of secondary education has likewise been pragmatic and a reaction to social and economic pressures.

Future Possibilities: The Year-Round School

Still another possibility for secondary education is that posed by the year-round school. The year-round school represents two different concepts. The first is the idea of extending schooling for all students year-round, and the second is to extend the school year from 180 days to at least 225 days or more, but reduce the total number of students in school at any time. In the first instance there are few savings if year-round schools allow all students to be educated beyond the 180(+) day year. In the latter, however, some segment of the school population is withdrawn from a portion of the extended school year, thereby allowing the teaching staff to be similarly reduced and buildings to be utilized more effectively. There are several variations of year-round education. (41)

Various forms of year-round schooling were actually used in the early 1800s in major Eastern cities such as New York, Chicago, Buffalo and Cincinnati. (42) In 1913 New York State established the school year at 180 days. The rationale for this length of time was that it represented essentially a compromise between those who desired year-round schooling, and the farmers who wanted their children in school only when they were not needed on the farm. By 1915, the 180 day school year had become standard across the nation.

The most famous year-round school model attempted was that in Aliquippa, Pennsylvania from 1929 to 1938. The Aliquippa approach was developed as a response to mushrooming school attendance and the fact that the school system had reached a bonding limit to finance new schools. As a response, Aliquippa instituted a mandatory four quarter model which was abandoned nine years later with the reduction of the manpower demands at local steel mills. (43)

According to George Jensen, year-round school advocated the Aliquippa Plan demonstrated the following:

1. Year-round schools can save money;
2. The employment of the teaching staff posed no particular problem;
3. Academic achievement of the students did not fall off in the summer months;
4. There were no mental or physical health hazards for either teachers or pupils;
5. Average daily attendance was not affected by year-round schooling, in fact, summer attendance was higher than for any other period;
6. Families were not frustrated in vacation planning due to a mandatory attendance pattern. (44)

Types of Year Round Schooling

The 45-15 Plan

The 45-15 model derives its name from the fact that while students attend 180 days of school they do so on the basis of 45 days of school and 15 days of vacation all year long. At any one time the school system would only be three-fourths full. This allows a school district to increase its student population by one-fourth without building new schools. (45)

The Quinmester Plan

The Quinmester Plan has been developed in Dade County (Miami), Florida and divides the 52 week calendar into five quins or terms. Each quin is 45 instructional days. At the termination of each quin, one-fifth of the students go on vacation. The curriculum must be rewritten into shorter segments since two quins equal one semester. Once again, districts can utilize existing buildings more effectively. Teaching staff may be hired to teach anywhere from one to five quins. The actual employment period may therefore vary according to desire and demand for certain courses.

The Four Quarter Sixty Day Plan

The four quarter plan dates back to 1904 where it was tried in Bluffton, Indiana. The Newark, New Jersey system operated a four quarter plan from 1912 to 1931. In the four quarter plan a student attends school three of the four quarters. If educational enrichment is desired a student might attend all four quarters. Under the four quarter plan or any other plan, voluntarism is a major consideration. If students and their parents are allowed to volunteer for which quarters they prefer, there is a tendency to select the traditional three quarters, fall, winter, and spring, leaving a decreased and unbalanced enrollment for the summer quarter. This has been the case in the Atlanta, Georgia Public Schools four quarter plan.

Very little hard core research data are available showing either savings accrued from year-round schooling or pupil achievement. A savings of 2 percent in the total budget was claimed by Valley View, Illinois on the 45-15 plan. (46) A report prepared by Education Turnkey Systems for the Prince William County Public Schools, Virginia, comparing the 45-15 plan at Godwin Middle School showed that the overall costs were 9.6 percent lower than they would have been under a traditional nine month school year. A savings was reported in the utilization of classroom personnel costs by eliminating all nonteaching (in-service and preparation) days for teachers. Instead of actually reducing costs, teachers were asked to teach on the days they had previously been allotted for in-service. (47)

Whether or not there are any real savings for the year-round school is still being debated. If the plan does advance education by enriching the educational program the implications for curriculum development for the 45-15, the quinmester and the sixty day four quarter plan still remain. The plans do promote a reexamination of the curriculum of the secondary school. In some cases the reexamination has prompted the development of a more assessable and visible curriculum which has become less time based than before and more student performance oriented.

However, in some cases the curriculum has become more rigid and even more compartmentalized than before. The length of the school year, the degree to which that year is broken into constitutent parts exercises a powerful influence on curriculum shaping. Time has been equated as a measure of learning in the schools and has been standardized with the adoption of the Carnegie Unit. Standardization of time exercises a pervasive influence on curriculum thinking and planning.

The Administrative Climate for Curriculum Development

The administrative climate of the secondary school, that is, the atmosphere and the quality of interpersonal relationships is also an important factor in curriculum development. The development of a healthy and positive climate is the responsibility of the school administration. School climates which are characterized by high anxiety, fatigue, and cynicism are not conducive to maximum participation in curriculum development. There is a great deal of human interaction in the creation of revised or new curricula. If teachers or other educational personnel are fearful of their jobs, afraid of public scrutiny or criticism, they will not objectively examine the pitfalls of their school's curriculum. Instead, such analyses will mean a defense of the status quo, a rationalization of current practice rather than a probing and careful revising of areas deemed to be missing or inadequate.

Sometimes the use of test data as a lever to curriculum improvement has been employed. Usually what occurs is that the test items are pirated into the lesson plan and substitute for an objective examination of the school's curriculum. Punitive school climates cannot be the successful breeding grounds for the long range improvement of the curriculum of the secondary school. More than a mere consideration of the type of organization or its assumptions, the modus operandi of the school administration will have more to say about how curriculum development actually takes place than any other single factor.

Innovations such as the Program, Planning, Budgeting System (PPBS) in which educational objectives are linked to establishing dollar costs for achieving those objectives, have been a controversial subject and leave unanswered questions regarding the validity of the curriculum. Prorating the cost of achieving certain educational objectives within the curriculum can be deceiving. School systems also do not have at their disposal complete control of all of the cost variables such as teacher salaries. PPBS can provide useful and informative data to decision making groups within a school or school system if it is clear that costly objectives are not necessarily "bad" and cheap ones "good." Schools and school systems should know how many organizational resources are required to obtain some types of educational outcomes. Budget allocations should follow validated priorities. The concept of beginning with a zero budget base (ZBB) each year in school budget planning can serve as a method to reexamine what is really important in the school curriculum. The zero base merely implies that beginning the budget cycle each curriculum area must compete anew for organizational resources based upon changing priorities rather than beginning with the previous year's expenditures as the base for establishing a new budget. ZBB means that the budget is a more accurate reflection of changing curricular priorities.

The linkages between pupil performance, teacher behavior, school climate and curriculum construction and revision are very vague, not to mention extremely complex. Efforts to establish clearer relationships among these factors are essential if educational improvement of the nation's schools is to be attained. However, the mere application of PPBS may be a short-sighted approach if it is not accompanied with a clear understanding that the curriculum has in too many cases followed the addition of an organizational and administrative plan and therefore an assessment of its strengths and weaknesses via PPBS may really be a test of organizational strengths and weaknesses and have little to do with the curriculum per se.

The history of technological innovation in the schools as a reform strategy has been rather disappointing. Such innovations have tended to subvert means for ends and reinforce outmoded curricula. They have also tended to downplay or ignore the critical human dimensions of school life. While curriculum, too, is a means to an end, school organizational patterns should follow curriculum development rather than exercise the function of shaping curriculum to fit its own needs for bureaucratic tidiness. Curriculum development cannot be improved if it is continually made subservient to organizational requirements.

CHAPTER REFERENCES

1. Michael B. Katz, *The Irony of Early School Reform* (Boston: Beacon Press, 1968).

2. As cited in Colin Greer, *The Great School Legend* (New York: Basic Books, 1972), p. 123.

3. See Edward A. Krug, *The Secondary School Curriculum* (New York: Harper and Row, 1960), pp. 14-19.

4. See Lester W. Anderson and Lauren A. Van Dyke, *Secondary School Administration* (Boston: Houghton Mifflin, 1963), pp. 49-52.

5. Ellwood P. Cubberley, *The History of Education* (Boston: Houghton Mifflin, 1920), pp. 699-700.

6. Ibid.

7. J. B. Edmonson, Joseph Roemer, and Francis L. Bacon, *The Administration of the Modern Secondary School*, 4th ed. (New York: Macmillan, 1953), p. 9.

8. Anderson and Van Dyke, *Secondary School Administration*, p. 53.

9. Ibid., p. 55.

10. Harl R. Douglass, *Organization and Administration of Secondary Schools* (Boston: Ginn and Co., 1945), p. 5.

11. From James B. Conant, *Education in the Junior High School Years* (Princeton, New Jersey, 1960), p. 11.

12. Jonathan P. Sher and Rachel B. Tompkins, "Economy, Efficiency, and Equality: The Myths of Rural School and District Consolidation," National Institute of Education, U.S. Department of Health, Education, and Welfare, Washington, D.C., July 1976, p. 3.

13. Leonard P. Ayers, *Laggards in Our Schools* (New York: Russell Sage Foundation, 1909), p. 57. Cited in Samuel H. Popper, *The American Middle School* (Waltham, Massachusetts, 1967), p. 15.

14. Ibid., p. 11.

15. Ibid., p. 41.

16. Anderson and Van Dyke, *Secondary School Administration*, p. 84.

17. Conant, *Education in the Junior High*, p.11.

18. Joseph Bondi, *Developing Middle Schools: A Guidebook* (New York: MSS Educational Publishing Co., 1972).

19. Popper, *The American Middle School*, pp. 295-98.

20. "Middle Schools in Theory and Fact," *NEA Research Bulletin*, 47, no. 2 (May 1969): 49-52.

21. Patrick F. Mooney, "A Comparative Study of Achievement and Attendance of 10-14 Year Olds in a Middle School and in Other School Organizations" (unpublished doctoral dissertation, University of Florida, 1970).

22. Edward M. Trauschke, Jr., "An Evaluation of a Middle School by a Comparison of the Achievement, Attitudes, and Self-Concept of Students in a Middle School with Students in Other School Organizations" (unpublished doctoral dissertation, University of Florida, 1970).

23. Jack L. Hillyer, "A Comparative Study of Maturity Factors of Elementary and Middle School Pupils with Implications for School Grade Organization" (unpublished doctoral dissertation, University of Missouri at Columbia, 1972). Hillyer used the *Otis Quick Scoring Mental Ability Test*, the *California Test of Personality* interest and activity portion, and the same test to determine personal adjustment.

24. Cameron D. Gateman, "A Comparative Study of Fifth and Sixth Graders' Academic Achievement, Self-Concept and School Attitudes in New Jersey Elementary Schools and Middle Schools" (unpublished doctoral dissertation, Teachers College, Columbia University, March 1974).

25. Mauritz Johnson, Jr., "The Magic Numbers of 7-8-9," *NEA Journal* 52 (March 1963): 50-51, as cited in William M. Alexander, *The Emergent Middle School* (New York: Holt, Rinehart, Winston, 1968), p. 103.

26. Cubberley, *The History of Education*, p. 42.

27. B. Othanel Smith, William O. Stanley, and J. Harlan Shores, *Fundamentals of Curriculum Development* (New York: World Book Co., 1950), p. 396. Actually, this was a point made earlier by John Dewey in his writings.

28. Hilda Taba, *Curriculum Development* (New York: Harcourt, Brace and World, 1962), p. 186.

29. See W. W. Charters, Jr., "An Approach to the Formal Organization of the School," in *Behavioral Science and Educational Administration,* Sixty-Third Yearbook of the National Society for the Study of Education, Part 2, ed. Daniel E. Griffiths (Chicago: University of Chicago Press, 1964), pp. 243-61.

30. See Arno A. Bellack, "History of Curriculum Thought and Practice," *Review of Educational Research* 39, no. 3 (June 1969): 283-92.

31. From a survey of the U.S. Office of Education, "The Junior High School: A Survey of Grades 7-8-9 in Junior and Junior-Senior High Schools, 1959-60," by Grace S. Wright and Edith S. Greer, Bulletin 1963, no. 32 (Washington, D.C.: Government Printing Office, 1963), p. 20, as cited in Gordon F. Vars, "The Core Curriculum: Lively Corpse," in *Education for the Middle School Years: Readings, eds. J. Hertling and H. Getz* (Glenview, Illinois: Scott, Foresman and Co., 1971), pp. 144-49.

32. Robert N. Bush and Dwight W. Allen, *A New Design for High School Education* (New York: McGraw-Hill, 1964).

33. Donald C. Manlove and David W. Beggs, *Flexible Scheduling* (Bloomington, Indiana: Indiana University Press, 1965).

34. Judith Murphy and Robert Sutter, *School Scheduling by Computer: The Story of GASP* (New York: Educational Facilities Laboratories, 1964).

35. J. Lloyd Trump and Dorsey Baynham, *Guide to Better Schools* (Chicago: Rand McNally, 1961).

36. See Fenwick W. English and Donald K. Sharpes, *Strategies for Differentiated Staffing* (Berkeley, California: McCutchan Publishing Corp., 1971).

37. W. W. Charters, Jr., and Roland Pellegrin, "Barriers to the Innovation Process: Four Case Studies of Differentiated Staffing," *Educational Administration Quarterly* 9, no. 1 (Winter 1972): 3-14.

38. Fenwick W. English, "Assessing Teacher Attitudes towards Staff Differentiation" (unpublished doctoral dissertation, Arizona State University, September 1971).

39. A. S. Neill, *Summerhill* (New York: Hart Publishing Co., 1960).

40. In a sample of school board members in November, 1975, the National School Boards Association indicated that alternative secondary schools existed in only 13 percent of the districts responding. See *Alternative Schools,* Research Report No. 1976-3 of the National School Boards Association, 1976, Evanston, Illinois.

41. Parts of this section have been extrapolated from a report partially written and edited by Fenwick W. English, "A Feasibility Study of the Year Round Utilization of School Buildings (YRS) in Sarasota County," Sarasota County Schools, Florida (October 1973). (Mimeographed.)

42. Michael Y. Nunnery, "Status of the Extended School Year in 1972," College of Education, University of Florida, November 1972.

43. H. R. Vanderslice, "What One Town Learned in 10 Years of Year Round School," *U.S. News and World Report* (August 2, 1957): 48-52.

44. George M. Jensen, "The Calendar—Underdeveloped Educational Resource," speech delivered to Third Annual National Seminar on All Year Education in Cocoa Beach, Florida, March 1971.

45. See Leonard Servetter, *Year Round School Program: A Case Study* (Chula Vista, California: People Education and Communication Enterprises, Inc., 1973).

46. See "Year Round Schools: The 45-15 Plan," U.S. Department of Health, Education and Welfare (OE-72-9), p. 15.

47. The study was accomplished in October, 1972. See "45-15 and the Cost of Education," Education Turnkey Systems, Washington, D.C.

3   Establishing
Understandable
Objectives

Objectives merely represent the outcomes that one hopes to achieve as a result of a given program or enterprise. Boards of directors of corporations establish goals set on the basis of such factors as the availability of natural resources, labor supply, production costs, potential markets, and methods of distribution. Goals establish directions toward specified conclusions and, to the degree defined, suggest means of attaining those conclusions.

In education such words as objectives, aims, goals, purposes, priorities, and ends have been used interchangeably. Any standard dictionary of the English language uses all of these words in attempts to define each of the others. Thus, end becomes object or purpose. Purpose is seen as object, aim, or result. Objective is identified with end, aim, and goal. Goal is perceived as synonymous with such words as purpose, end, and aim. Efforts to distinguish meanings among the words move in circles. Both in standard English usage and in the professional language of education the words used to identify outcomes overlap and are used synonymously.

Even so, the immediacy of the outcome to be achieved may be appropriate as a means of distinguishing professional use of the word *objective* from all of the others. That is, if the outcomes are long range, such words as aims, goals, ideals, and purposes, accurately identify relatively undefined, not immediately attainable ends. If the outcomes are short range, well-defined, and attainable, the word objective applies most directly. In this sense, the more general words apply to the ends sought for American education and secondary education, to the outcomes identified by state departments of education, and to the priorities and philosophies phrased by school systems and individual schools. The more specific word, objective, applies to the outcomes of instruction, to the ends identified by teachers as objects to be achieved by pupils.

It is in this sense that the various words used to identify outcomes are used in the remainder of this chapter and throughout this volume. Such words and phrases as objectives, instructional objectives, and teaching objectives are used to refer to outcomes planned by teachers. National, state, and local educational outcomes are given as aims, goals, or any of the other nearly synonymous words used to indicate long-range ends.

In classroom teaching, if there is one truth, it is that professional teachers begin their work with the establishment of objectives. Without a specific understanding of the outcomes to be achieved, teachers can do no more than flounder toward unknown ends. Well-defined objectives help the teacher select subject matter appropriate to the students, assist in the determination of proper learning activities, and directly determine the means of evaluation. Phrasing objectives is the first step in organizing subject matter, in planning learning activities, and in constructing tests.

The need for national and state goals for education, for school system and school building objectives, and for clear understanding by teachers of their own instructional ends is not questioned by the overwhelming majority of educators. In fact, large chapters in the history of education during this century have been given to statements of general educational goals as well as to ways of organizing and stating the outcomes of instruction.

Goals for American Education and Secondary Education: Historical Perspective

The first and most copied statement of goals for secondary education produced during this century is the famous definition of the role of the secondary school proposed in 1918 by the Commission on the Reorganization of Secondary Education of the National Education Association. Sponsor of numerous reports, starting in 1913 and continuing into the 1920s, the Commission's 1918 statement of Cardinal Principles recommended that the major aims of secondary education should encompass seven areas:

1. Health
2. Command of the fundamental processes
3. Worthy home membership
4. Vocational efficiency
5. Civic competence
6. Worthy use of leisure time
7. Ethical character (1)

Although such general aims may seem commonplace today, they represented a sharp departure from the tradition of the secondary school. The idea that the high school curriculum should include programs related to such areas as health, home membership, use of leisure time, and vocation, broke sharply with tradition. As late as 1893 another committee of the National Education Association, The Committee of Ten on Secondary School Studies, had reaffirmed the function of the high school as a college-preparatory institution. (2) The Committee of Ten also recommended that the number of years given to elementary education be reduced to six and that the years of secondary education be extended to include grades seven and eight. Although this recommendation eventually led to the formation of the three-year junior and senior high school pattern of secondary education, there is little doubt that the purpose of the Committee was to find two additional years for college preparation. The same program of studies was expected for all students. Those whose academic talent allowed them to succeed passed on to universities and positions of professional leadership. Those who failed dropped out to the farm or factory.

Thus, the Cardinal Principles suggested a totally new direction for secondary education in this country. Indeed, the comprehensive nature of these seven brief phrases has never been surpassed. Later statements have been more detailed and definitive, have reaffirmed or reemphasized one or another of the Principles, but have added little that could not be classified within the 1918 phrases.

The durability of the Cardinal Principles is suggested by a reaffirmation of their applicability published nearly sixty years after their appearance. With due regard for the expansion of meaning resulting from six decades of experience, a distinguished panel of educational leaders and scholars reaffirmed the Principles as appropriate guidelines for education for the foreseeable future. (3)

Through the years other influential statements on educational purposes have appeared, either to reinterpret or expand some aspect of the Cardinal Principles, or to stress some economic social, military, or purely educational problem facing the nation at a given time.

In 1938 the Educational Policies Commission of the National Education Association joined with the American Association of School Administrators to produce a statement of goals centering on the purposes of education in American democracy. (4) Holding that education is concerned with the development of the learner, with home, family, and community life, with economic demands, and with civic and social duties, this Commission proposed forty-three aims grouped under four major headings: self-realization; human relationship; economic efficiency; and civic responsibility. As an example of the type of aims grouped under each of these headings, those listed under civic responsibility included social justice, social activity, social understanding, critical judgment, tolerance, conservation, social applications of science, world citizenship, law observance, economic literacy, political citizenship, and devotion to democracy. Each aim, in turn, was defined in a single complete sentence and explained in following essays.

Taken as a whole, the forty-three aims proposed by the Commission as the purposes of education in this republic represented a considerable refinement of the meaning of the Cardinal Principles and are further evidence of national commitment to universal, comprehensive, secondary education. The emphases given to economic matters and to citizenship is understandable in the context of a time when aggressive totalitarian states in Europe and Asia were rising to threaten world peace. Further, the nation was in the latter stages of the Great Depression, and there was doubt whether or not the government possessed the capacity or the will to rise from that depression. Under such circumstances the attention given to democratic ideals and economic considerations may be seen as an educational adjustment to matters of national concern.

The same Commission phrased another comprehensive commitment in a 1944 publication. Set forth in terms of the needs of all youth under the general heading, "The Common and Essential Needs That All Youth Have in a Democratic Society," the Commission proposed ten goals that became commonly known as the Ten Imperative Needs of Youth. (5)

1. All youth need to develop saleable skills and those understandings and attitudes that make the worker an intelligent and productive participant in economic life. To this end, most youth need supervised work experience as well as education in the skills and knowledge of their occupations.
2. All youth need to develop and maintain physical fitness.
3. All youth need to understand the right and duties of the citizen of a democratic society, and to be diligent and competent in the performance of their obligations as members of the community and citizens of the state and nation.
4. All youth need to understand the significance of the family for the individual and society and the conditions conducive to successful family life.
5. All youth need to know how to purchase and use goods and services intelligently, understanding both the values received by the consumer and the economic consequences of their acts.
6. All youth need to understand the methods of science, the influence of science on human life, and the main scientific facts concerning the nature of the world and of man.
7. All youth need opportunities to develop their capacities to appreciate beauty in literature, art, music, and nature.
8. All youth need to be able to use their leisure time well and to budget it wisely, balancing activities that yield satisfactions to the individual with those that are socially useful.
9. All youth need to develop respect for other persons, to grow in their

insight into ethical values and principles, and to be able to live and
work cooperatively with others.

10. All youth need to grow in ability to think rationally, to express their
thoughts clearly, and to read and listen with understanding. (6)

As can readily be perceived, the Ten Imperative Needs are all
inclusive and closely related to the earlier statements cited. It requires no
great intellectual exercise to see that the needs repeat such goals as good
health, vocation, understanding of fundamental processes, worthy use of
leisure time, civic responsibility, and the like. Perhaps the special emphasis upon science is understandable for those writing at the dawn of
the atomic era. However, the major distinction of the Imperative Needs
is that they focus directly upon the needs of youth.

This focus was brought into even sharper clarity in a publication of
the United States Office of Education, variously dated 1947, 1948, and
1951. (7) *Life Adjustment,* as it came to be known, centered on the
needs of youth whom the high school had failed to serve adequately,
estimated to include some 60 to 75 percent of all those of high school age
at the time. The report was prepared by a group called the Commission
on Life Adjustment Education. Named to membership by the United
States Commissioner of Education, the Commission attempted to translate previous reports and recommendations into action.

Although subject to varying interpretations and described in different ways at various places in the report, one of the clearest statements of
its meaning is as follows:

> The Commission defines Life Adjustment Education as that
> which better equips all American youth to live democratically with
> satisfaction to themselves and profit to society as home members,
> workers, and citizens. (8)

This definition was then related to such general goals as ethical
living, the fundamental skills, recreation, and work. The bulk of the
report was given to applications of life adjustment under these headings:
Guidance and Pupil Personnel Services; Ethical and Moral Learning;
Citizenship Education; Home and Family Life; Self-Realization and Use
of Leisure; Health and Safety; and Consumer Education. A brief description of practical arts appears in an appendix, and a passing reference is made to vocational education.

Imperfectly understood, criticized for being antiacademic, and seldom put into action as the Commission had hoped, Life Adjustment
nevertheless continued the ongoing effort to adjust secondary education
to the real needs of students, contributed to the development of block-

time or core curricular offerings, and furthered the development of guidance as an essential secondary school service for students.

Then, in 1952, almost as a return to the 1890s, the so-called Harvard Report appeared. (9) This report was prepared by a committee composed of faculty members from Harvard, Princeton, and Yale Universities and several prestigious private, college-preparatory academies. In brief, it called for an integration of the work of the last two years of high school with that of the first two years of college in the area of general preparation. The report focused upon the needs of the academically talented, and its concern was for the superior student.

Perhaps the concern for quality evident in the report was well taken. It is hard to quarrel with a call for an end to curricular repetition, waste of time, and lack of motivation. By 1952 some concern for the needs of the college-preparatory student was long overdue.

However, the Harvard Report did not stem the tide toward enormously ranging objectives for secondary education; in fact, it only added to the lists by recalling the particular needs of the academically capable. By 1956, a committee for The White House Conference on Education appointed by President Eisenhower produced a statement of educational objectives as broadly conceived as any of its predecessors. Fifteen major objectives for American schools were defined as follows:

1. A general education as good as or better than that offered in the past, with increased emphasis on the physical and social sciences;

2. Programs designed to develop patriotism and good citizenship;

3. Programs designed to foster moral, ethical, and spiritual values;

4. Vocational education tailored to the abilities of each pupil and to the needs of community and nation;

5. Courses designed to teach domestic skills;

6. Training in leisure-time activities such as music, dancing, avocational reading, and hobbies;

7. A variety of health services for all children, including both physical and dental inspections and instructions aimed at bettering health knowledge and habits;

8. Special treatment for children with speech or reading difficulties and other handicaps;

9. Physical education, ranging from systematic exercises, physical therapy, and intramural sports, to interscholastic athletic competition;

10. Instruction to meet the needs of abler students;

11. Programs designed to acquaint students with countries other than their own in an effort to help them understand the problems America faces in international relations;
12. Programs designed to foster mental health;
13. Programs designed to foster wholesome family life;
14. Organized recreational and social activities;
15. Courses designed to promote safety. These include instruction in driving automobiles, swimming, civil defense, etc. (10)

Note the reemphasis on the needs of abler students as well as the recommendation for special programs for the handicapped, the indentification of particular kinds of health services and recreational activities, and the naming of particular instruction under safety education. Without belaboring the point, it is obvious that most schools and school systems, many years after this report, are still struggling to implement some of the expectations. Courses in swimming cannot be offered where facilities are lacking. Programs for the handicapped are only now pushing to a priority position at state levels and slowly appearing in practice in schools and school systems.

The reports persisted and persist today. Only two years following the White House Conference a special report of the Rockefeller Brothers Fund (11) was given entirely to consideration of programs for the academically superior. The report emphasized the need for excellence, high performance, and talent for the perpetuation of democracy. Curricular reform based upon traditional liberal arts doctrine was recommended for all those of considerable academic ability.

A later entry in the long history of goals for education and secondary education appeared in 1973. The report was prepared by a National Commission on the Reform of Secondary Education established by the Charles F. Kettering Foundation. (12) The major portion of the book concerns thirty-two recommendations for reform in secondary education covering such matters as community participation in reform, career education, affirmative action, alternate educational routes, uses of television, school security, sexism, corporal punishment, student activities, the terminal age of compulsory attendance (recommended by the Commission to be dropped to age fourteen), and interscholastic athletics for girls. The many recommendations will be discussed and debated through the years that are now upon us. Some will become reflected in school practice, others modified for adoption, and others rejected, as is the fate of all reports which attempt to cover the entire range of school matters.

Unfortunately, the goals for secondary education stated by the Commission do not correlate closely with the recommendations. Thirteen goals, defined as long-range directions, are given as follows:

Content Goals

Achievement of Communication Skills
Achievement of Computation Skills
Attainment of Proficiency in Critical and Objective Thinking
Acquisition of Occupational Competence
Clear Perception of Nature and Environment
Development of Economic Understanding
Acceptance of Responsibility for Citizenship

Process Goals

Knowledge of Self
Appreciation of Others
Ability to Adjust to Change
Respect for Law and Authority
Clarification of Values
Appreciation of the Achievements of Man (13)

These goals almost seem to have been tucked into the body of the manuscript as an afterthought, repeating, as they do, generalizations common for at least fifty years. Even as defined in the report, the goals seem to have been conceived with little thought to the recommendations and vice versa. For example, the goal, development of economic understanding, seems to be reasonable and is defined clearly in the report. However, none of the thirty-two recommendations relates directly to economic understanding. Surely, the need for reform in this area is at least as great as the need in occupational competence. Yet, three of the recommendations concern the need for career opportunities, career education, and job placement, all of which relate to the goal of occupational competence. The text lays great stress on school security, terming the situation critical and giving an entire chapter to the crisis. Additional remarks on the high schools in crisis appear in the introductory pages. However, as a goal, a platitude about respect for law and authority is offered. If the situation is as critical as the report suggests, perhaps even a long-range goal related to it should be stated more specifically.

The report as a whole, however, is an important document and succeeds in doing what all the others have done, namely, to focus the attention of educators and the public upon the purposes of the secondary school. It also suggests the need to provide courses and programs to achieve those aims, and it clarifies the issues confronting those whose task it is to implement such programs.

The Kettering Report was followed in 1976 by a semiofficial report of a national panel on secondary education which suggests strongly that the comprehensive high school cannot achieve all of the goals set for it. (14) Appearing as a logical extension of concepts of career education, the report calls for the high school to be reestablished as an intellectual institution. Comprehensive opportunity would be provided by the school in cooperation with other community agencies, public and private. Actual time spent in school would be reduced but educational and work experiences in other settings would be expanded. The report calls for federal funding to implement its numerous recommendations.

None of the reports cited here was intended to provide final answers nor to cement general goals in place for all time. They were intended only to stimulate thought about the purposes of education and to indicate the kind of school that could result from the acceptance of particular kinds of objectives. As noted at the beginning of this chapter, general national goals are necessary to establish directions and commitments. They do not substitute for action. They hardly resemble instructional objectives. National goals for schools relate to instructional objectives in the same way that national goals for transportation relate to the day-to-day travel of the urban commuter. One group talks and writes about the need for such things as better mass transportation, more limited access highways, the need to conserve energy, plans for car-pooling, alternatives to the internal combustion engine, decentralization of industry, and other general possibilities. The other group faces reality and adjusts to the bus, train, or subway schedule, adapts to the dimensions of the automobile, motorcycle, or bicycle, or walks.

The Hierarchy of Educational Outcomes

Descriptions of educational outcomes range from general to specific as they move from those recommended by national sources, through statements of philosophy adopted by state and local school systems, and on to instructional outcomes planned by teachers. For the most part, state level plans, designs, and statements, set forth as goals, merely repeat or paraphrase such sources as those previously cited in this chapter with, however, the limitations and reservations made necessary by particular state needs and resources. School aims are necessarily derived from and somewhat more specific than those set forth at the school system and state levels. And, it follows that even the general objectives for a given course of study should be more specifically stated than the philosophy of education adopted for a whole school.

Thus, the single word *health* may suffice as a national goal for education. However, the word must be subjected to increasing definition as it is perceived relevant by state departments of education, local school boards, and eventually, school faculties. Ultimately, individual teachers must decide what specific facts, concepts, skills, attitudes, appreciations, and behaviors, derived from an analysis of health are appropriate to their courses and to their students.

As we turn to consideration of instructional objectives, it is pertinent to mention that all national goals are not equally applicable to all subjects and to all teachers. Consideration of the probable content derived from analysis of health as a goal, for example, suggests direct applications to such fields as physical and health education, home economics, and biology. More general, but still proper topics for study, may be perceived in the social sciences. However, it strains the imagination to find subject matter and valid learning activities related to health in such subjects as algebra and typewriting. This says only that one studies anything in order to attain what is logically and psychologically related to the given field.

Thus, a fundamental task facing teachers in each subject field is to decide which of the many alternative general goals suggested for secondary education are applicable to the field under consideration. Beyond this, as teachers work at departmental and individual levels, is the task of formulating objectives derivable from analysis of the content of particular subject areas and specific courses of study.

Toward Specificity in Stating Instructional Objectives

The key issue in formulating objectives for classroom use has always been the need for teachers to state their objectives in specific, definitive terms rather than as generalizations, usually in infinitive form. Until the 1930s it was commonly assumed that an objective, even one designed for teacher use, represented something to be attained. Hence, it seemed natural for objectives to start with the word *To*. Objectives, even those appearing as models in textbooks on teaching, appeared typically as follows:

To develop appreciation for good design.
To encourage creative thought.
To develop understandings of the culture of Brazil.
To teach the major classifications of plants.
To understand the principles of good citizenship in a democracy.
To understand the development of the United States as a world power.
To understand the hazards of habit-forming drugs.
To review the fundamentals of algebra.
To understand terms in poetry.

During the late 1930s and in increasing numbers during the 1940s and 1950s, educators pointed out that such infinitive statements furnish few, if any, clues as to what is actually taught and learned. The illustrations above, for example, do not suggest what is meant by such words and phrases as *appreciation, good design, creative, culture, major classifications, democracy, good citizenship, world power, hazards, fundamentals,* and *terms.* Infinitive phrases make agreeable-sounding generalizations but do not indicate what is taught or learned, do not illustrate the teacher's mastery of subject matter, and do not suggest appropriate learning activities. That which two teachers plan for learning about the development of the United States as a world power could lead to entirely different results because of differing content, methods, resources, and possibly even differing attitudes of the teachers toward the concept, world power. The objective, as stated, is meaningless as a guide to curriculum content and classroom method. The real curriculum is masked and hidden behind infinitive phrases rather than brought into the open for examination.

Although infinitively stated objectives still appear in teacher's guides and textbooks on education, the prevailing expectation for instructional objectives is that they be stated in complete, declarative sentences. The use of sentences does not guarantee specificity, but allows for it, which is much more difficult with the infinitive. Sentences permit the teacher to demonstrate mastery of content. The objective is stated as something already attained and not as something dimly perceived, *to be* attained. Sentences may more accurately identify content and method. And, finally, sentences translate directly into objective means of measurement.

Two factors, among others, contributed directly toward the evolution of the instructional objective in specific, declaratively stated form. As implied above, the first was the increasing use of objective tests and measures by classroom teachers. The content of the objective examination certainly reflects the real curricular objectives of the course of study in which it is given. If not, the test should be rephrased because the teacher's obligation is to measure for the attainment of stated objectives. Objectively stated purposes correlate easily with objectively organized examinations. As soon as teachers perceived that the first step in evaluation is the formulation of specifically worded objectives, use of the infinitive became a useless exercise.

The second major factor toward specificity was the emergence of various forms of unit plans for teaching and learning proposed by leading educational writers. With variations in form and style, the unit plan is a written plan for integrating subject matter, teaching and learning activities, learning resources, and methods of evaluation. The unit is built typically around a logical block of subject matter but psychologically constructed in terms of the abilities and needs of students, community and school resources, and the strengths of the teacher. As a minimum, all unit variations require: statements of general and specific objectives for the unit; a listing of individual and group activities for students, both required and optional; and, a means of evaluation, typically one or more achievement tests. Additional paraphernalia sometimes include statements of indirect, but probable learning outcomes, course outlines, study guides, lists of references and other resources, and daily plans in one form or another. (15)

The emphasis given to the delimitation of objectives by exponents of unit teaching produced large number of teachers who are fully capable of writing explicit, clear, measurable and understandable objectives for their courses. Even as we turn to consideration of more recent developments, it is well to remember the continuing presence in the schools of many teachers and administrators who are highly skilled in the task of formulating specific objectives for their own schools and classes. It is well to keep in mind, also, that the key issue in preparing instructional objectives continues to center on *generality versus specificity*. Those who forget this are apt to become mired in terminology and to fill their files with beautifully classified statements of objectives which bear little or no relationship to classroom work. Phrasing objectives is part of planning for teaching. It is not the act of teaching.

Behavioral Objectives: Performance

To the degree that the purpose of instruction is to modify behavior, it is logical to expect students to be able to do something following a meaningful period of instruction that they could not do before. Any outcome involving *doing, performing,* and *demonstrating* is a behavioral objective. For years teachers in such areas as physical education, industrial arts and vocational education, business education, and in some aspects of the physical sciences, have defined objectives behaviorally, whether or not such objectives were so labelled. The ability to type forty words a minute without error is a behavioral objective. So is the ability to run fifty yards in six seconds and such physical skills as are necessary to bake a cake, repair a two-cycle engine, hit a golf ball, drive an automobile, dance the polka, use a microscope, and perform an experiment in the chemistry laboratory. Analysis of course content and formulation of objectives in terms of performance expectations is a reasonable and long-standing aspect of planning by teachers in many subject areas. (16)

We run into difficulty when we attempt to apply behavioral terms to all educative experience, because to do so is to ignore that which is not implied by the phrase, *to do.* This includes values and value systems and includes whatever is suggested by such words as ideals, appreciations, and attitudes. Unless one assumes that knowing and behaving are the same process, much of knowledge is excluded from behavioral analysis. The behavioral objectivist assumes that all the outcomes of instruction can be defined in behavior change and that outcomes so defined can be observed and measured with standardized precision. This assumption is true only to the degree that doing constitutes a logical and psychological objective to the course of study. Whenever knowing, understanding, believing, valuing, and appreciating enter into consideration of outcomes, it is illusory to believe that outcomes phrased in terms of doing are meaningful. To effect meaningful change in human behavior is a long-range process that involves all the resources of society including those of the school. During this process, the work of every teacher may include the formulation of objectives directly related to immediate performance. This is especially true where fundamental intellectual processes need to be mastered and demonstrated and where physical, motor, and mechanical skills are demanded.

The effort to persuade teachers to define all objectives behaviorally has resulted in the ludicrous practice of heading several pages of undefined material with the statement, "The student will . . . " as though, by so doing, the material will automatically be converted to student behavior. The student will consider information contained on nutrition labels. The student will recognize basic health practices used in the preparation of food. The student will demonstrate understanding of the concept of area. Such statements flood educational literature and they are no improvement over the infinitive statement. How much better it would be if the people who phrase these pseudobehavioral statements would take the time to describe the information contained on nutrition labels, to identify basic health practices, and to define area. Then, and only then, we might be assured that they, as teachers, have a solid grasp of the specific outcomes they project for students. (17)

On the other hand, well-stated behavioral objectives do tend to be specific and measurable. Where they are applicable, behavioral objectives can describe expected outcomes in a clear, understandable and precise manner. Such objectives can be stated in terms of particular students, can suggest the conditions for teaching and learning, and can indicate the degree or level of attainment that is expected before advancing to new or more difficult material. All of these characteristics are desirable, regardless of the form of the objective.

Ultimately, as is discussed in chapter fourteen, the so-called *behavioral* outcome should be identified as a *performance/operational* objective. Criteria set on performance expectations, after all, are part of every course of study regardless of its nature or grade level. Expectations set in terms of performance are less likely to be identified with the emotional, almost political, atmosphere that has been associated with discussions of behavioral change. Performance, also, as a reasonable expectation in all courses of study, is less likely to be automatically identified with all of the far-reaching tenets of the school of behavioral psychology. (18)

Criteria for Evaluating Instructional Objectives

The previous discussion has suggested a number of criteria for evaluating instructional objectives. Among the more important are these. (19)

Instructional Objectives Should:

1. *Be measurable.* Measurability implies the avoidance of infinitive phrases and dependent clauses. As much as possible the specific instructional objective should be written in complete, declarative sentences. The means of evaluation is implied by the objective.
2. *Indicate that the teacher understands what he expects students to learn.* Basic vocabulary words are identified. Definitions are thought through. Terms and concepts are analyzed.
3. *Be achievable.* The statement of objectives is not so far reaching or inclusive that achievability is doubtful. Reasonable limits for the achievement of most students has been defined.

4. *Be appropriate to the students and the course of study.* Attention has been given to the needs of students and to their age-grade-experience levels. Students are ready for the work to be done. The objective represents material that is normally perceived as part of the course of study. General objectives set forth for all of education are not merely repeated.

5. *Suggest probably learning activities.* Whether stated in terms of knowing, understanding, demonstrating, showing, using, comparing, computing, reading, stating, describing, or any other of the words commonly affixed to statements of objectives, the objective suggests probable learning activities. If the objective is well stated, the appropriate learning activity follows.

6. *Be expressed in performance or other terms as determined appropriate by the teacher.* This means that the teachers and or curriculum workers who work at the cutting edge of curriculum planning are able to judge how objectives should be stated. The profession does not need a class of educational planners to formulate objectives for teachers. Teachers need to formulate their own instructional objectives or to find them in published materials prepared expressly for use by students.

Objectives that meet these criteria are neither difficult to write nor to locate in published sources. Those illustrated below, although presented under a variety of titles, represent well thought through instructional outcomes.

Illustrative Instructional Objectives

A. From a course in business law

Terminal Objectives

1. Given the following list, the student will be able to explain these terms correctly:
   a. Constitutional law
   b. Statutory law
   c. Common law
   d. Case law
   e. Administrative law.

2. Given a set of samples of contracts and noncontracts, the student will be able to identify correctly the samples that are legal con-

tracts and be able to tell why the remaining samples are not legal contracts.

3. From a list of legal terms, the student will be able to define and interpret correctly in writing, a minimum of 80 percent of the list. (20)

B. From a course in English

Key Ideas

a. The verb *set,* meaning *to put or place something,* requires an object, except when used in connection with the sun, the moon, or a setting hen.

b. The verb *sit,* meaning *to rest,* requires no object.

c. The verb *lay,* meaning *to put or place something,* requires an object.

d. The verb *lie,* meaning *to rest,* requires no object.

Behavioral Outcomes

As the pupil studies this lesson, he may be expected to develop behavioral traits such as these.

a. Uses *set* or *lay* when he means *to put or place something.*

b. Uses *sit* or *lie* when he means *to rest.* (21)

C. From a social studies course

Objective

The child will demonstrate his ability to distinguish between fact and opinion statements by correctly categorizing a given set of statements.

Items

a. King Francis I of France was bold and fun loving.

b. One of the reasons the French came to the New World was for adventure.

c. Champlain traveled to the Caribbean and Mexico as well as America.

d. The Algonkian Indians were a very friendly tribe.

e. The most important reason for French settlements in America was the rich fur trade.

    f. New France was sparsely populated.

    g. The Company of New France was organized to trade and colonize in America.

    h. The French were better colonists than the English. (22)

    Note: The above items are from eighteen pages of sets of similar items, all intended to measure for the stated objective. Also included are directions for each set of items and reading sources suggested for students.

D. From a source in literature

    Insights to Be Gained

As the students read this cluster, they will discover that:

1. Each of the main characters creates an image for other people that is different from what he or she really is.

2. Some of the characters are "forced" by circumstances to become something else; others create a public image to fulfill a personal need; still others do it for sheer enjoyment.

3. The creation of a "false front" can produce problems as well as satisfactions.

4. Some of the selections are realistic; others are not. But in all cases, the authors are successful in achieving the effects they wish. (23)

    Note: The above insights represent objectives to be achieved by students as a result of reading and studying a cluster of four literary selections. Study questions, suggested procedures, related language study, and recommended related activities in such areas as art, writing, and discussion are built into the complete plan for teaching the cluster.

    As models for instructional objectives, the examples given are infinitely better than the vague generalizations frequently set forth as teaching objectives. Whether stated behaviorally or as concepts, insights, understandings, key ideas, and similar terms, such objectives are measurable, appropriate, achievable, suggest the probable learning activities, and indicate that the teacher understands what the students are to learn.

    The criterion of measurability, of course, suggests that relatively hard-to-measure outcomes identified with such words as ideals, attitudes, and appreciations are not defined as objectives within the context of the present discussion. This is true. However, as previously emphasized, such values are extremely important and should not be overlooked. It is suggested that instructional objectives be supplemented with descriptive statements identifying such long-range outcomes for courses or for units within courses. Among the headings which might be used to identify these outcomes are general objectives, indirect objectives, goals, specific terms such as attitudes, appreciations, and so on; or, in the terminology of the following section, *affective objectives.*

Taxonomies of Objectives

The classification of educational objectives into standard categories ranging from simple to complex results in a *taxonomy of objectives* similar to that in biology in which biological knowledge is logically organized. The first published work in this area appeared in 1956 as the *Taxonomy of Educational Objectives, Handbook I: Cognitive Domain.* (24) The second taxonomy was published in 1964 as *Handbook II: Affective Domain.* (25) The third, *A Taxonomy of the Psychomotor Domain,* (26) came out in 1972. The taxonomies are not difficult to understand, provided that the terminology is mastered.

The *cognitive domain* includes knowing facts, recalling knowledge, generalizing, and applying generalizations. As such, it includes thinking, problem-solving, and creating. These are the things that occupy most of the time of teachers and students. Well-stated cognitive objectives are understandable, measurable, and derivable from analysis of subject content. Probably nine-tenths of the instructional objectives ever written by teachers could be classified as cognitive.

The *affective domain* includes objectives implied by such words as attitudes, ideals, values, and appreciations. Such objectives are difficult to measure and normally perceived as important long-range outcomes rather than as specific objects of instruction. Curriculum workers and teachers should be able to state and describe probable course outcomes in terms of values and corollary judgments, but they can seldom be certain that the values identified actually were achieved. Written tests are inadequate as measures of such a quality as "appreciation." And, although behavior may provide some clues, it would be naive to assume that *good* behavior, e.g., that which is cooperative, responsive, and attentive may mean more than driving desire for high marks, compulsion to be first in achievement, or willingness to acquiesce in order to achieve some goal entirely apart from school matters. Naturally, teachers prefer sportsmanlike, friendly, cooperative behavior among students. However, such behavior is not direct evidence that particular ideals, attitudes, values, and appreciations have been accepted.

Even so, values are important long-range goals of education. Hence, the effort to classify objectives within this realm is at least as valid as the effort to classify cognitive goals.

The *psychomotor domain* involves objectives which require movement. This includes muscular and motor skills and manipulations of materials and objects. The taxonomy includes six levels of psychomotor behavior, ranging in complexity from simple reflex movements to forms of nonverbal communication.

For brevity, the entire continuum of subcategories is not reproduced here. The major classification levels in each domain are:

Cognitive (Knowledge)

1.00 Knowledge (Intellectual Abilities and Skills)
2.00 Comprehension
3.00 Application
4.00 Analysis
5.00 Synthesis
6.00 Evaluation (27)

Affective

1.00 Receiving (Attending)
2.00 Responding
3.00 Valuing
4.00 Organization
5.00 Characterization by a value or value complex (28)

Psychomotor

1.00 Reflex movements
2.00 Basic fundamental movements
3.00 Perceptual abilities
4.00 Physical abilities
5.00 Skilled movements
6.00 Nondiscoursive communication (29)

Remember, the taxonomies are no more than attempts to classify categories of objectives into levels of difficulty from simple to complex. As such, they may assist teachers and curriculum workers to agree upon the essential facts, concepts, skills, and resulting attitudes, appreciations, and other values that derive from analysis of course content. The taxonomies provide standard meanings for terminology in this area, thus allowing for more effective communication among those concerned with curriculum development. The classifications suggest types of objectives that might be overlooked if not recalled to attention. Movement analyses falling within the psychomotor domain suggest objectives and consequent learning activities in English, foreign languages, and the social studies, particularly for oral and group activity, that might be forgotten as teachers in these areas concentrate on cognitive matters. Intellectual abilities are as important in so-called skill subjects as they are in any other. Indeed, knowledge is basic to any advanced skill. Finally, the very arrangement of the classifications, simple to complex, suggests the sort of arrangement that should prevail for unit and topical statements of objectives and correlating learning activities.

The separate taxonomies do not suggest that sets of instructional objectives fall exclusively within one or another of the domains. The interrelatedness of all categories of objectives is obvious. Objectives for any fully developed plan for teaching include cognitive, affective, and psychomotor outcomes as they are perceived to be appropriate by the teacher.

Furthermore, the taxonomies are not handbooks on how to write instructional objectives. Even a cursory examination of illustrative objectives in the three volumes reveals many that are, themselves, so in need of definition that they are totally useless as models. They serve only as guides to the establishment of objectives. This comment merely recognizes that the concern of the editors and authors was with the classification scheme and not with the task of phrasing specific instructional objectives.

Summary

Objectives are needed in order to identify expected outcomes, to suggest directions, and to determine means of evaluation. Goals recommended for national and state purposes may be very general in nature because such goals represent ideals and expectations toward which the nation continuously strives. Instructional objectives must be specifically stated because they represent outcomes already achieved by the teacher and set forth as objects of instruction for the student.

Numerous statements of national purpose in education and secondary education have appeared during this century starting with the tradition-breaking *Cardinal Principles* in 1918. For the most part, these statements have expanded the purposes of secondary education. Those contributing to this expansion include *The Purposes of Education in American Democracy,* 1938; the *Ten Imperative Needs of Youth,* 1944; the *Report of the White House Conference on Education,* 1956; and the *Kettering Report,* 1973. From time to time, more specialized recommendations have appeared, such as the call for *Life Adjustment* education in 1948 and arguments for renewed emphasis on college-preparatory and or intellectual curricula typified by the *Harvard Report* in 1952, the *Rockefeller Report,* 1958, and the *Martin Panel Report,* 1976.

Throughout the years, the key issue has been how to translate the general goals of education into understandable instructional objectives. This cannot be done by repeating all the general goals for all courses of study. It can only be accomplished by applying appropriate general goals to specific, appropriate areas, and by analysis of academic content followed by formulation of content-related objectives in terms of the aptitudes, abilities, and needs of students. The trend toward more specific delimitation of instructional objectives was furthered during the 1940s by the widespread adoption of objective tests and measures and by by the emphasis placed on definition of objectives by proponents of unit teaching.

More recent efforts to classify educational objectives by type, e.g., cognitive objectives (knowledge and intellectual abilities), affective objectives (value), and psychomotor objectives (movement), have provided useful tools for those studying the nature of objectives. However, they have not provided models for those who must write instructional objectives.

Performance objectives, centering on what the student is to be able to do, to demonstrate, to perform, or to practice, are, for the most part, specific and measurable. However, attempts to apply behavioral terms to all educative experience omit outcomes that cannot be observed and measured with standard precision. Hence, the practice of heading statements of objectives with such phrases as "The student will . . . " is, at best, a waste of time and, at worse, a departure from other, more central goals of instruction.

In the final analysis, the key issue remains one of generality versus specificity. Instructional objectives should be stated as specifically as possible and, to that end, should be measurable, achievable, appropriate to the students and to the course of study, and expressed in performance or other terms as determined appropriate by the teacher. Objectives which meet these criteria will suggest probable learning activities and indicate the teacher's grasp of that which students are expected to learn.

CHAPTER REFERENCES

1. National Education Association, Commission on the Reorganization of Secondary Education, *The Cardinal Principles of Secondary Education* (Washington, D.C.: U.S. Office of Education, Bulletin 35, 1918).

2. National Education Association, *Report of the Committee on Secondary-School Studies* (Washington, D.C.: U.S. Government Printing Office, 1893).

3. Harold G. Shane, "The Seven Cardinal Principles Revisited," A Bicentennial Project, *Today's Education* 65, no. 3 (September-October 1976): 57-72.

4. Educational Policies Commission, National Education Association and American Association of School Administrators, *The Purposes of Education in American Democracy* (Washington, D.C.: National Education Association, 1938).

5. Educational Policies Commission, National Education Association, *Education for All American Youth* (Washington, D.C.: National Education Association, 1944).

6. Ibid., pp. 225-26.

7. The Commission on Life Adjustment for Youth, *Life Adjustment Education for Every Youth* (Washington, D.C.: U.S. Office of Education, Bulletin 22, 1951). (Issued in offset print in 1948 with the same title and published in mimeographed form in 1947 with the title *Every Youth in High School—Life Adjustment for Each.*)

8. Ibid., p. 9.

9. A Committee Report, *General Education in School and College* (Cambridge, Massachusetts: Harvard University Press, 1952).

10. Committee for the White House Conference on Education, *A Report to the President* (Washington, D.C.: U.S. Government Printing Office, April 6, 1956), pp. 11-12.

11. Special Studies Report V, *The Pursuit of Excellence: Education and the Future of America,* Rockefeller Brothers Fund (Garden City, N.Y.: Doubleday & Co., 1958).

12. B. Frank Brown, Chairman, The National Commission on the Reform of Secondary Education, Charles F. Kettering Foundation, *The Reform of Secondary Education* (New York: McGraw-Hill, 1973).

13. Ibid., pp. 32-34.

14. John Henry Martin, Chairman, National Panel of High School and Adolescent Education, *The Education of Adolescents* (Washington, D.C.: U.S. Department of Health, Education, and Welfare, 1976).

15. For a description of unit teaching, see Leonard H. Clark and Irving S. Starr, *Secondary School Teaching Methods,* 3rd ed. (New York: Macmillan, 1976), Chapter 6, "Planning Courses and Units."

16. As an example of an early argument for objectives stated in terms of behavior, see William L. Wrinkle, *Improving Marking and Reporting Practices* (New York: Rinehart and Co., 1947), Chapter 10, "How Should Objectives Be Stated?"

17. For a critical analysis of behavioral objectives, see David N. Campbell, "Behavioral Objectives—The Grande Charade," *Today's Education* 65, no. 2 (March-April 1976): 43-44.

18. See Chapter Fourteen, "The Translation of an Educational Goal into a Performance Objective."

19. Developed from criteria illustrated in Frank L. Steeves, *Fundamentals of Teaching in the Secondary School* (New York: Odyssey Press, 1962), p. 95.

20. *A Handbook for Business Education in Iowa,* The Iowa Business Education Association and the State Department of Public Instruction (Des Moines, Iowa: Department of Public Instruction, 1972), p. 113.

21. Harold G. Shane et al., *English 6: Language, Linguistics, Composition,* Teachers' Edition (River Forest, Illinois: Laidlaw Brothers, 1967), p. T270. Reprinted by permission of Laidlaw Brothers, A Division of Doubleday & Company, Inc.

22. Les Brown, ed., *Secondary School Social Studies: Evaluation for Individualized Instruction,* rev. ed. (Downers Grove, Illinois: Public School District 99, January 1972), pp. 35-36.

23. Leland B. Jacobs and Shelton L. Root, Jr., *Teacher's Handbook for Ideas in Literature,* Book 3, *Dimensions* (Columbus, Ohio: Charles E. Merrill Publishing Co., 1966), p. 21.

24. Benjamin S. Bloom, *Taxonomy of Educational Objectives, Handbook I: Cognitive Domain* (New York: David McKay Co., 1956).

25. David R. Krathwohl, Benjamin S. Bloom, and Bertram B. Masia, *Taxonomy of Educational Objectives, Handbook II: Affective Domain* (New York: David McKay Co., 1964).

26. Anita J. Harrow, *A Taxonomy of the Psychomotor Domain* (New York: David McKay Co., 1972).

27. Bloom, *Cognitive Domain,* pp. 201-07.

28. Krathwohl, Bloom, and Masia, *Affective Domain,* pp. 176-84.

29. Harrow, *Psychomotor Domain,* p. 32.

FOR FURTHER READING

Atkyn, J. Myron. "Behavioral Objectives in Curriculum Design: A Cautionary Note." *The Science Teacher* 35 (May 1968): 27-50.

Billett, Roy O. *Improving the Secondary-School Curriculum.* New York: Atherton Press, 1970. See Chapter Two, "The Secondary School Curriculum: Objectives, Values, and Value Systems."

Conant, James B. *The American High School Today.* New York: McGraw-Hill, 1959.

Davies, Ivor K. *Objectives in Curriculum Design.* London, England: McGraw-Hill Book Company (UK) Limited, 1976.

Gagne, Robert N. "Behavioral Objectives? Yes!" *Educational Leadership* 29 (February 1972): 394-98.

Kneller, George G. "Behavioral Objectives? No!" *Educational Leadership* 29 (February 1972): 397-400.

Krathwohl, David P. "Stating Objectives Appropriately for Programs, for Curriculum, and for Instructional Materials Development." *Journal of Teacher Education* 16 (March 1965): 83-89.

Mager, Robert F. *Preparing Instructional Objectives.* Palo Alto, California: Fearon Publishers, 1962.

——————. *Goal Analysis.* Palo Alto, California: Fearon Publishers, 1972.

——————. *Analyzing Performance Problems.* Palo Alto, California: Fearon Publishers, 1972.

Lange, Phil C., ed. *Programed Instruction.* The Sixty-sixth Yearbook of the National Society for the Study of Education. Chicago: University of Chicago Press, 1967.

Popham, W. James, and Baker, Eval L. *Systematic Instruction.* Englewood Cliffs, N.J.: Prentice- Hall, 1970.

PROLOGUE:

*Skills for
Survival*

II Evolution
and Reform
in Subject
Areas

It is no secret that subject matter organization is central to the curriculum of American secondary education, especially during the senior high school grades. This was fundamental to the establishment of the high school as an educational institution in the United States. It is true today. It will be true tomorrow.

The commitment to subject organization is reflected in the administrative structure of secondary schools, where teachers are grouped into departments, each with its own chairperson, schedule, laboratories, classrooms, and resources. School buildings are designed to accommodate the particular needs of the subjects to be taught, and a walk through the corridors of any junior or senior high school reveals areas designed specifically for learning one subject or another. Language and science laboratories, business education areas, gymnasiums, art and music facilities, vocational wings, swimming pools, athletic fields, and areas designed for homemaking, are all examples of architectural and educational testimony to the subject as the basic resource for teaching and learning. Books and materials in school libraries and teaching resources centers are classified and filed by subject. Teachers, themselves, are certified to teach only if their college level work includes large blocks of specified subject matter. And, once employed, teachers read journals published in their own subjects, and they affiliate with national associations dedicated to better teaching in these subjects.

At the same time, it is obvious that acquisition of subject matter is not the uppermost goal in the minds of most students. Nor, indeed, is imparting subject matter the sole responsibility of the secondary school. Persistently, from the time of Johann Pestalozzi, eighteenth century Swiss education reformer, to the present, educational writers have emphasized the need for individualized instruction, for curricula based on the needs of students, and for due regard to such matters as social development, adjustment to life, to democratic processes, and to societal needs. None of these things can be ignored by those who teach in and administer schools. Goals broader than the transmittal of subject matter are accepted by the American people and are subscribed to by most students of education. Consequently, the total curriculum of the school is now perceived to include structures for guidance and counseling, support for student organizations, processes for individualized instruction, and such developments as various plans for integrated course offerings, independent study, modular scheduling, open plan schools, and team teaching. All of these, one way or another, resulted from the acceptance of goals for secondary education set beyond the content of formal courses of study.

Certainly, also, following the elementary school years, it is very difficult to identify courses of study which are essential to the future well being of all students. For example, all students do not need to study French, or chemistry, automobile mechanics, or commercial law. It might be argued that all citizens should have an understanding of what these and other major fields involve. Some knowledge of chemistry might be useful to all of us, if only because of the medications we take and the mass-produced food that we consume. Auto mechanics is not appropriate for everyone for vocational purposes, but as drivers and owners of automobiles, some understanding of the vehicle might make life easier, and less expensive, for most people.

Even though subject matter is and must be at the heart of the secondary school curriculum, the same subject matter cannot be prescribed for all students. Even within given subjects such as English, content must be differentiated to meet very real and very apparent individual needs. All students do not need to study Milton's poetry. Many citizens lead good and useful lives with no concrete knowledge of John Milton, his poetry, his life, or his times. However, it is crucial to remember that, for others, the study of Milton is essential to happiness, well being, and productivity as human beings at the levels of their personal understanding. For a few, penetrating knowledge of Milton and his writings may become an occupational and or intellectual necessity. The same comments could be made about secondary school studies as diverse as instrumental music, Latin, physics, business organization, or mathematics.

The principle involved is long standing and in the forefront of current argument about reform in secondary education. Can the secondary school preserve its academic function and, concurrently, meet the needs of its individual constituents and of society in general? The answer is that the school must do so. Regardless of alternatives to the formal structure for education, the core of any nation's educational process must be that structure. In the United States this means a system of secondary schools based upon assumptions involving multiple goals, diversity, independence, and individualization.

This does not mean dilution of subject matter as the fundamental vehicle for learning in secondary education. Far from it. Knowledge of mathematics contributed to the development of all the nations and empires in human history and, as a discipline, has survived although many of the political structures have disappeared. Mathematics will be mastered by its citizens or any nation will disappear. Other studies, for example, biology, may prove to be equally enduring as the history of the race proceeds into the future. The curricular problem focuses as it always has on the questions of what level of mathematics or biology, for whom, at what time, for what reasons, and in what ways.

Nothing more is called for than the shift of emphasis highlighted by all leading American educators of this century. Blocks of subject matter are not fixed in place eternally, to be mastered regardless of individual desire, talent, or need. Subject matter must be deliberately organized to meet the needs of those who study in school. Otherwise, the needs of society will be served badly.

Neither do these observations imply that course-of-study manipulation is any certain road to curriculum improvement, especially where such manipulation ignores the psychological readiness of students to assimilate the material. Financed by federal and foundation sources during the 1950s and 1960s in such subjects as biology, physics, mathematics, English, and geography, widely publicized course-of-study revisions have produced doubtful long-range improvement.

What needs to be recognized is that although course revision is no panacea for curriculum ills, neither is retention of present course structures without revision or, worse, going through the motions of teaching and learning without much of either taking place.

The task of organizing subject matter into courses of study as indicated herein must be faced by all educators and implemented primarily by those identified as subject matter specialists. It is with this task in mind that we approach the chapters centered on evolution and reform in each of the major subject areas. The issues confronting those who teach in these areas and those who administer the schools provide ample challenge. Reform in secondary education, where truly needed, will be accomplished when that challenge is met.

4 Traditional
Academic
Subjects

Traditional and Fundamental

The traditional academic subjects of English, mathematics, science, social studies, and foreign languages became so because of their central role in preparation for college. Universities established entrance requirements set in terms of expectations in each of these major subject divisions. High schools made certain that students bound for college completed the expected courses, even to the point of meeting the admissions requirements of specific colleges. Thus, for many years college expectations influenced and shaped the secondary school program of studies.

This was not unreasonable in 1900 when all or nearly all high school graduates planned to enter college, and when the high school existed primarily for purposes of college preparation. Even well into the century the college-bound constituted a significant segment of the high school student population, and the curricular patterns set for this group dominated high school programs. Realistically, of course, one of the functions of the high school is to prepare for college. Therefore, college entrance requirements continue to exert a force upon the subject selections of many high school students.

However, the total secondary school program of studies continued to expand throughout the century. Vocational programs, including home economics, were established to meet the needs of students who did not perceive college in their future. Business and commercial programs, traceable to the earliest years of the nation, expanded rapidly during the depression years of the 1930s when sales and distributive occupations became important to the well-being of society. Physical education became an established requirement in all the states. New courses and programs such as driver education were thrust upon the schools.

One result of curricular expansion was that more attention was given to needs which all youth share in common. Junior high schools, especially, were organized on the assumption that students would participate in exploratory studies deemed to be important for all. Each major subject division became accepted as having a contribution to make to general education. Industrial arts, homemaking, physical education, and the fine arts were, to a degree, built into the programs of students during the early secondary school years. Ultimately, high school programs became more flexible, partly by permitting elective opportunities which had previously been denied. Typewriting, for example, became a respectable skill for college-preparatory students as well as a marketable tool for those entering jobs. Biology came to be recognized as having value for all students and not merely a course of study for those seeking college entrance.

Concurrently, the country built a system of higher public education based upon each state university, the land-grant colleges and universities, and a separate system of public universities that evolved from the several hundred teachers' colleges founded during the first half of the century. Now supplemented with a growing system of two-year community colleges, higher education in the United States offers a variety of opportunities for entrance. No single pattern of high school preparation is necessary in order to get started. What the student takes in high school may still rest with the particular expectations of a specific college, but, more fundamentally, relates to general occupational and career goals accepted by the student. One who attends college in order to learn how to manage hotels does not need the same high school preparation appropriate to someone who hopes to practice dentistry. And, for the majority who do not enter college, the high school itself becomes the institution responsible for both general education and some degree of preparation for work and careers.

Each of the traditional subject areas under consideration in this chapter is fundamental to the general education of all students. Ability to communicate in English is basic for success in any occupation or endeavor undertaken by American citizens. A degree of mathematical skill is as basic to all of the skilled trades as it is for the engineer. All citizens, regardless of career, share responsibility for shaping and re-shaping the society and its institutions. All should be involved with the political process of the republic. All enjoy the benefits of scientific advances and face together the concerns and ethical choices forced by scientific applications in such areas as military weaponry, population control, and food processing. Finally, foreign language, that old standby for entrance to college, perhaps may have a more significant meaning when perceived as a skill needed by more citizens in order to communicate in an increasingly pluralistic culture.

English: A Language

Traditionally, the study of English has been concerned with the various elements of communicating in the language: reading, writing, speaking, and listening.

Reading, for example, is a fundamental skill in and of itself. If reading is not mastered, very little else can be learned efficiently. However, one learns to read for larger purposes. The ability to read leads to the ability to read with comprehension, in order to understand the mass of informational material produced for general consumption in any modern society. The sheer volume of reading matter put before the public also demands that selectivity in choice of reading material be part of the learning process. And, beyond reading as a basic skill, beyond reading for comprehension, and beyond selectivity in reading, lies the entire world of literature and reading for enjoyment, for appreciation, and for more complete understanding of humanity. Thus, courses and experiences built upon reading include both the basic skill as a means of selecting and comprehending contemporary information, and also the literature of the language.

In the same manner, courses and experiences planned to achieve writing, speaking, and listening skills are part of the English program. Writing by students should reflect generally accepted standards of grammatical construction, form, and usage. Speaking and listening skills necessary to meet life's challenges should be part of the equipment of every adult educated through high school.

Primary responsibility for achievement in these areas rests with English departments. This point is emphasized because English teachers, more than teachers in any other area except for the social studies, have been called on to work in correlated, problem-centered, and core-type programs, the objectives of which are separate from the content of English. Hence, English teachers are perennially criticized for the failure of students to achieve reasonable proficiency in English skills. The criticism is unfair if teachers of English have been pushed or assigned to topics that more properly belong in personal and occupational guidance. The criticism is equally unfair if English teachers are not trained properly for the charge given to them.

The preparation of English teachers is a matter of concern if communication in the language as a goal is taken seriously. Most college and university major programs for future teachers of English consist of little more than a year of general composition, a concession to linguistics by way of a course or two, and a very large dose of literature. Consequently, most English departments are not populated with teachers able to deal effectively with reading or with verbal problems. English departments will become effective units for instruction in language communication only when two conditions prevail: When specialists in speech and reading are routinely added to the secondary school staff; and when colleges place more emphasis on reading, speech, and written composition in the academic programs planned for secondary school English teachers.

For the first half of this century the student entering the seventh grade became exposed to a subject called "English" which he was required to take each year through grade eleven. Those in college-preparatory programs were expected to survive the requirement through the twelfth grade. English was scheduled as a daily class and identified simply by grade level as, for example, English 10. Some provision was made to distinguish among course sections at each grade level on the basis of ability or assumed ability. In addition to English designed for college-bound students, courses were established in *commercial* English and *general* English. In all instances, however, the course was required, met daily, and proceeded through sequences of academic topics planned in advance by the teacher, the department, the school system, or established by the sequence of chapters in one or more textbooks.

Content focused on literary selections classed as "good" and generally recommended for school reading and study. Much time was given to the study of grammar and its rules. Some attention was given to written composition. In general, English courses designed for students not going on to college were watered-down versions of work planned for the academically talented.

The work was repetitious through the grades, based on the illusion that the study of formal grammar improves English usage, isolated from work going on in other courses, and unrelated to the real needs of students, either while in school or out. Even the study of literature, presented in terms of the plots, themes, and characters of a few hoary classics, was out of step with literary development and production of the twentieth century. By 1950, many English departments recognizing these deficiencies, were experimenting with correlated English-social studies courses, and devising courses to reflect precepts set forth by proponents of such concepts as life adjustment, common learnings, and integration. For better or worse, what was planned as the core curriculum usually included English teachers along with social studies teachers among the planners. Unfortunately, while such experimental efforts may have been more interesting for students, they provided no evidence of better learning in the subject field. If the elements of English were taught and learned, it was by accident.

Through the 1960s English teachers continued to experiment. Structural linguistics was conceived as a substitute for traditional grammar, a substitution abandoned by many schools within a few years. The terminology of linguistics proved to be baffling and difficult for teachers and students. Worse, it soon became obvious that neither the old nor the new grammars contributed much to the improvement of English usage and style. If anything, linguistics contributed less to understanding in these matters. (1) Learning by *inquiry* and by *discovery* became key words to describe the English program in the 1970s, and a wide variety of elective offerings and minicourses replaced the old, standard full-year offerings. The meaning of *literature* was expanded to include current writings, including science fiction, (2) newspapers, comic strips, and magazines. *Viewing* was added to the elements of reading, writing, speaking and listening as a concern of English teachers, adding film and film making and television analysis and production to English programs. (3)

The transformation of English from the deadening, repetitious, college-oriented program of only a few years past was long overdue. However, concerns with what has resulted continue to be expressed.

The central problem, as ever, is to make certain that the essential content of English, set forth as fundamental skills in reading, writing, speaking, and listening, and their derivatives, are not lost in a hodge-podge of electives and minicourses. (4) A program based upon transitory notions of relevance and student interest may not be as meaningful as one established upon accomplishment and scholarship.

The trend toward elective minicourses scheduled for periods of time from a few weeks to a few months allows students to select work to meet their needs and interests and may be defended on this basis. (5) However, unless students elect such courses, under guidance, with a view to correcting real deficiencies or building upon existing strengths, it is hard to see how the new English program can result in a sequential and cumulative learning experience. At the very least, elective programs in English should be constructed with attention for existing guidelines and suggestions for assessment. (6) (7)

Whatever else may be included, the English language is central to the English curriculum. (8) Related study in arts and humanities, film and television techniques, journalism, and career education should not be allowed to become the central or identifying elements in any program calling itself a program in English. A reading of the titles of courses currently offered in only a few high schools leaves one with the uneasy feeling that anything that can be learned in English has been conceived by someone, somewhere, to be part of the content of English curriculum.

Comprehensive texts in English teaching continue to focus on the content of English and on the processes for dealing with that content. (9) (10) Vigorous argument within the profession about the need for basic instruction in English suggests that all concern for the basic skills is not voiced by critics outside the schools. (11) (12) We are continually reminded that English is a process of communication, a process which includes the ability to express oneself through writing and speaking, the ability to read and listen with comprehension, and the ability to understand and use a linguistic system of grammar and composition. (13)

Perhaps no more needs to be offered here than the reminder that English does have parameters of its own. It was not life adjustment or the whole of common learnings when these things were the current curriculum fads. It is not career education today. The best contribution that English can make to career education is to provide the communications skills necessary for success in careers and in life. If this task is neglected in favor of minicourses on finding jobs and getting along with other people, both English and career education will be badly served.

Other Languages

In 1900 when foreign languages, especially Latin, were required for entrance to nearly every college, languages occupied a central place in the program of studies. The proportion of students taking Latin declined as colleges substituted modern languages for admission, but the shift of emphasis merely moved a higher proportion into modern languages. Total enrollment held steady both in Latin and in such modern languages as French, Spanish, and German. In addition to college-entrance requirements, local efforts to preserve the culture and language of immigrant neighborhoods resulted in the appearance of Hebrew, Italian, Norwegian, Russian, and other languages in the nearby schools. However, no modern languages other than French, Spanish, and German gained status approaching national acceptance, and even these were grounded in regional history. Thus, Spanish evolved from the history of the Southwest and West, French from the history of the Northeast and of Louisiana, and German from the settlement of Wisconsin, Minnesota, and other central states.

When colleges began to drop foreign language requirements for entrance, the popularity of language study diminished. The decline was steady for a half century. Whereas 80 percent of high school pupils were enrolled in a language course in 1900, no more than 20 percent were so enrolled by the early 1950s. Other factors for the trend included the emergence of commercial and vocational programs in which a second language was not perceived necessary. Many children of immigrant parents were not interested in learning the language of the old country. Many sons and daughters of immigrants resented programs designed to preserve foreign identification.

However, even as the proportion of students enrolled in language courses declined, the total number of students taking language, including Latin, increased because of the growing population and the higher percentage of those remaining to complete high school. Further, although colleges no longer required a language for admission, most college-preparatory programs included languages as strongly recommended options.

Unfortunately, even though millions of secondary school students enrolled in foreign languages, few managed to come out of their courses with anything resembling proficiency in using second or third languages. Until at least the 1940s, language study focused on grammar and rules with little or no emphasis on speaking. The process was dull and uninteresting for most students, who looked upon the foreign language as just another hurdle on the way to college. That, of course, is what it was.

National crises have brought about peculiar results in the teaching of foreign languages. For example, German, which was the most popular modern language prior to 1914, nearly disappeared as a result of World War I. Prevailing notions of patriotism held that it was somehow disloyal to learn the language of the enemy. Even during World War II, when military and diplomatic needs in language became obvious, some schools discontinued courses in German and other "enemy" languages.

World War II military sentiment, however, emphasized the need to communicate with members of opposing military forces and to understand the communications of these forces. The global nature of the conflict made the need for communication even more pressing as the armed forces of all the involved nations came into contact with little-known languages and cultures. Whoever could communicate had the advantage. Whoever could not was disadvantaged. The need to learn dozens of both well-known and relatively unknown languages provided a powerful incentive for the military to undertake the teaching of languages.

Turning from the time consuming, indirect, and ineffective method of approaching language by study of grammar, the army concentrated on aural-oral competence as the priority goal. Using a variety of audiovisual aids and native speakers, the army was able to teach languages in from three to nine months. The language skills of the soldier-students surpassed the achievement of those students exposed to the language for up to six years in high school and college. Even though this was intensive full-time study by carefully selected and strongly motivated students, the results were impressive. Following the war, schools moved to implement what had been illustrated by the armed forces.

The language laboratory, built around applications of the tape recorder and individualized opportunity for listening and practice in speaking, was developed as an adjunct to the regular classroom. At the same time, audiolingual methods based on dialogues and practice drills emerged. (14) Listening to taped dialogues became the order of the day in thousands of language laboratories during the 1950s, an activity hardly calculated to arouse the enthusiasm of students. As the crisis of war faded into history, the reasons for learning foreign languages became less urgent. Enrollments continued to decline, this time in total numbers.

Then, in response to Sputnik I, the National Defense Education Act of 1958 authorized the expenditure of more than one billion dollars in federal money and an equal amount of matching funds to improve teaching in science, mathematics, and foreign languages, and to upgrade guidance services. The injection of this huge amount of money, earmarked specifically for particular subject areas, contributed nothing to national defense and little to education. However, it did focus much attention on content and method in the subject areas named and resulted in the acquisition of vast amounts of hardware and remodelled electronic facilities. For a time, during the early 1960s, programs artificially stimulated in the name of national defense cast an illusion of well-being about the programs. The future suggested increasing enrollments and achievement. The history of the intervening years illustrates the opposite, steadily declining enrollments throughout the 1970s and no evidence of better achievement.

The present mood of foreign language specialists and educators about the status of languages is one of crisis and uncertainty. Deeply concerned about declining enrollments since 1970, an editorial called for an effort to make the case for foreign languages with the public. (15) Some 650 respondents to a survey in New York suggested that the decline in enrollments is due directly to the fact that language is no longer mandated for college entrance. The author of a published report interpreting the survey pleads for colleges to reestablish language as an entrance requirement. (16) This is unlikely to happen. Colleges not only do not require foreign languages for entrance, they do not require languages for graduation. Even in colleges of liberal arts, where a language expectation is traditional, substitutions for language are common and proficiency examinations accepted in lieu of formal course work. Through one's doctorate work, substitutions for foreign language are permitted, including such examples as computer language, advanced statistics, and various other research tools and techniques. It would seem that secondary school language study must be justified for reasons more defensible than college requirements.

One studies a foreign language in order to be able to communicate in that language, primarily by speaking, secondarily by reading and writing. Language plurality in American culture is a reality for millions of citizens. Contact with Americans whose native language is one other than English is more and more a reality. Spoken contact with foreigners, either as they visit this country or as Americans travel abroad, is an increasing possibility. As Ziegler points out, language is relevant to the conditions of today. (17)

Language is studied also because it helps to understand humanity, human cultures, and ethnic differences. Cultural reasons for language study are emphasized in educational literature. (18) For example, social problems such as sexism can be found in foreign language textbooks as well as in texts written in English and are equally offensive wherever located. (19)

And, although experts in language argue whether goals for language should be established in such terms as careers, tourism, cooking, artistic and musical interests, hobbies, and the like, perhaps what is actually being argued is not whether some goals are valid and others invalid but, rather, what priorities among goals for language instruction pertain to all students and what priorities pertain to the selected few. Programs built on the needs of students and society do not have to reflect equally important goals. The needs of students for language study vary widely and the needs of society change with the years.

To ask how many years a language should be studied or by whom is like asking how large an apartment should be. The only answer rests with the needs of the occupants. A nine-week exploratory course in a language may be all that some students want, need, or can profit by. Several years of continuous study in high school and college may not be sufficient to meet the needs of someone, for example, preparing to be a teacher of the language. Years of graduate study involving multiple languages may be needed by the serious student of world languages.

Which students should study languages in the secondary school? Here, again, experts differ but the present writers perceive no fundamental differences. True, serious language study is not for everyone as Gaarder argues. (20) Nothing that people learn is for everyone, from playing the flute to quarterbacking the football team. Equally true is Grittner's position that all students can profit to a degree from language study, even from an exploratory course. (21) If foreign language study is as important to human understanding as its proponents maintain, at least this much is due to all students.

The writers suggest that language instruction is well established in American secondary education. Language programs oversold in the name of national defense need not be abandoned just because enrollments stabilize as curriculum balance returns. Language study is needed for more valid reasons.

Exploratory courses in language are needed for all students during the early secondary school years, roughly ages eleven through thirteen, grades six through eight. The purpose of such courses is to help decide the future directions of personal study in language. The methodology should be centered on speaking and listening rather than on grammar and writing. Content should focus upon cultural problems of common concern. (22) (23)

Short courses for particular purposes are needed, both at exploratory and advanced levels. Language teachers should not be afraid to organize minicourses oriented toward culture, careers, student interests such as art, music, cooking, travel, or whatever else seems pertinent. The key to the future of foreign languages in the total school program rests with service and diversity. It is the job of foreign language teachers to meet the challenge. (24)

In all of this it is necessary to keep in mind the special needs of the language-talented student and to maintain the opportunity for advanced individual and group study that this student needs. It might be well to remember that the purpose of all language study is communication and that this purpose has never been achieved by any means other than speaking, listening, reading, and writing. And, if the current call for individualization in language instruction is to take on meaning, take care that such individualization does not take the form of isolated students sitting in lonely booths, working their individual ways through even more canned courses.

And, finally, it would not be amiss if an innovative school here and there broke down the artificial wall of departmentalization separating English from the other languages. Why not a single unit dedicated to the improvement of all language teaching, including English?

The Social Studies

The term *social studies* refers to those courses in secondary education which examine society and social institutions, past and present. Traditionally, in junior and senior high schools, the most common sequence of offerings included physical geography in grade seven, United States history in grade eight, civics in grade nine, world history in grade ten, United States history again in grade eleven, and problems of American democracy in grade twelve. Each of these courses was presented in several sections grouped by academic ability.

Both civics and problems of democracy were organized as courses in the broad field intended to acquaint students at introductory and advanced levels with problems of government. Civics, which during the century gradually supplanted ancient history as the ninth-grade offering, focused on the problems of local government. Although ancient history disappeared as a separate course, its content was retained in the world history course. Problems of democracy touched upon a wide variety of national and international problems where it was actually organized as a course dealing with the nation's problems. However, the course was given frequently as a study of the legislative, executive, and judicial structures of the federal government.

Dominated by history for three of the six years and most often oriented toward government in two of the remaining three, the typical social studies program into the 1960s offered only an exploratory introduction to geography and drew little from such disciplines as anthropology, economics, psychology, and sociology. Obviously, in a world beset by both cold and hot wars, and in a society whose moods ranged from unrest to rebellion, organization of the social studies had to be altered. History and political science, important as both may be to the social studies, do not offer adequate opportunity to study local or national problems when these problems are sociological or economic.

Efforts of social studies educators to devise programs responsive to national, local, and student needs have resulted in offerings reflecting influences from at least three differing viewpoints. First, courses in the formerly college level disciplines of anthropology, economics, psychology, sociology, and political science, have become generally available as electives in grades eleven and twelve. Second, in a move away from the separate disciplines toward problem-centered courses characterized by such words and phrases as *self-discovery, inquiry, conceptual,* and *process,* all essentially the same in practice, an awesome assortment of electives has been devised for all secondary grade levels. Third, and also based on problem-solving, are elective courses using interdisciplinary approaches. Each of these movements, any or all of which may be reflected in the program of a given school, has its proponents and its critics.

Civics and problems of democracy have all but disappeared as separate courses. However, the units formerly included in these offerings are now elective minicourses. As such, students pick and choose from the social studies smorgasbord and may, during the process, fail to attain a balanced social studies diet. The charge is made that the proliferation of short courses in the social studies has made knowledge trivial. (25) Although the diversity of courses was a necessary move from formerly rigid requirements, the result may be a disunity in which the subjects taken have little relationship to each other. (26)

The separate disciplines are defended as capable vehicles for fostering intellectual skills and studying social institutions, qualities lost in elective, fragmented, discovery approaches. (27) At the same time, suggestions are made to avoid overspecialization in secondary education in favor of interdisciplinary, problem-centered courses. (28)

The picture in social studies is not depressing to those who have studied and observed the history of this field. Instead, the variety of social studies programs and courses merely reflects the vitality and challenges of the society which is studied. Anything less would be truly trivial.

History, although no longer the dominant force in the social studies that it once was, is still a potent and frequently required subject. Its presence bolstered by state laws and its place among the social sciences secure, history has both remained and changed. A major influence affecting the teaching of history goes back to demands made by black Americans during the late 1960s for accurate ethnic history. Surely, history was distorted from the points of view of those whose ancestors were Africans, Japanese, Chinese, Native American Indian, Cuban, Mexican, Filipino, or, for that matter, Irish, Italian, Polish, or German. The demand for ethnic study in history and other social studies (29) is no more than a demand for accuracy.

The teaching of history has moved from a straight chronological presentation to counterchronological or theme-centered approaches during which students move back and forth through history as they investigate the same problem at different times. Although it is argued that such approaches may lessen the student's understanding of historical cause and effect (30), they have the advantage of starting where the student is, thus offering a better chance of motivation for wanting to learn history.

Global issues have been brought into the content of history, geography, government, and other courses in the social studies, to help students face the reality of a world of independent nations, each dependent upon others for survival. The need in one nation may be for food; for another, metals; for a third, wood; and for a fourth, oil. In each instance the implication is the same. No nation can stand alone. This is a world of interdependent nations, and the social studies should be taught and learned so as to reflect that fact. (31)

The social studies have changed to reflect general educational argument for more clearly defined objectives (32) and for competency in both cognitive and affective learning. (33) Concept and discovery learning were applied to the social studies because of sound argument for their applicability. (34)

In the final analysis, however, it is social studies teachers themselves who have changed their field from a series of rigid and timeworn requirements to a flexible, fluid, and relevant elective program. This might have been expected because social studies teachers have always been in the forefront of experimentation with such concepts as correlation, the core curriculum, and integrated offerings. Many of the trends noted in the social studies today are no more than extensions and reapplications of earlier ideas that never quite passed away.

The writers suggest that those concerned with the development of the social studies take seriously the possibility that the current movement toward elective minicourses may have resulted in trivial programs for some students. If, indeed, students are electing all their work from a particular viewpoint, for example, black studies; if students are failing to learn that the social studies are derivations of the social sciences; and if students are not learning something about historical cause and effect, attention needs to be given to the problem. The failure of students to find sequential and cumulative programs for learning in the social studies is as crucial here as it is in English. In both instances the failure would be that of the school and not of the student. The remedy is either to reduce the number of electives or to make certain that courses elected do combine into meaningful, coherent, worthwhile patterns for each student.

Science and Mathematics

Science and mathematics, along with the foreign languages, fell heir to the content reform stemming from the National Defense Education Act and extensive foundation support given for change in these areas during the 1960s. Teachers in these fields were also subjected to the catch words of the decade—process, inquiry, individualization, discovery, elective minicourses, and the like. The results have been mixed.

If one looks at the findings of the National Assessment of Educational Progress (NAEP) which, in 1975, reported on mathematics and science achievement between 1969 and 1973, the figures are not discouraging. Achievement levels in biological and physical sciences declined slightly between these years but only by about two percentage points. (35) Although the figures bear watching, this is hardly a trend and probably reflects no more than a return to normalcy after the undue emphasis given to science after Sputnik. The assessment of achievement in mathematics suggested that students age thirteen could compute about as well as adults, and seventeen year-olds even better than that. (36) Despite public criticism of content change in mathematics, the *new* math of the 1960s apparently had no harmful effect on achievement.

On the other hand, after an expenditure of more than a billion dollars for reform in these areas, the results should have been more encouraging. The fact is that neither youth in school nor adults in general have ever demonstrated much ability by way of computation. Neither youth nor the general citizenry have shown much understanding of scientific principles or the ability to apply such principles to daily life. Certainly, by now, more progress should be evident. Turning to what actually has happened in each of these areas again illustrates a mixed pattern of progress and accomplishment, set off against traditional, relatively unchanged programs.

Science

The traditional standard program in science consisted of a sequence of year-long courses including general science, biology, chemistry, and physics, scheduled from grades nine through twelve. Advanced biology was sometimes available as an alternative to chemistry and physics. The program was designed for the college-bound who were expected to take all of the courses with the possible exception of physics. Students not planning to enter college did not continue in science beyond the general, exploratory, ninth-grade course. Even there, they were segregated into sections designed for students of lesser academic ability. How much change has been effected as a result of the massive efforts to reform the science curriculum? Some, one must conclude, but not nearly enough.

Science programs are still designed for students going on to college, and most course sequences still focus on biology, chemistry, and physics. There is little evidence of integration with other subjects and little individualization. (37) Science is not part of the general education of significant numbers of high school students.

However, some progress is evident and some changes stand out, especially for college-preparatory students. Exploratory courses, including general science, appear in the eighth grade, followed by biology, chemistry, physics, and organic chemistry or other advanced electives in the succeeding grades. More science is being covered, and advanced students commonly earn college credit for some work completed while still in high school.

Further, at least three levels of courses ranging from those planned for the academically talented to those designed as *general* or *applied* (38) are found in many schools. At least, this opens the opportunity for elective work in science for noncollege students.

A variety of elective, short courses have been made available from grade seven and beyond, including courses intended for understanding in life science, earth and space science, science values, and science in everyday life. One promising project sponsored by the National Science

Foundation, the Individualized Science Instructional System (ISIS), has been planned to produce minicourses primarily for nonscience oriented students and to provide broader options beyond traditional biology, physics, and chemistry. (39) In progress, the project ultimately will produce year-long courses in the traditional subjects as well as a complete range of short courses for grades seven through twelve.

Calls for emphasis on values in science, especially values related to social problems and human welfare, appear regularly in the journals of science education. (40) (41) As previously noted, science teachers have made efforts to adjust methods to the process, inquiry, and discovery approaches, that cut across subject divisions. In fact, one assessment of recent trends in science (42) presented trends as *emphases,* nearly all of which reflect social and educational priorities outside science. Included were such emphases as using community resources, emphasis upon basic skills, developing reading skill, preparing for accountability, using behavioral objectives, and diagnostic and prescriptive teaching. If, in fact, such phrases describe trends in science teaching, the field is clearly in tune with what is going on in the rest of secondary education.

Mathematics

The traditional sequence of courses in mathematics consisted of algebra or general mathematics in grade nine, Euclidian geometry in grade ten for those who had taken algebra, advanced algebra in grade eleven, and trigonometry and solid geometry in grade twelve. The program was planned to prepare for college, and little mathematics was available for the majority of students. General mathematics led to nothing except for the students who moved into courses in commercial or shop arithmetic.

Although still strongly oriented for college preparation, current mathematics programs may offer as many as four or five course choices at each grade level from the eighth grade through the twelfth. Selections range in difficulty from those designated as accelerated or honors courses to applied, general, or even remedial sections. Algebra-algebra-geometry has replaced the algebra-geometry-algebra sequence and may start as early as grade eight. Precalculus enters grade eleven and calculus in grade twelve. College credit for advanced students in mathematics is a common arrangement. Elective courses for students of adequate ability may include number theory, computer programing, and analytic geometry.

Clearly, more mathematics is available today, although content changes of the 1950s and 1960s did not appear to result in significantly improved student achievement. Little encouragement may be perceived from the inconclusive results of the first National Assessment of Educational Progress. Steadily declining scores on the Scholastic Aptitude Test suggest to many writers that a return to basics is necessary. Although the college preparatory student is being well served, the majority who enroll in general and applied courses are still not mastering basic computational skills to a satisfactory degree.

In the opinion of the present writers, it would be a mistake to blame the new mathematics e.g., structure, logic, sets, numeration systems, axiomatic systems, transformations, for any lack of progress that might be perceived. Modern mathematics is here to stay and will evolve further. Computational skills will not be taught better by returning to an outmoded content. If renewed emphasis on fundamental skills is needed, the emphasis should be set within the advances of the past twenty years, not as a substitute for this progress. (43) The infusion of new mathematics was needed. However, too much rigor and formality combined with little understanding of how much of anything can be absorbed at a given time characterized early course revisions. (44) The scholarly mathematicians who devised content revisions simply did not understand the learning process, especially in elementary education and early secondary education. Input by teachers and educators through the years and modification of courses on the basis of experience has corrected much of the initial difficulty with modern mathematics.

Classroom use of the inexpensive pocket calculator also has caused concern among those who worry about the ability of the population to perform fundamental arithmetical computations. Will people in the future be able to do arithmetic, or will they just be able to push buttons and read answers? The point to emphasize is that there is no argument about the need for computational skill. Arithmetic is essential for all business and industrial occupations, fundamental for professions based on science, and necessary for consumers. The issue centers on the method of calculation to be employed, pencil and paper vs. the calculator. (45) Currently, use of the calculator is widely accepted, and no evidence has surfaced to indicate decrease in the ability to compute by paper and pencil as a result.

The writers view the argument somewhat as a horse and buggy versus automobile, or sailing vessel versus steamship category of concern. The calculator is here and will become an integral part of classroom problem-solving in mathematics, science, social studies, consumer education, and all other areas where computation is necessary. (46) Mathematics teachers could be criticized by their colleagues and by the public if they failed to keep pace with the technology represented by the calculator.

Renewed concern for human values through science and mathematics should be reflected in all courses. These things are taught because they are part of human experience. Mathematical and scientific principles govern much of the physical and social world (47) and help to explain the universe. Every child should be given a chance to understand this world.

When words such as *process* and *inquiry* are used to identify an emphasis in teaching, take care that the words are used with common meanings, at least on a schoolwide or school system basis. Evidence suggests that such words have no generally accepted meaning among science teachers. (48) Yet, excellent sources are available which can assist toward understanding. (49) (50) Remember, also, that concepts such as *individualization* do not mean that the student works in isolation untouched by human teachers as he or she pursues mechanical processes. Opportunity to work and interact with others may be part of true individualization and, certainly, is preferred by students. (51)

Finally, in both science and mathematics, as in other subjects, each school must find the fine balance between exploratory courses and programs needed in the beginning secondary school years and the structure necessary for advanced work. Too much formality and structure, too soon, can be harmful. Too little structure and rigor in advanced courses betrays the education of advanced students.

CHAPTER REFERENCES

1. Don M. Wolfe, "Grammar and Linguistics: A Contrast in Realities," *English Journal* 53, no. 2 (February 1964): 73-78, 100.

2. See Elizabeth Calkins and Barry McGhan, *Teaching Tomorrow* (Dayton, Ohio: Pflaum/Standard, 1972). This is a handbook of science fiction for teachers.

3. See Thomas R. Giblin, ed., *Popular Media and the Teaching of English* (Pacific Palisades, California: Goodyear Publishing Co., 1972).

4. Mary M. Dupuis, "Undeceiving and Decision Making: Some Thoughts on Electives and Mini Courses in English," *English Journal* 63, no. 4 (April 1974): 29-33.

5. See G. Robert Carlsen, "Some Random Observations—About the English Curriculum," *English Journal* 61, no. 7 (October 1972):1004-1009.

6, 7. See, for example, Larry Palmatier and Millie Martin, "Ten Guidelines for Establishing an Elective Program," *English Journal* 65, no. 4 (April 1976):28-31.

8. A point made by Allan E. Dittmer, "Curriculum Trends: One Year Later," *English Journal* 63, no. 4 (April 1974):72-74.

9, 10 For example, see J. N. Hook, *The Teaching of High School English,* 4th ed. (New York: The Ronald Press Co., 1972). Theodore W. Hipple, *Teaching English in Secondary Schools* (New York: Macmillan, 1973).

11, 12. See "Back to Basics," Forum Section, *English Journal* 64, no. 9 (December 1975):12-14. Also, see in the same publication, "What's Happening to Basic Skills?" 65, no. 5 (May 1976):16-20.

13. Peter O. Evanechko, "Reading Is Only One of the Language Arts," *Language Arts* 52, no. 6 (September 1975): 839-40.

14. Mary H. Jackson, "Foreign Languages—Yesterday, Today, and Tomorrow," *Today's Education* 63, no. 4 (November-December 1974): 68-71.

15. Joint National Committee for Languages, "The Case for Language Study: Taking It to the Public," *The Modern Language Journal* 60, no. 4 (April 1976): 149-50.

16. Norma Enea Klayman, "Views of Secondary School Educators on the Foreign Language Requirement in Higher Education," *The Modern Language Journal* 59, no. 4 (April 1975): 168-73.

17. See Carl Ziegler, "The Language Teacher and the Amateur Language Student," Chapter 8 in Frank M. Grittner, ed., *Student Motivation and the Foreign Language Teacher* (Skokie, Illinois: National Textbook Co., 1974), pp. 107-18.

18. Robert C. Lafayette, Howard B. Altman, and Renate Schulz, eds., *The Culture Revolution in Foreign Language Teaching* (Skokie, Illinois: National Textbook Co., 1975).

19. See Betty Schmitz, "Sexism in French Language Textbooks," Chapter 9 in Lafayette, Altman, and Schulz, *The Culture Revolution,* pp. 119-30.

20. A. Bruce Gaarder, "Elitism, Teacher Training, and Other Forbidden Topics," *The Modern Language Journal* 60, no. 4 (April 1976): 150-55.

21. Frank M. Grittner, "Foreign Languages and the Changing Curriculum," *NASSP Bulletin* 58, no. 384 (October 1974): 71-78.

22. Judith C. Morrow, "Exploratory Courses for the Middle and Junior High School," Chapter 9 in Grittner, *Student Motivation,* pp. 119-43.

23. See Dwayne Adcock, "Foreign Languages in Elementary and Emerging Adolescent Education," Chapter 9 in Gilbert A. Jarvis, ed., *An Integrative Approach to Foreign Language Teaching: Choosing among the Options* (Skokie, Illinois: National Textbook Co., 1976), pp. 289-325.

24. See Robert C. Lafayette, "The Minicourse: A Viable Curricular Alternative," in Jarvis, *An Integrative Approach,* pp. 81-128.

25. Robert B. Anthony, "Changing the Social Studies Curriculum: Some Suggestions and Aids," *The Social Studies* 66, no. 5 (September-October 1975): 208-10.

26. George Sykes, "The Decline of Social Studies: Changing Perspectives in Social Studies Education in the 20th Century," *The Social Studies* 66, no. 6 (November-December 1975): 243-46.

27. Herman F. Eschenbacher, "Social Studies, Social Science, and School Reform," *Intellect* 102, no. 2358 (May 1974): 507-09.

28. Robert B. Anthony, "Rationale for an Interdisciplinary Approach in the Social Studies," *The Social Studies* 65, no. 4 (April 1974): 150-51.

29. James A. Banks, "Teaching Ethnic Studies: Key Issues and Concepts," *The Social Studies* 66, no. 3 (May-June 1975): 107-13.

30. Robert Pearson, "Beyond the New Social Studies," *The Social Studies* 64, no. 7 (December 1973): 315-19.

31. Jayne Millar Wood, "Adding a Global Outlook to Our Secondary Curriculum: Classroom Teaching Strategies," *Social Education* 38, no. 7 (November-December 1974): 664-71.

32. Dale L. Brubaker, *Secondary Social Studies for the 70's: Planning for Instruction* (New York: Thomas Y. Crowell Co., 1973). See Chapter 5, "Stating Your Own Social Studies Objectives."

33. William C. Merwin, Donald O. Schneider, and Lester D. Stephens, *Developing Competency in Teaching Secondary Social Studies* (Columbus, Ohio: Charles E. Merrill Publishing Co., 1974). See Chapter 2, "Setting Conditions for Cognitive Learning," and Chapter 3, "Setting Conditions for Affective Learning."

34. Lee Ehman, Howard Mehlinger, and John Patrick, *Toward Effective Instruction in Secondary Social Studies* (Boston: Houghton Mifflin, 1974). See Chapter 5, "Teaching the Use of Concepts."

35. J. Stanley Ahmann et al., "Science Achievement: The Trend Is Down," *The Science Teacher* 42, no. 7 (September 1975): 23-26.

36. Martin S. Wolfe, "Mathematics—Programs and Trends," *NASSP Bulletin* 60, no. 396 (January 1976): 91-96.

37. Gerald H. Krockover, "Science Education for the Future: Tomorrow Never Comes," *School Science and Mathematics* 75, no. 7 (November 1975): 639-44.

38. Bernard Uzelak, "Why, What, and How—Senior Electives in Science," *The Science Teacher* 40, no. 7 (October 1973): 28-29.

39. Ernest Burkman, "Unhooking High School Science: The ISIS Project," *The Science Teacher* 41, no. 7 (October 1974): 30-32.

40. David J. Kuhn, "Value Education in the Sciences: The Step beyond Concepts and Processes," *School Science and Mathematics* 74, no. 7 (November 1974): 582-88.

41. Paul DeHart Hurd, "Science, Technology, and Society: New Goals for Interdisciplinary Science Teaching," *The Science Teacher* 42, no. 2 (February 1975): 27-30.

42. Paul B. Hounshell and Edwin L. West, Jr., "Trends in the Teaching of Science: A Mid-Decade Analysis," *The High School Journal* 59, no. 5 (February 1976): 218-22.

43. See Wolfe, "Mathematics—Programs and Trends."

44. Vincent J. Glennon, "Mathematics: How Firm the Foundations?" *Phi Delta Kappan* 57, no. 4 (December 1975): 302-05.

45. Donald R. Quinn, "Calculators in the Classroom," *NASSP Bulletin* 60, no. 396 (January 1976): 77-80.

46. Jon L. Higgins, "Mathematics Programs Are Changing," *The Education Digest* 40, no. 4 (December 1974): 56-58.

47. Herbert J. Greenberg, "The Objectives of Mathematics Education," *The Mathematics Teacher* 67, no. 7 (November 1974): 639-43. See also, Kuhn, "Value Education in the Sciences."

48. John F. Newport, "A Comparison of Viewpoints in Process-Centered Instructional Objectives," *School Science and Mathematics* 74, no. 7 (November 1974): 614-20.

49. For example, see Paul DeHart Hurd, *New Directions in Teaching Secondary School Science* (Chicago: Rand McNally, 1970).

50. See Robert B. Sund and Leslie W. Trowbridge, *Teaching Science by Inquiry in the Secondary School,* 2nd ed. (Columbus, Ohio: Charles E. Merrill Publishing Co., 1973).

51. Jack A. Reed, "Individualized Instruction—A Positive Experience?" *School Science and Mathematics* 74, no. 5 (May-June 1974): 366-70.

5 Physical
Education
and
Health

Introduction

With the exception of English, physical education is the most required program in the secondary school, central to general education, an expectation of all students. Hence, it is well to develop an understanding of the contributions of physical education to the academic program and to appreciate the potential of physical education as a vehicle for realizing meaningful educational goals.

To many observers, physical education is and traditionally has been merely free play or highly organized recess. Indeed, the recollection which many adults have of their physical education experience is that of a loosely organized group program centering on games such as volleyball and basketball. Sandwiched in the schedule between academic classes, little time was allowed for actual participation. Surely many readers can recall gym classes of fifty or sixty minutes each where no more than half the time was actually given to instruction and participation. Surely, most can remember rushing from physical education, sans shower, to escape tardiness in some academic class. Fortunately, such recollections identify programs which, in most schools, no longer exist. Current emphases toward individualized instruction, lifetime sports and recreational activities, and the program flexibility made possible by modular scheduling, have combined to work major changes for the better.

This chapter will examine and provide, in capsule form, an insight into what physical education is today, how it came to be what it is, and how it fits into the framework of the total educational processes of American society during the final quarter of the twentieth century.

Historical Perspective

In a broad sense, one might consider that physical education has been part of the customs, mores, and needs of all societies, ancient and contemporary. However, modern physical education is little more than a hundred years old, traceable to 1861 when Edward Hitchcock initiated the Department of Physical Education and Hygiene at Amherst College. (1)

This chapter is adapted from an original, unpublished article written by Dr. William F. Stier, Jr., administrative assistant to the vice president, Cardinal Stritch College, Milwaukee, Wisconsin. However, where Dr. Stier's article considered interscholastic athletics to be the apex of the total physical education program, the present volume treats interschool athletics as being more akin to the cocurriculum than to the program of studies. (See chapter ten.) Included by permission of Dr. William F. Stier, Jr.

The original professional organization for physical education was the American Association for the Advancement of Physical Education. This organization was founded in November, 1885, by a group of thirty-five men under the leadership of William G. Anderson, who later became its first president. (2) The first official professional publication of this organization appeared in 1896, the *American Physical Education Review*. Commencing as early as 1885, the *Proceedings* of the association had been published in reports to the membership and the profession.

It was also in the early 1880s that Swedish gymnastics were introduced to the American public by Hartwig Nissen, who in 1883 was the vice consul to the United States for the countries of Norway and Sweden. Nissen was the prime mover behind the opening of a Swedish Health Institute in the nation's capital. (3) With the advent and influence of the Swedish and Norwegian style of physical education and gymnastics, as well as imports from other European countries, the foreign influence within this country was supreme and continued dominant until the time of the first world war. For example, in 1886, the Nordamerikanischer Turnerbund (North American Turner Society) was established to promote a method of German gymnastics based upon movements derived from turning various parts of the body. Importation of fully developed systems of physical activity and gymnastics into the United States negated any apparent need for an American version of physical education until after the turn of the century.

Ten years later in 1893, Harvard College became the first institution of higher learning to confer an academic degree in the discipline of physical education. Prior to that date, and even for some years to follow, professionals actively involved in the study of physical education were often medical physicians and/or scientists in biological areas. Only much later did the profession provide for the preparation of physical educators via a specialized preparation program which differed significantly from that of medical physicians and biologists. (4) (5)

In 1903, the American Association for Advancement of Physical Education changed its name to the American Physical Education Association (APEA). Thirty years later there was an additional name change. Specifically, on June 28, 1937, as a result of a merger between the American Physical Education Association and the Department of School Health and Physical Education of the National Education Association, the American Association for Health and Physical Education was born and operated as a department of the NEA. A year later the organization assumed yet another name, American Association for Health, Physical Education and Recreation. This change reflected the culmination of years of work and effort for professional unification by health educators, physical educators, and leaders in recreation. From that point on, HPER (health, physical education, and recreation) operated under one roof, a fact which provided no small amount of difficulty in later years in terms of individual identity and professional respectability for those persons actively involved in health science education and recreation as well as the various subcomponents of physical education.

A major change occurred in 1973 when the American Association for Health, Physical Education and Recreation, through its representative assembly at its annual convention in Minneapolis, ordered a reorganization of the Association (AAHPER). The following year, at its next annual convention in Anaheim, California, the AAHPER was reorganized, and the name of the organization was altered to reflect the reorganization. The name was changed to the American Alliance for Health, Physical Education and Recreation. It was at this time that health education, within the AAHPER, gained final recognition as a separate, distinct, although closely related, area of study. The umbrella of the AAHPER still stretched over health, physical education, and recreation, but each area was officially recognized, in name and in fact, as a distinct field of study.

An Overview of Physical Education

What, exactly, is physical education? Where does it fit into the educational structure of secondary schools? What does it include? How can physical education meet or help to meet the general goals of the educational system?

Physical education is education of, by, and through human movement. It is that facet of general education which contributes to the total growth and development of the individual primarily by means of selected movement experiences and physical activities. The general goals of education and of physical education are indeed identical, the greatest possible development of each individual, and education for responsible democratic citizenship. (6)

It is essential to recognize that there is no conflict between the goals of general education and those of physical education. The product, objectives, and program of physical education are in harmony with those of general education. The reason why any discipline or area is retained or added to a curriculum is because of the belief that the discipline conforms to common goals which the educational system and the general public view as truly significant.

Physical education is education through the physical. Yet, it is more than the acquisition of manipulative or motor skills and deals with considerably more than physical well-being. The activities of physical education require cognitive knowledge and result in values, attitudes, and appreciations that are consistent with the cognitive and affective outcomes defined for any subject area.

Physical education is commonly pictured as a triangle, the base of which is taken to represent basic instructional classes or services. This is the level at which all, or nearly all, students participate. Moving up the triangle and involving a fewer number of participants is the intramural program where various forms of competition are scheduled on an in-school basis. Still higher, and with still fewer participants, is the extramural program where the best intramural teams from one school may compete with their counterparts from other schools. Finally, the apex of the triangle locates the interscholastic program where the most highly skilled individuals represent their schools in competitive activities. Content at each level may be described as follows.

Basic Instructional Level

Physical education activity classes provide opportunities for students to be introduced to selected physical activities and/or to improve upon skills and competencies already possessed. Such activities include:

a. Recreational or lifetime leisure activities—i.e., bowling, golf, tennis, yoga;

b. Individual or dual sports—i.e., fencing, bowling, gymnastics, handball;

c. Combative sports—i.e., wrestling, fencing, judo, karate;

d. Team sports—i.e., football, baseball, softball, soccer, field hockey;

e. Developmental physi al activities—i.e., gymnastics, weight lifting, free exercise.

It should be noted that specific physical activities may be classified under more than one heading, such as wrestling being classified as an individual or combative or even developmental physical activity. The important point is that individual physical activities may be classified or categorized under one or more specific headings so that the physical education program can be molded to meet the needs of individual students.

It is at the bottom of the triangle that one finds the basic instructional or activity program offered within the physical education curriculum. It is here that the largest number of students, either in a required or elective program, are exposed to the fundamental and basic physical skills involved in physical movement experiences as well as the more functional and structured activities involving the physical nature of humanity. It is here that the student is introduced to those fundamental skills necessary to successfully master more advanced and sophisticated physical manipulations.

Intramural Activities

Further up the triangle, one views the intramural activity program. It is here that students, usually fewer in number, elect and freely choose to participate in recreational, competitive, or developmental physical activities within the confines of one's own school against and/or with his or her peers. Participation in physical activities at the intramural level is usually on a higher plane in terms of difficulty, skill proficiency, and sophistication. Additionally, the physical activities are usually in the form of games, sport activities, or contests rather than individual execution of a specific fundamental skill, although the latter is not precluded from taking place.

Thus, the student is introduced to, taught, and exposed to specific and general physical skills and activities in the basic instructional or activity class. He is allowed to practice and improve under the watchful eye of the physical educator. Having obtained some degree of skill proficiency, regardless of whether or not it was obtained or refined in the basic activity level program, the student is able to practice and participate in the activity under the auspices of the school intramural director. The intramural director serves not as a coach but rather as an administrator, facilitator, and organizer. His task is to provide opportunities for students within the school setting to experience meaningful success through participating in individual and/or group activities, games, and sports. It is well to remember that, on both the basic activity and the intramural levels, the needs of beginning, intermediate, and advanced skill proficiency can be served. Both the intramural program and the activity or basic instructional program have the potential for serving a wide spectrum, from one end to the other, from the "no skill" situation to the most "highly skilled" situation. (7)

Extramural Activities

Moving up the triangle, and again involving a smaller number of participants, one finds the extramural activity program. This program is very similar to the intramural program but involves participation in activities not only within one's own school but also with and against individuals and teams from other schools. Although there are no professional coaches on this level, there are planned physical activities, both recreational and competitive in nature, among participants representing two or more educational institutions. Often, the champions of the intramural program in a specific activity or sport from one school may compete against their counterparts from another school.

Interscholastic Athletic Competition

The apex of the triangle, involving the fewest number of participants but also involving the highest level of proficiency, represents the interschool or interscholastic athletic program. It is here that the most highly skilled individuals in a particular activity are selected to represent, on a voluntary basis, their school in a competitive physical activity, under the watchful and critical eye of a professional athletic coach. (See chapter 10.)

Selected Areas Within Physical Education

Physical education is generally conceded to contribute to a number of broad areas within which both long-range goals and specific instructional objectives may be formulated.

Physical Fitness. Many persons confuse physical *fitness* with physical *education.* Physical fitness received a boost in awareness by the general public as well as by educators during both world wars. However, these eras of semipopularity were totally overshadowed by the fitness craze which followed publication of the results of the Kraus-Weber Tests. (8)

In 1953 a comparison study of back and abdominal strength and flexibility of European children and children in the United States was brought to the attention of the national press. The poorer performance of American children was concluded to be a result of a lack of the various types of formal exercises which are thought to build up the body in specific areas. In response to the uproar of the nation's educators and general populace, President Dwight D. Eisenhower in 1956 called a White House Conference of outstanding leaders to examine the problems brought to light by the study. (9)

A result of the conference was the establishment of a Citizens Advisory Committee on Youth Fitness to which was given the responsibility of finding acceptable ways of improving the physical fitness of our young people and techniques of implementing such plans as soon as possible. This committee was later replaced (1968) by a group which is known as the President's Council on Physical Fitness and Sports.

Charles B. (Bud) Wilkinson served as Special Consultant on Youth Fitness under President John F. Kennedy. From 1964 to 1967, Stan Musial served as consultant, succeeded by Captain James A. Lovell, Jr., USN, astronaut, in 1967.

The President's Council on Youth Fitness and Sports has recommended that children in grades kindergarten through twelve be required to take part in daily physical education programs which emphasize the development of physical fitness. (10) Physical fitness has indeed assumed a very prominent position within the physical education curriculum in our schools during the past two decades. (11) (12)

Skill And Knowledge Development. Physical education is concerned with more than mere physical fitness. The development of useful skills, hopefully, those that can be practiced on a lifelong basis, is of paramount importance. So, also, are the acquisition of knowledge and the formation of consequent concepts, attitudes, ideals and appreciations. Without such long-range outcomes, the physical education experience is of only momentary value as training or conditioning. Such training, while excellent in terms of short-range objectives, e.g., to get into good physical condition, does nothing in terms of long-range goals.

Social And Psychological Development. A program of physical education should be judged in terms of how well it meets the biological, psychological, social, and mental needs of students. Physical education and sports activities can be viewed as a microsociety within which social values such as cooperation, teamwork, respect for the rights of others, and the like, may be experienced and internalized. It should be noted, however, that true change in behavior (meaningful and sustained change) does not usually occur unless planned for in depth and achieved through acceptable and conscious effort to modify attitudes. (13)

Physical Activities as Tools for Curriculum Improvement

Physical activities must be considered as means utilized to accomplish a variety of purposes and objectives. The manner in which these "tools" are utilized as well as when and where they are to be used will have a great effect upon ultimate goals. Criteria for the selection of activities must also be carefully determined to insure that the use of a specific activity, in reality, aids in reaching a specific objective for individual students.

In early grades, emphasis is on self-awareness and *movement education* or *movement exploration* type activities. In the higher grades, students are instructed in sports techniques. Additionally, lifetime sports type activities are included in the junior and senior high grades. Physical fitness emphasis is usually maintained throughout the individual student's educational experience. (14)

The curricular elements (activities) must be evaluated as to their worth (as tools) in terms of physical, intellectual, social, emotional, psychological, safety, and recreational contributions. Activities traditionally have been allocated to appropriate grade levels to correspond with the peak of natural interest by participants. Determining factors to help decide whether any particular activity is suitable or acceptable in the program include:

1. Whether the activity is best suited for fall, winter, spring, or all seasons,
2. Whether such activity could be classified as recreational, individual, dual, combative, team, or developmental in nature,
3. Whether the activity will be provided for boys, girls, or both,
4. Whether there exist sufficient facilities, adequate amount of equipment, qualified number of staff, enough time, acceptable natural environment, and sufficient budget and financial support.

Further evaluation of potential activities on the basis of student needs and compatibility with the educational philosophy of the school, the school system, and the community will aid significantly in determining the final desirability of any specific physical activity.

Health Education

Health as a subject in the school curriculum has been claimed by many different disciplines. Health has been and is being taught by the school nurse, the athletic coach, the biology teacher, the home economics teacher, the history teacher, the physical education teacher, and by almost any other teacher willing to assume the task and able to perceive a degree of correlation between some topic in health and the subject matter of a course of study. As a consequence, many schools and school systems have failed to implement a meaningful plan of attack for providing health programs and experiences for students.

In addition, the area is frequently perceived to include personal and community health, mental health, alcohol, tobacco, and drug education, and safety education. (15) Thus, concepts about the content of health overlap with similar content set forth for safety education, in which the same topics may be recommended. And, even more complicating, comprehensive texts on physical education typically include sections and chapters on health topics and may even extend discussion into various aspects of safety education.

The result of this is that no ones knows what health concepts are being taught, to whom, or why. No one knows what is being learned. No one really knows what is being retained. Health, despite its status as a major national goal in American education, is simply not being dealt with adequately by the schools. Obviously, health taught on the basis of correlation with other subjects, even if taught well, will reach only the students enrolled in those subjects. And, except for English, physical education, and the combined social studies, this means a significant minority of the student population. Thus, for example, health, even taught well in home economics classes, will reach less than a quarter of the students; as a related topic in chemistry, even fewer. As a means of organizing for health education, correlation leaves much to be desired. (16)

The most thorough research into the status of health education and the needs of youth was initiated in 1961 and was brought to a head in 1965 by the School Health Education Study. The findings of this investigation indicated that the health content then available in the schools of this nation was both repetitious and boring throughout the grades without consideration for the real problems of youth. Further, universally neglected content areas included consumer education, sex education, venereal disease, noncommunicable disease, smoking, alcohol and drugs, community health programs, environmental hazards, mental health, and nutrition and weight control. (17) (18)

The background of the School Health Education Study (SHES) can be traced back to 1960 when the NEA-AMA Joint Committee on Health Problems in Education recommended a survey of the nation's school children to determine the status of health education in the schools. Under a grant from the Samuel Bronfman Foundation (1961) the School Health Education Study was initiated. Its purpose was to discover the status of health instruction and to gain support from the public for reform measures. (19) (20)

The SHES brought together health education specialists, supervisors, and classroom teachers to develop a sample experimental curriculum and materials based on a *concept* approach. In 1966, SHES received support from the Minnesota Mining and Manufacturing Company (3M) to continue the development and publication of curriculum materials which had been previously started during the 1964-65 academic year in various organizational meetings. In 1967, packets of materials pertaining to the concepts were made available commercially. Further nationwide examinations and investigations in 1967 again revealed glaring weaknesses in health education in large, medium, and small school districts in the United States. Curriculum was repetitious, and specific areas within health education were being completely ignored, either by design (too controversial) or by ignorance. (21)

Although SHES is not regarded as a national curriculum, it is to be thought of as a suggested approach to curriculum development based on big ideas or the conceptual approach. The SHES curricular approach revolved around three large concepts supported by ten central concepts, and these, in turn, were supported by various subconcepts. (22) (23)

It seems to the present writers that the first step toward improving instruction in health education is to take advantage of the interdisciplinary nature of the field. There are ample opportunities, or at least there should be, for health learning situations in physical education, biology, chemistry, the social studies, home economics, and other subjects. The fact that health concepts are not learned at present in these subject areas does not mean that the concepts are unimportant. Rather, it means that the school itself is not organized to deal effectively with interdisciplinary concepts. Hence, the first step suggested here is to organize an appropriate, broadly based planning or curriculum committee and charge it with the task of framing educational outcomes in health education that are essential to the well-being of all students. If possible, such a committee should include a certified teacher in health education; a representative of the health professions, preferably a nurse; three or more teachers from areas such as home economics, physical education, and the natural sciences; and, where feasible, community and student representatives.

The second step is for the committee to get at the work of defining goals as outcomes of health instruction. Since health instruction is so broad, encompassing everything from sex education to the problem of metabolic disturbance resulting from movement through various time zones, it is essential that priorities be established on the basis of importance, relevance, and need.

Once goals are established and priorities listed, the next step is to translate them into performance objectives. Creating performance in health is necessary although oftentimes difficult. For example, most objectives in health education involve present or future behavior or choice of behavior. Yet, specific evaluation in health courses still rests on testing and evaluating facts. How does one evaluate and grade on health habits and health behavior? Utlimately, it is health habits, behavior patterns and health choices which educators are attempting to influence and direct.

The inconsistency between the objectives and evaluations in health is compounded by the following fact. One of the objectives in health education is that individuals act on the basis of their own knowledge about health. Hence, knowledge is important. However, it is abundantly clear that simply informing people about health matters is not generally sufficient to alter specific behavior patterns, reinforced .by months or years of habit, particularly if problems of psychological or physical dependency or social approval are involved.

Following a definition of performance objectives, it is necessary to determine the best or best available vehicle for attaining them, that is, either within existing curricular disciplines or by way of a separate course or courses in health instruction. At this point individual teachers, either as members of the committee or working with the guidance of the committee, should proceed to devise learning activities appropriate to the stated objectives and, ultimately, carry out evaluations to determine the degree of achievement for each objective.

This procedure assures that the school has organized for instruction in health education and that it is at least equally concerned with learning as well as with planning in the area. The procedure is consistent with the major expectations of the needs assessment process and is perceived here as the most certain route to curriculum improvement in health education. (See *A Proposed Model for Curriculum Development,* chapter fourteen.)

A Word about Recreation Education

As is true with health, education for recreation or leisure is also associated closely with the general field of physical education. For example, the emphasis upon lifetime sports in physical education, represents an effort by physical educators to adjust programs to the needs of students after they have left school. Yet, reflection about the recreational and/or leisure-time needs of adults suggests that such needs are by no means met solely by physical or sports activity.

Recreational preferences vary widely. In addition to sports activities such as golf, tennis, and bowling, which are among the major "lifetime" sports, leisure activities of adults include all sorts of hobbies, from bird watching to woodworking; outdoor recreation, including hiking, camping, skiing, hunting, and fishing; a variety of art, arts and crafts, and music undertakings; cooking and sewing; reading and writing; and many, many others. A specific listing of recreational interests of Americans could fill several pages. Hence, it is evident that education for recreation is also an interdisciplinary problem if schools are to organize to achieve generally accepted national goals such as "worthy use of leisure time." The same processes recommended for curriculum improvement in health education would seem to apply to recreation education.

The general goal has been established and accepted for a half century or more. The need has become increasingly obvious because of such factors as shorter working hours, earlier retirement ages, longer vacation periods, less personal satisfaction from work as jobs become more and more mechanized, and the development of transportation which opened areas of new activity to the general population. Unless the need is met, and the schools have a major role to play, Americans will, more and more, fall into the habit of being entertained during their leisure hours. And, it is suggested, passive entertainment is neither as worthwhile nor as productive as active participation in constructive, self-educating, leisure-time enterprises.

Summary

Of the ten problems confronting the public schools, the Gallup Poll in 1974 indicated poor curriculum as holding the ninth position. (24) This fact, coupled with the statement by the American Alliance for Health, Physical Education and Recreation that only about one in four schools offers a sports and physical education program designed to bring out each student's physical best, is somewhat a poor commentary on the present status of the physical education curriculum in the United States. (25) This is even more significant when one realizes that physical education has never before been more acceptable in the general curriculum nor more highly successful in meeting the needs of students. Improvements have indeed been made. In some instances giant steps have been taken. However, much remains to be done in terms of making the physical education learning experience truly meaningful and significant for each and every secondary school student.

To achieve goals set for health and recreation education demands the central participation of physical educators because of the close relationship of these areas to physical education. However, both health and recreation involve considerable input from other disciplinary areas if general goals in these areas are to be realized. Consequently, it is recommended that interdisciplinary committees be established in both health and recreation in order to establish goals, to determine priority among goals, to translate goals into performance outcomes, to identify content areas and/or other means of achieving outcomes, and to proceed on to the means of evaluating achievement. In all of this it should be understood that what is recommended will become a continuous process of curriculum adjustment and not a one time method of achieving temporary improvement.

CHAPTER REFERENCES

1. Robert N. Singer and Walter Dick, *Teaching Physical Education—A Systems Approach* (Boston: Houghton Mifflin, 1974), p. 18.

2. Greyson Daughtrey and John B. Woods, *Physical Education and Intramural Programs: Organizations and Administration* (Philadelphia: W. B. Saunders Co., 1976), p. 14

3. "Notable Events in Physical Education 1823-1973," *Journal of Health, Physical Education and Recreation* (November-December 1973): 10.

4. William F. Stier, Jr., *The Development of an Instrument and Procedures to Accompany the Bookwalter-Dollgener Score Card for Evaluating Undergraduate Professional Programs in Physical Education* (Vermillion: USD Press, 1972), p. 2.

5. William F. Stier, Jr., "Professional Preparation of Physical Educators," paper presented at National Convention of AAHPER, April 15, 1973, Minneapolis, Minnesota.

6. Victor P. Dauer and Robert P. Pangrazi, *Dynamic Physical Education for Elementary School Children* (Minneapolis: Burgess Publishing Co., 1975). p. 2.

7. William F. Stier, Jr., "The 1970 Status of Programs Offered by Departments of Physical Education in Junior Colleges Possessing an Athletic Program," paper presented at National Convention of AAHPER, April 3, 1971, Detroit, Michigan.

8. Hans Kraus and Ruth P. Hirschland, "Muscular Fitness and Health," *Journal of Health, Physical Education and Recreation* (December 1953): 17-24.

9. "Operation Fitness—USA," *Journal of Health, Physical Education and Recreation* (January 1959): 25.

10. President's Council on Physical Fitness and Sports, *Suggestions for School Programs, Youth Physical Fitness* (Washington, D.C.: U.S. Government Printing Office, 1973), p. 3.

11. American Alliance for Health, Physical Education and Recreation, *Youth Fitness Test Manual*, rev. ed. (Washington, D.C.: American Alliance for Health, Physical Education and Recreation, 1975), p. 1.

12. John F. Kennedy, "The Vigor We Need," *Sports Illustrated* (July 10, 1962): 12.

13. Thomas Sheehan and William L. Alsop, "Educational Sport," *Journal of Health, Physical Education and Recreation* (May 1972): 41-45.

14. Kate Keating and Edwin Kiester, Jr., "The 'New' Physical Education—And Why We Need It," *Better Homes and Gardens* (October 1976): 11.

15. See Cyrus Mayshark and Roy A. Foster, *Health Education in Secondary Schools* (St. Louis: The C. V. Mosby Co., 1972).

16. Marion B. Pollock and Edward B. Johns, "Health Education," Chapter 8 in *Curriculum Handbook for School Executives* (Arlington, Virginia: American Association of School Administrators, 1973).

17. Elena M. Sliepcevich, "Health Education: A Conceptual Approach," (Washington, D.C.: School Health Education Study, 1965), p. 5.

18. School Health Education Study Advisory Committee, *Health Education: A Conceptual Approach to Curriculum Design* (St. Paul, Minnesota: 3M Press, 1967), p. 9.

19. Elena M. Sliepcevich, *School Health Education Study: A Summary Report* (Washington, D.C.: SHES, 1964), p. 3.

20. School Health Education Study, *School Health Education: A Call for Action* (Washington, D.C., 1965), p. 1.

21. Teaching-Learning Guides, together with basic document *(Health Education: A Conceptual Approach to Curriculum Design, Grades K-12)* and printed originals and overhead projection transparencies, are available from Visual Products of 3M Company.

22. Carl E. Willgoose, *Health Education in the Elementary School* (Philadelphia: W. B. Saunders Co., 1974), p. 189.

23. School Health Education Study, *Health Education: A Conceptual Approach to Curriculum Design*, p. 20.

24. George H. Gallup, "Sixth Annual Gallup Poll of Public Attitudes toward Education," *Phi Delta Kappan* (September 1974): 21.

25. Keating and Kiester, "The 'New' Physical Education," p. 8.

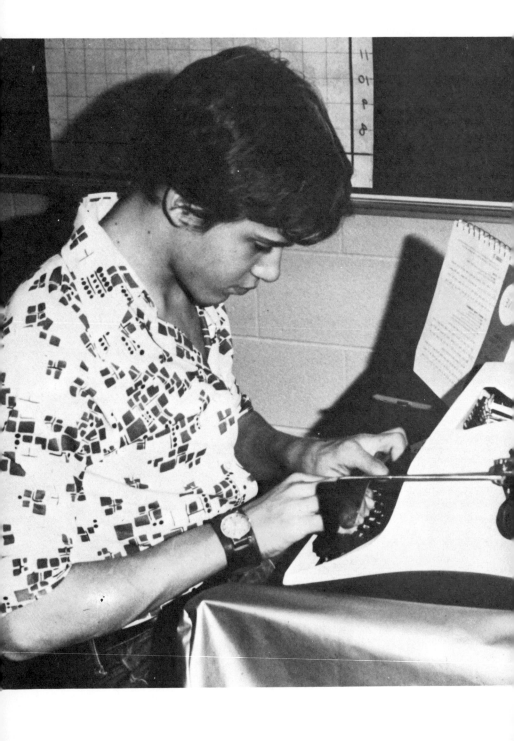

6   Vocational Education and the Practical Arts

A secondary school serving a predominately agrarian society with a low level of technological development does not require extensive occupational offerings in its curriculum. In such a society students are trained within classical and traditional disciplines for the university. As they leave the secondary school prior to graduation they assume a place in the workaday world in which manual labor is dominant.

This was the nature of American secondary schools well into the nineteenth century as it pertains to vocational education and the practical arts. Vocational education in the United States was prompted largely by federal efforts to upgrade the quality of skilled labor pools beginning with the Morrill Act of 1862 and culminating in the first Vocational Education (Smith-Hughes) Act of 1917. According to Grant Venn, the Morrill Act brought the preparation of professional manpower to higher education. Later federal efforts would attempt to stimulate the role of the high school and junior college to develop the skilled technical training required for nonprofessional manpower. (1)

As a curricular concept vocational education encompasses the idea that the secondary school should provide for specific skill training so that those students not entering college can enter the world of work. This differs from the practical arts which include home economics, industrial arts and business courses which assume that the skills learned in them will be helpful mostly in the home, and not necessarily for occupational preparation specifically.

Vocational education and the practical arts educators in the secondary school have encountered great difficulties. These have ranged from finding both good teachers and skilled craftsmen for classroom teaching to discovering that guidance departments conceived of these curricular areas as "dumping grounds" for the nonmotivated, alienated, noncollege bound student. The stigma attached to occupational preparation in the secondary school and the failure of curriculum developers to overcome formal and informal tracking of students was one of the stimuli toward career education as an alternative or offshoot. (see chapter seven)

Vocational Education

It has been estimated that 80 percent of the jobs in the nation do not require a college education. Yet more than 50 percent of the graduates from high school enter colleges and universities each year. (2) In her scathing indictment of overtraining and mistraining of American youth, Caroline Bird reported that in 1975 the U.S. Department of Labor had estimated that there would be 4,300 jobs for psychologists. Colleges were going to graduate 58,430 students with undergraduate degrees in psychology. She stated that in a followup study of thirty psychology majors at Vassar College, only five had jobs in which their college training was remotely related, while others were working as teachers, waitresses, typists, secretaries, a delivery driver and diet technician. (3)

For millions of secondary school students, vocational education therefore represents not only a viable curricular place of some importance and interest, but an avenue to a productive place in society and the world of work. The popularity of career education is not expected to diminish support of basic efforts in vocational education but add to them.

The vocational education curriculum is limitless, bounded only by the demand for various types of occupations in which training can be housed in the secondary school. One of the problems with vocational education is that as courses of study are established for specific occupations, the advancing technology within those occupations or fields either diminishes or eliminates the need for the skilled manpower. Following is a table showing two lists of occupations over a thirty-five year period in the United States, from 1941 to 1976. A cursory analysis will indicate that some occupations no longer exist, others have changed remarkably and others are relatively unchanged. Some occupations have not been changed radically by technology. Some have moved slowly. The real possibility of placing or trining students for dead end or marginal jobs is one of the concerns of maintaining a viable vocational education program. (6)

In an effort to combat some of the problems, vocational educators have taken to preparing vocational surveys which attempt to pinpoint the kinds of jobs available within a specified radius of the training facility. The rise of separate vocational-technical high schools represents a further effort to maintain the viability of vocational education. Such schools reduce the necessity to duplicate expensive equipment and provide the means to insure that only the most qualified professional staff members are giving the most up to date advice and training possible. Traditional efforts in vocational education such as cooperative work study programs which combine secondary schooling in general courses and on-site work training are still important facets for the comprehensive secondary school.

David Jepsen and Josiah Dilley examined various types of vocational decision-making models. (7) Utilizing psychological decision theory as a framework, Jepsen and Dilley constructed a paradigm which located vocational decision-making approaches along two continua: amount of information (and comprehension of that information) and an approach which demanded a long range or short range effect upon the

Table 6-1

A COMPARISON OF PARTIAL LISTS OF
OCCUPATIONS IN THE UNITED STATES,
1941-1976

1941	1976
secretary	computer operator (console)
telephone operator	cosmetologist (all around shop operator)
slubber tender*	dental assistant
welder	nurse
farmer	landscaping designer
forest ranger	air conditioning mechanic
waiter	welder
dietitian	aviation mechanic
maid	acountant
lab technician	auditor
bank teller	millwork operator
bank page	finish carpenter
buyer	designer
shipping clerk	secretary
cable splicer	pulp and paper specialist
salesperson (4)	chef (5)

*A *slubber* is a partly twined woolen thread. The *slubber tender* worked in the woolen mill and tended the machine that produced the slubber. Within a few years after 1941 as technology advanced, this step was eliminated and the job became obsolete.

decision-maker. High school curriculum choices on a day to day basis would be an example of a short range change which would not require a great deal of information or understanding. This can be contrasted with a selection by the student of future occupational goals as a life style which may have far reaching consequences and require a maximum type of information and understanding about self and society. Decision-making theory appears to be one way of approaching the vocational education problem of choice, and of linking counseling and that curricular area more closely together.

Industrial Arts

Industrial arts has been a secondary curriculum area which has traditionally included drawing (drafting), electricity, graphic arts, metals, photography and woods. Recently there has been emphasis on including ceramics, plastics and power mechanics as additional curricular units/ areas. A course of study in introductory plastics might include the following units: (8)

molding (injection, compression, molds, cycling)
thermoforming (molds, vacuum, blow, finishing)
extrusion (profile, shapes, molds, dies)
foams (beads, expansion, styrene, urethane, catalysts)
rotational molding (organisols, plastisols, cycling)
encapsulation (resins, molds, catalysts)

A critical curricular problem in the industrial arts areas is the identification of key skills contained in various processes of manual application. The curriculum developer in industrial arts often begins with a list of processes in a general area and then attempts to isolate various types of pupil projects which call for the learning of the skills required to complete them. Industrial arts course designers create charts to analyze the operations involved in making book ends, ash trays, utility boxes or tackle boxes. For example, a tackle box may require nineteen different operations or skills in sheetmetal work such as making a lap seam, drilling holes, cutting metal on squaring shears, etc. (9)

While the analysis of operations is important for the curriculum developer to ensure that the important skills in each area are covered in various pupil projects, the result has sometimes been a stultifying progression of trivial activities. Some industrial arts teachers present a series of projects which have little personal relevance to their students. Choosing between constructing a sugar scoop, toy pail, ash tray, canteen or book ends, may not be very exciting or meaningful for modern secondary school students.

A more pragmatic approach would require a more sustained examination of the curriculum in which shop situations reflected real life problems and potential applications. While few students would miss building a sugar scoop, many might need to know how to install a ventilation duct for a home dryer. Repairs in the home can encompass many basic industrial arts skills, from plumbing to wiring, and involve carpentry skills as well.

Thinking about approaching the industrial arts has been the subject of some change in secondary schools since 1881. At first the Russian system of skill development was employed. This consisted of training pupils in a graded series of exercises without any practical application. A rival system from Sweden called the *sloyd* approach became very popular. The sloyd system had students building whole objects from models.

This too came in for criticism on the grounds it was too formal and rigid for meaningful secondary school shop situations. (10)

The industrial arts have remained a strong curricular area in general, but have been downgraded in some communities which emphasize college preparation and envision the area as only important for school dropouts or for those who find the rigors of academic preparation unrewarding or difficult. This is an unfortunate circumstance particularly if the industrial arts are geared to later life skills for all students and not merely seen as entry into a manual vocation.

Home Economics

Perhaps no area of the practical arts is so visibly preparing students for later life skills than home economics. Home economics includes study in family living, nutrition and foods, home management, care and safety, health and personal grooming, entertainment and manners, and textiles and clothing. (11) Modern home economics in the secondary school have gone beyond the stereotyped sewing and cooking classes to include instructional units on self, personal care, interpersonal relationships and a study of group dynamics, consumerism, and in some cases sex education and reproduction.

A sample of home economics learning modules for grades five through eight in New York includes attention to the following topics:

using allowances	crafts from nature
pack yourself a lunch	fire safety
toy safety	perfect party foods
"I am me"	kitchen safety
making friends	eating out
wrapping gifts	special diets
face facts	to see ourselves as others see us
cooking outdoors	making your clothes more personal
keeping children safe	analyzing food labels (12)

Home economics has become one area of the secondary school curriculum which has been responsive to societal changes and the impact of the growing teenage market in clothes and personal grooming items. It is not difficult to identify future survival skills that relate to the home, kitchen, safety and consumer protection as valuable and necessary. Home economics is therefore not faced with the same kind of stigma problems as industrial arts or perhaps business education.

Business Education

Business education is one of the practical arts which can lead to almost immediate employment if such skills as accounting, shorthand, or typing have been learned proficiently. If not, students may have to attend business school to increase competency in an attempt to enter a business occupation. One area of business education which has enjoyed great success in universal appeal to students is personal typing. Typing has become an important academic skill for students continuing their education, and it is not unusual for high school teachers to request papers to be typed. Typed reports, essays, and term papers in college are the rule rather than the exception. For this reason, typing in the business curriculum has enjoyed a wider appeal than many other more narrowly defined business courses such as law, merchandising, or business math. The latter can become a way of meeting secondary math requirements in less academic settings for those students who must meet a general math requirement for graduation.

One of the most exciting approaches to learning office practice procedures and skills in business education is to create an office practice laboratory. (13) In the lab are located all of the modern office machinery that a business student might encounter in a real office. These may include various models of typewriters, duplicating equipment and copiers, adding machines and electronic calculators, dictating machines and filing equipment. Such labs may also include a keypunch machine, collator, varityper, postage meter and computyper. Within the lab students are systematically expected to learn the skills related to office practice. Students may then be expected to log a required number of hours of school service in various offices or in the local business community. (14)

Improving the Viability of the Practical Arts in the Secondary School

Some secondary schools are reporting declining enrollments and student apathy in the practical arts. The oversold college preparatory courses and the publicity of career education as a renewed emphasis upon vocational preparation have served to detract from the appeal of the practical arts. What can be done other than to simply eliminate the practical arts piece by piece from the secondary curriculum? The following dialogue attempts to highlight both the nature of the problem and current perceptions about it, to a possible solution or approach toward changing this trend.

Meeting of the Washington School District Curriculum Council Sub-Committee on the Practical Arts

PERSONS IN ATTENDANCE

Dr. Doris Blavitt, director of curriculum
Mr. Raymond Morris, principal, Washington High School
Mrs. Lois Holmes, principal, Washington Middle School
Mrs. Rita Gavin, chairperson practical arts, five through twelve

DR. BLAVITT: If you will recall our last meeting we expressed growing concern with the declining enrollment in the practical arts curriculum, particularly at the high school. I've developed some data which indicate our overall enrollment loss over a three-year period. As you can see over the time period we've suffered a 38 percent decline in business education, a 12 percent decline in industrial arts, and a 5 percent decline in home economics.

MRS. GAVIN: I'm terribly worried because I don't want to have to cut another teacher in the business education department. In all probability this will be Fred Stevens in the distributive education program. He has the least seniority and that will mean the end of that program. We've worked so hard to get that program and these are the kids who must go to work. The loss of that program will severely curtail our offerings. It means some students won't have any other alternatives at the high school.

MRS. HOLMES: I don't understand what is happening. The practical arts used to be one of the most popular areas of the secondary school when I was a student.

DR. BLAVITT: I think we have to face facts here. It's true that in the past this area of the secondary curriculum was one of the best, but what has happened is that our equipment has become obsolete and some of our teachers have not kept up. They're still teaching the way they were taught in college. Obsolete equipment and outdated teaching means that the practical arts can't compete for students on an elective basis. The kids are voting with their feet. They don't have similar options in English or math, but in the practical arts they can say something to us that perhaps can't be said any other way.

MRS. GAVIN: We've worked hard to overcome the problems. We applied for a small federal grant in vocational education but I couldn't get anyone to help me with it. Nobody seemed interested at the time.

DR. BLAVITT: Until, that is, until we cut a business teacher.

MRS. GAVIN: Yes, then the whole department got frantic.

MR. MORRIS: We have to look very hard at this situation. We don't want to lose the practical arts, but something is wrong. I suspect it's a combination of things. But I'm troubled by the fact that we aren't coming at this problem correctly. We are looking at business, industrial arts, and home economics as separate areas, each with its own problems. This may be true to a certain extent, but I think the fact that we have not thought about the practical arts per se as an entire area may be part of the problem. I've prepared this chart which indicates our enrollment grade by grade in all of the practical arts areas in grades five through twelve. The configuration shows the percentage of students of the entire student body by grade that enrolls in practical arts. The peak grades for enrollment by percentage of grades is seven and eight and then there is a declining percentage to the senior year at the high school.

MRS. HOLMES: Seven and eight are where the exploratories are pursued in the practical arts areas. In grades five and six they are merely receiving preliminary instruction in home economics and industrial arts.

MR. MORRIS: I know that in grade nine many are finishing a second year of personal typing so that's why that grade is the highest of the high school years. After that it's all downhill.

DR. BLAVITT: You know, Ray, I think perhaps we have not been thinking about the practical arts per se but as a collection of separate entities in the two secondary schools. What's happening to the practical arts that isn't happening elsewhere in the total curriculum?

MR. MORRIS: Well, I think that the combination of obsolete equipment and stodgy instruction which the kids see first hand in grades seven and eight convinces them they don't want any more when they have a chance to select courses from the ninth grade on.

DR. BLAVITT: You mean we should have put our best foot forward there and we don't.

MR. MORRIS: That's right. Pounding on old manual typewriters from old Nate Rogers doesn't excite middle school kids and they don't forget when it comes to high school.

MRS. HOLMES: We should lead with teachers who really can make the subjects interesting and we've got to do something about the equipment problem.

DR. BLAVITT: In addition to the personnel and staffing questions, I believe we should develop overarching objectives for the practical arts by which we can take this curriculum configuration developed by Ray and make systematic and valid changes in it. What is it that the practical arts should be doing for our students that is unique to this curricular area? I mean, why couldn't a student learn the skills offered in the practical arts in science or social studies as opposed to home economics or business courses?

MRS. HOLMES: We haven't been giving this enough thought I know, but we've got some immediate problems with possible staff reductions. Where can we find the time to do this and how will it help us?

DR. BLAVITT: How can we propose reductions when we don't know what impact it will have on the total practical arts area in the future? We aren't paying any attention to the future, we're only reacting to the pressures of the moment. What if a staff reduction means that five years from now several important objectives can't be reached and won't be picked up by any other curricular area? Will we be shortchanging our students in ways that we can't anticipate right now? We don't have any idea what the long range impact of these reductions means because we don't know what we have to do in the future. Maybe we should be consolidating staff to reach those objectives, or moving the practical arts around in the school day differently or at varying grade levels. Without any objectives any solution is probably as valid as any other. We don't have any criteria by which to meet this problem.

MR. MORRIS: That's management by crises.

DR. BLAVITT: Right. By not approaching this holistically and with ample forethought we may be doing the wrong thing.

MRS. HOLMES: What kind of configuration should we want instead of the one we have?

MR. MORRIS: Well, I for one would like to see greater enrollments and exposure at the earlier middle school years in all the practical arts. And I agree with what's been said earlier. Practical arts must go with its best teachers at these early years. The advanced courses have been parcelled out like favorites to the best teachers. The crux of the long-range problem lies at the middle school. I'd have to say, however, I don't want some of the duds at the high school, though. They will kill the program there even if the middle school kids are excited.

MRS. HOLMES: I've been saying that for years, Ray, middle school teachers must like middle school kids. They are a breed apart from either elementary or high school students. They can't be taught by tired old teachers who would really rather be at the high school.

DR. BLAVITT: We've got objectives from the state education department in all of the separate subject areas for the practical arts, but none as a collection of curriculum disciplines. In order to solve some of our staffing problems, we've got to pool our resources within a bigger curriculum pie. That means joint sharing of staff, supplies, and budget resources. Maybe by expanding the boundaries like this we can replace some of that old equipment in the business department.

MRS. HOLMES: The curriculum configuration question is crucial, I believe. We should be developing practical arts objectives for that area and then work back into the separate disciplines. I don't see how we can survive in that area without seriously rethinking priorities, and it's only with clear objectives that we can actually prioritize.

DR. BLAVITT: What we have here is a curriculum configuration by default.

MRS. GAVIN: The district took the first step when it abolished three separate chairperson positions and created just one chair for practical arts. That hasn't set too well with the one person who was a chairperson last year. It was fortunate that the other two retired when they did. I still wonder whether I can talk to the business teachers the same way I work in home economics. I just don't feel as comfortable outside of home economics.

DR. BLAVITT: It will come and maybe you will never feel totally comfortable. It seems to me that the overall responsibilities for coordination in the two schools demand more of your time anyway. Remember that we have a social studies chairperson now and nobody thinks anything about it. Twenty years ago there was a history and geography chair here. That has been changed as sociology, economics, and anthropology have been added. The academics have really led the way.

MRS. GAVIN: Well, what do we do now, I mean, where do we go from here?

DR. BLAVITT: It seems to me that we've got to do several things. First, I'd like the two school principals and you, Rita, to review staffing assignments with an eye to placing younger more recently trained staff up front with the middle school students. Then, I'd like Ray to take a crack at developing a short range curriculum configuration with whatever rationale he thinks will pertain. I'll try to develop some overarching objectives for the practical arts in terms of survival skills for students. Perhaps this will lead to lashing the separate disciplines a little more closely together to give us the flexibility to be more responsive to our situation.

MR. MORRIS: We could also make the practical arts a requirement rather than an elective.

DR. BLAVITT: That's the easy way out and I suspect it wouldn't be solving the problem anyway. The competition for the kids gives us an edge and an immediate method for determining how well we are really doing in meeting the problem. Besides, I don't think a college-oriented community like Washington would stand for required courses in industrial arts which kids found boring, or business or any other area. Boring college prep courses are more easily tolerated by parents because they value college. No course should be boring, but I suspect that the backlash would not do the practical arts as a valid subject in the secondary school curriculum any good. If our students flock to these curricular areas maybe the academic teachers will begin to see the need to revitalize their own houses too. I think we have the right opportunity here to lead the way.

MR. MORRIS: I don't know what other options we or the district has except to accept the budget cuts which I just can't bring myself to propose. But I see the need for change and we don't have all the time in the world.

DR. BLAVITT: Our options do seem small. I suggest we get to work.

The problems with practical arts discussed in this hypothetical dialogue are not unique to that area of the curriculum alone. Indeed, they apply to most of the curricular areas of the secondary school. The continuing problem with technical and skill obsolescence is one which will continue to plague the practical arts and vocational education. Under conditions of declining enrollment the lack of relevancy becomes acute and the need to reconceptualize the curriculum emerges as a theoretical and practical necessity.

The lack of appropriate overarching curriculum objectives by which to make decisions about curriculum organization will be the discussion of several later chapters. Every secondary school has a peculiar configuration. Most, however, occur by default and without adequate planning or consideration of alternatives. When elective courses begin losing enrollment, the pressure builds for a planned rather than a haphazard response.

In secondary schools, the practical arts are faced with most of the problems recounted in this chapter. The fact that curricular offerings in these areas are disappearing from course catalogs means that the loss of the concept of the comprehensive high school has begun. It is a trend which deserves the most serious, sustained and searching analysis possible in secondary education.

CHAPTER REFERENCES

1. Grant Venn, *Man, Education, and Manpower* (Arlington, Virginia: American Association of School Administrators, 1970), pp. 145-84.

2. Miriam Hecht and Lillian Traub, *Alternatives to College* (New York: Macmillan, 1974).

3. Caroline Bird, *The Case against College* (New York: David McKay Co., 1975), p. 83.

4. Extrapolated from Mildred Davy, Elizabeth Smith, and Theodore Myers, *Everyday Occupations* (Boston: D. C. Heath Co., 1941).

5. All of these occupations are part of the secondary school training program in vocational education and are explained in "Guidance Counselor's Handbook," Mid-Westchester Center for Occupational Education, Board of Cooperative Education Services, New York, 1976.

6. See Marvin J. Feldman, "The Reformed Curriculum in Vocational Education," in *High School 1980*, ed. Alvin C. Eurich (New York: Pitman Publishing Co., 1970), pp. 193-206.

7. David Jepsen and Josiah Dilley, "Vocational Decision-Making Models: A Review and Comparative Analysis," *Review of Educational Research* 44, no. 3 (Summer 1974): 331-50.

8. The course of study was taken from "Secondary Industrial Arts: An Instructional Planning Guide," State Education Department, Bureau of Industrial Arts, Albany, New York, 1973, p. 7.

9. See J. W. Giachino and Ralph O. Gallington, *Course Construction in Industrial Arts, Vocational and Technical Education* (Chicago: American Technical Society, 1967)

10. See Edward A. Krug, *The Secondary School Curriculum* (New York: Harper and Row, 1960), pp. 361-84.

11. *Home Economics Education: Syllabus for a Comprehensive Program* (Albany, New York: State Education Department, Bureau of Home Economics, 1965).

12. Module unit titles taken from "Home Economics Education: Curriculum Planning Guidelines, Level I and II, Grades 5-8," State Education Department, Bureau of Secondary Curriculum Development, Albany, New York, 1974.

13. The description of the office practice laboratory was extrapolated from Chapter 3, "The Office Practice Laboratory," in *Office Practice 1 and 2 Syllabus* (Albany, New York: State Education Department, Bureau of Secondary Curriculum Development, 1972 revision), pp. 13-18.

14. For a thorough review of almost all areas of business education, see Calfrey C. Calhoun and Mildred Hillestad, eds., *Contributions of Research to Business Education* (Washington, D.C.: National Business Education Association, Yearbook Nine, 1971).

FOR FURTHER READING

Burkett, Lowell A. "The Role of Vocational Education in Career Education." *NASSP Bulletin* 57 (March 1973): 73-81.

Fibel, Lewis R. "Should Schools and Industry Train Technicians?" *Industrial Education* 62 (November 1973): 107-08.

Huffman, Harry, and Welter, Clyde W. "Updating Business Education Programs." *Business Education Forum* 30 (January 1976): 5-13.

Lee, Jeanette. "The Future of Home Economics: A Delphi Study." *Journal of Home Economics* 65 (October 1973): 23-27.

Malsbury, Dean R. "Business Education" (Curriculum Update). *NASSP Bulletin* 59 (January 1975): 95-100.

Morgan, Barbara. "The Home Economics Program in a Model School." *Journal of Home Economics* 64 (January 1972): 43-45.

Peterson, Sterling D. "Can Industrial Arts Fit into Vocational-Career Programs?" *Industrial Education* 62 (September 1973): 35-37.

Prediger, Dale J.; Roth, John D.; and Noeth, Richard J. "Career Development of Youth: A Nationwide Study." *The Personnel and Guidance Journal* 53 (October 1974): 97-104.

Severino, Sister Carolyn. "Business Education in the Academic High School." *Business Education Review* 22 (Spring 1971): 46-56.

Wells, Carl E. "Will Vocational Education Survive?" *Phi Delta Kappan* 54 (February 1972): 369, 380.

Wray, Jerome A. "Vocational Education—Of What Value?" *NASSP Bulletin* 60 (December 1976): 60-62.

7 Career
Education

Career education is less than a decade old, but already it has made significant inroads in the thinking of secondary school educators. A survey for the U.S. Office of Education in the late 1970s revealed that while only three percent of the country's 16,000 school districts had completely implemented the concept, more than half were engaged in gearing up for some type of future implementation. (1) The demand by educational leaders, politicians, and industrial and business executives for reinforcement of the requirement for skilled workers in the American economy has ebbed and flowed since the 1880s. (2) The inability of efforts in vocational education to satisfy this demand was a major impetus in the rise of career education.

Vocational education did not meet the needs of many secondary school students who found the academic, college-oriented curriculum unsuited to their abilities or interests, and the general curriculum a "sop" which left them unprepared to enter the job market and secure gainful employment. Vocational education had acquired a stigma within the secondary school curriculum as a place for misfits, dropouts, or for those with limited intellectual abilities, who were satisfied to leave school as early as possible for deadend jobs.

Vocational education also suffered from underfunding when programs with outdated equipment sent students to jobs which required knowledge and skill with newer equipment. Some jobs students were trained for in school simply did not exist or were rapidly disappearing from the occupational scene. Even after training, students still had to receive additional training in apprenticeships and could not find immediate employment.

The first national assessment of career occupational development was administered during the 1973-74 school year to 100,000 persons. The results indicated that one-third of the adults and more than half of the seventeen-year-olds had difficulty writing a job application and figuring a finance charge. Less than half the seventeen-year-olds had taken an aptitude test and only 16 percent discussed the results with a school counselor. In one test exercise only 24 percent put a return address on a job application letter assuring them that they would not get a job. The study also found that those subjects with the least education and from the lowest income levels of society were the ones most lacking employable skills. Perhaps most disturbing was the fact that 44 percent of the seventeen-year-olds wanted a professional career. National figures show that of all the jobs available, only 20-25 percent were professional or managerial in nature. (3) (4)

Sidney P. Marland, as United States Commissioner of Education, almost singlehandedly ushered forth the cry for career education in a series of widely publicized speeches that decried the general curriculum of the secondary school as a "dumping ground" for students leading to general unemployment. (5) (6) Marland cited the need to reestablish the moral qualities of work in American life and to relieve the general unemployment rate. (7)

Career education is an attempt to reinstate the world of work in the secondary school curriculum as something worthwhile for all students. It tries to reduce the elitism of the academic curriculum by insisting that preparation for college is nothing more than a different career and that all of education is ultimately career education in that it ends with a job.

More specifically, career education aims to create a "real world" job awareness in school students long before decisions about school curricula to reach those careers must be made. By beginning in the elementary grades more realistic personal and societal assessments could be undertaken by students so that they would understand their own capabilities. Career education also aims to identify and teach those skills and work habits which are required in the world of work.

The advocates of career education point out that the secondary schools have a responsibility for the total education of the student and that this most definitely includes some preparation for the world of work. Studies by the U.S. Department of Labor indicate that students in the general curriculum of the secondary school account for 70 percent of the high school dropouts, 78 percent of the inmates in correctional institutions, and 88 percent of the enrollees in manpower training programs. However, students in this high school population account for only 32 percent of all high school pupils. (8)

The secondary curriculum developer may well ponder the problem posed while trying to create studies which meet the needs identified and avoid the shortcomings of the efforts in vocational education. Some of these dimensions are as follows:

Jobs in the nation are not equally open to all, some require extensive training, preparation periods, degrees and certification;

Some jobs possess less qualifications, less training and preparation;

Some secondary school students do not appear to possess the interests, abilities, experiences and backgrounds to pursue extended and prolonged training (delayed gratification patterns) to jobs which require such training;

Some students in the secondary school appear to have no place, they are neither college oriented or motivated, nor interested in highly technical work;

The economic conditions of our society as well as its work values require a person to work to survive and acquire a sense of personal worth. (9)

Some of the ways the curriculum developer may approach the challenge may be cited below.

Change the Parameters or Definitions of Schooling

The National Commission on the Reform of Secondary Education established by the Charles F. Kettering Foundation recommended that compulsory education be dropped to the age of fourteen in order to free the secondary school from its demeaning and deadening custodial functions. (10) This would perhaps eliminate that segment of the student population which find school and its curriculum largely irrelevant, and the necessity for a general curriculum. The requirement for a "dumping ground" would therefore be reduced. Other social alternatives for these youth would have to be established. Still another solution would be to move completely away from the notion of the comprehensive secondary school by modeling a European approach to secondary education. This would return the secondary school to almost exclusively a college preparatory institution. In essence the social sorting function of students would occur at lower levels than the secondary school.

Change the Secondary Curriculum

Current secondary schools have between two or three "tracks" or general curricular paths. Broadly speaking these are college preparatory, vocational technical, and general. The general curriculum too often represents watered down basic college preparatory courses. In the place of Algebra 1, the course General Math is instituted and in the place of Biology 1, General Science or Basic Science.

Disciplinary problems, pupil absence and truancy most often run highest in the general courses in the initial school years of secondary education. Characteristics of the secondary pupils who have a high degree of school related problems may be one or all of the following:

a. They are most often representative of the poorer socioeconomic classes; (11)
b. They have a variety of problems in school such as reduced language utilization and efficiency, difficulties in handling abstract language and/or mathematic concepts;

c. They have shorter attention spans and find difficulty in functioning under delayed gratification patterns demanded in school work;
d. They lack "acceptable" social skills, courtesies and amenities. Many are physically aggressive and resort to violence easily;
e. Parental participation and interest are marginal in the school. Parental attitudes may be hostile towards school held values and authority. Parental authority in the home may often be totally absent;
f. They hold poor self-concepts and reflect negative social stereotypes held of them by the larger society. They are fatalistic;
g. They are "here and now" oriented rather than future-oriented.

Highly motivated college-oriented secondary school students present few school problems for secondary educators. Even if school is totally lacking in appeal, many, with positive reinforcement from the home, "make it through" the curriculum and head for the professions at the college or universities. Without reinforcement, facing failure and frustration, alienated youth come to resent school. Its ways are foreign and nonsensical. Possessing a low frustration level to handle anxiety, such students pose enormous problems for secondary schools. The school curriculum may be as irrelevant for all students as for these students. However, these lack the sophisticated and sublimated coping skills possessed by their wealthier, more parent-motivated peers. Violence, vandalism, and attacks upon teachers and each other have resulted in rising costs for protection because of the need for security guards in hallways, restrooms, and lunch areas.

Change the Existing Social Order

This alternative may not appear to be too practical for the secondary curriculum developer. After all, what power is possessed to engage in such radical change beyond the school? It is not suggested here that the curriculum developer engage in attempts to alter the existing social order, but rather to recognize that perhaps not even career education will be successful because of constraints imposed by the present social order.

The social order is hierarchically arranged. Prestige, status, power and wealth follow the lines of social and work hierarchies. Such hierarchies are intimately related to a capitalistic economy with primary emphasis upon the profit motive. Wealth is capital. In order to open up job opportunity it is necessary for the social order to undergo fundamental changes. Such concepts as establishing ceilings on what a person could ultimately earn and floors for a guaranteed living wage and income have been proposed by Christopher Jencks in his searching study of inequality in American life. (12) It is argued that once the social order is rearranged the functions of schools within that order can be more easily altered than at the present time. Meanwhile the schools and the curriculum within the schools can serve as a prod to such social reordering.

While such a strategy may seem farfetched at the present, the goals of career education may not be possible without some social restructuring. The educator cannot create jobs in the existing social order. To the largest extent the curriculum developer is captured by what jobs are available for students to fill as the next several sections in this chapter will amply demonstrate. If career education merely clarifies realistic aspirations for students, as it surely must attempt to do with 44 percent wanting professional jobs and such jobs available for only 25 percent, on what basis is this to be accomplished? The career education advocate would point out that the students need realistic career counseling in order to realize that not all of them have the aptitude to perform well or be happy at such jobs.

The contrary view is that aptitude is largely a matter of cultural conditioning and that the abilities to perform well at a professional or managerial level, as opposed to other levels, is the result of artificial barriers imposed by a discriminatory selection process for training and entrance. (13) Critics of career education point out that it will become another vehicle to channel the poor and the minorities into low paying, deadend jobs at perhaps an earlier age. (14)

Career education believers point out that the world of work will provide new meaning for many alienated students and if the curriculum is properly developed, students will be able to avoid being channeled into deadend jobs. Still another approach may be to alter the curriculum in significantly different ways by developing alternatives which are more in tune with the learning styles and experiences of the disadvantaged. This curriculum would be one which does not depend upon a lecture-recall teaching strategy, which does not require extended pupil inactivity in seat bound situations, and which can capitalize upon bilingualism. This would foster teaching methodologies which are immediate and couched within the life framework of the ghetto or barrio. School values which clash with the viewpoints of minority culture such as cooperation versus competition (as with certain Indian tribes or Mexican-Americans) would be harmonized.

Positive features of each minority culture would be highlighted in art, music, and the academics as well as the approach to life and living. The unitary structure of values in the secondary schools, now dominated by middle class values, will have to become more pluralistic. The "real" world is many worlds with many viewpoints. While it may be necessary to prepare students to live in the real world and earn a living, merely providing access to the skills of a job may not be enough. Happiness is not a deadend job on a marginal income which reinforces the social necessity for the existence of a ghetto, or welfare and handouts. The acceptance of the present job structure of the nation may be a value which is *not* fostered, depending upon the situation in which the individual worker may find herself or himself. If work is to become a meaningful activity students may have to be taught additional skills such as job enlargement and know where and how to engage in job advancement. In addition, racial and sexual barriers to union membership and work within the crafts and trades must be modified.

Schooling for some secondary students may have to be elongated beyond the present work experience approach. Students may be taught some job related skills and find work and maintain a student status beyond a three or four year time period. As such they may have "graduated" in one curriculum but graduate from school in another several years. The stigma of not having a high school diploma on the job market will have to be lessened or there may have to be several diplomas given at varying time periods.

Establishing Career Education Options for Job Training

The traditional secondary school curriculum at the junior high or middle school includes exploratory sequences in foods, home economics, typing, and industrial arts (which may include woods, metals, printing, drafting and electricity). At the high school level these same subjects may be pursued in greater depth in business education classes which may include courses in retailing, advertising, bookkeeping, shorthand, and advanced typing. Home economics may be broadened to include child psychology and child care, gourmet cooking, human relations and home hygiene. Industrial arts may include advanced woods, hobby woods, photography, advanced drafting, power mechanics, automobile repair and autobody work, furniture making, metal crafting and construction as well as drafting and architectural design. Large school systems may offer extensive vocational-technical training in specialized schools such as aviation mechanics, cosmetology, dental assistance, medical and legal secretarial training, air conditioning and appliance repair, carpentry and many others.

As the secondary school contemplates establishing curricular alternatives in which more of its graduates can move directly into the job market via career education, it is faced by the fact that it must have information about the available job markets in its surroundings. What are the jobs in which there is a shortage of skilled applicants? In addition, the curriculum planners should have some idea as to the stability of the jobs. Is it anticipated that while there may be a shortage at the present will the supply soon catch up with the demand? To plan intelligently for career education and job training in which secondary school students may either work in the community within simulated job situations in the school or on the job, the first steps towards establishing such options are securing data about the existing and future job markets for graduates.

Determining the Job Market by Developing a Community Profile from Census Data

Secondary schools located within urban areas or in suburban or rural areas will serve and be influenced by different job markets. It is important for school curriculum developers to secure a good picture of the possibilities of jobs in the local community, to have some idea of available human resources, and to know what the community's expectations in this area might be prior to actually developing a career education job training program. One excellent method for obtaining some answers to these questions is to develop a community socioeconomic-demographic profile. (15) An important source of data to construct such a profile is the United States Census. How this is done is shown in the next series of graphs and charts.

Let us suppose that Riverdell is a community of approximately 10,000 residents and it is composed of two census tracts, A and B. These tracts are located within a larger division called a county. Table 7-1 shows an ethnic breakdown of the population in Riverdell and its surrounding county. The county has more citizens of Italian, Mexican, and Puerto Rican descent than either of the two census tracts. On the other hand, Riverdell appears to have more descendents from the United Kingdom, Ireland, Sweden, Germany, Poland, Czechoslovakia, Austria, Hungary, Russia, and Canada than does the county. Riverdell is thus more heterogeneous than the county. A further examination of Table 7-I will show that the various nationalities have tended to cluster unevenly in one census tract. For example, there are more descendents from

Table 7-1

ETHNIC BREAKDOWN OF
POPULATION OF RIVERDELL

Item	County	Tract A	Tract B
1. Percent population who are natives	61.5%	59.3%	60.8%
2. Percent population of mixed percentage (one parent not a native)	26.4%	30.5%	29.6%
3. Percent foreign born	11.9%	10.0%	9.4%
Percent Foreign Stock			
United Kingdom	7.2%	8.0%	9.5%
Ireland	7.8%	12.2%	5.6%
Sweden	1.1%	.6%	1.8%
Germany	8.4%	8.1%	9.1%
Poland	5.7%	9.5%	4.6%
Czechoslovakia	1.8%	2.0%	2.4%
Austria	4.1%	5.5%	5.0%
Hungary	2.0%	10.9%	3.2%
USSR	7.9%	14.3%	15.7%
Italy	30.1%	12.3%	17.3%
Canada	3.3%	.8%	6.5%
Mexico	.1%	—	—
4. Percent black population	9.5%	2.1%	3.5%
5. Percent persons of Puerto Rican Birth	.006%	.001%	.003%

Ireland, Poland, and Hungary in Tract A than B. In Tract B there are more descendents from Sweden, Italy, and Canada. These uneven clusters may be descriptive of migration patterns both to and within the community. They may also indicate patterns of discrimination in housing as well.

Table 7-2 shows the varying classes of workers in Riverdell and the educational statistics of its population. Tract A has more private wage earners than the county and Tract B has fewer than the county. Tract B has more self-employed workers than either Tract A or the county. Table 7-3 shows that Riverdell (both tracts) differs from the county by having a lower percentage of nonhigh school graduates with quite a bit

Table 7-2

CLASS OF WORKERS IN RIVERDELL

Type of Work	County	Tract A	Tract B
Private wage earner	77.4%	79.5%	75.4%
Government worker	14.3%	14.7%	15.0%
Self-employed	7.8%	5.3%	9.5%
Unpaid family worker	.3%	.3%	——

Table 7-3

EDUCATIONAL STATISTICS OF RIVERDELL

Item	County	Tract A	Tract B
Percent age 16-21 not high school graduates and not enrolled in school	7.3%	4.7%	2.9%
Percent high school graduates	64.5%	63.4%	75.2%
Percent with 4 years or more of college	12.0%	12.0%	17.0%

fewer in Tract B. However, Tract A is homogeneous with the county in the number of high school graduates and the total percentage with four or more years of college. That educational differences account for income differences is strikingly illustrated in Table 7-4. Tract A's median income is below the county's and below in the income levels beginning in the range of $10,000. Tract A contains a larger percentage of families below the poverty level than the county and more people receiving Social Security income.

Tract B's greater income wealth pulls Riverdell above the county in median income, percentage of families with income in the $10,000-$24,000 range, and percentage of families with income in the $25,000-$49,999 range. Tract A's relative poverty puts Riverdell below the county's percentage of families with $50,000 or more in income, percent of families below the poverty level and percent of families receiving Social Security income. On the income level there appears to be great disparity within Riverdell. Table 7-5 indicates perhaps why the income

Table 7-4

INCOME STATISTICS FROM RIVERDELL

Item	County	Tract A	Tract B
Median Income	$13,784	$11,645	$18,712
Percent families with income in range of $10,000-$24,999	52.5%	48.4%	58.5%
Percent families with income in range of $25,000-$49,999	13.2%	10.3%	22.3%
Percent families over $50,000 in income	4.0%	2.0%	4.0%
Percent of all families below poverty level	4.5%	9.4%	1.9%
Percent of persons receiving Social Security income	22.8%	36.7%	28.2%

differentials are so striking. While both census tracts contain higher percentages of professional and technical occupationally employed compared to the county, Tract B is higher. In the numbers of persons in the managerial and administrative levels, Tract A has less than the county average and Tract B more. Both tracts contain greater numbers of clerical and secretarial personnel than the county, with Tract A being very much higher. Tract B has significantly fewer service workers (e.g. sanitation) than the county average and Tract A, as well as fewer private household workers.

Tables 7-6 and 7-7 show the relative age breakdown of the two census tracts. On the whole, Tract B contains more younger males and females except in the age range 20-24 than Tract A or the county, while Tract A contains more people in age ranges 55 and above than Tract B or the county. Tract A is a far older part of town with more established families. Table 7-7 shows a population pyramid constructed from the census data. The greatest percentages of population in the two tracts comprising Riverdell appear in age ranges 45-54, 35-44, and 10-14 respectively. The pyramid shows that about 50 percent of the total population of Riverdell is 34-years-old or younger, 28 percent between ages 35-54, and only 22 percent 55 and beyond. However a disproportionate number of these senior citizens live in Tract A.

Table 7-5

OCCUPATIONAL ANALYSIS OF TOTAL EMPLOYED
PERSONS 16-YEARS-OLD OR OVER, RIVERDELL

Occupation	County	Tract A	Tract B
1. Professional/technical	21.1%	26.4%	29.2%
2. Managers/administrative	12.6%	10.9%	16.6%
3. Sales	8.9%	6.4%	7.1%
4. Clerical/secretarial	21.0%	28.6%	22.4%
5. Craftsmen	10.7%	8.5%	8.4%
6. Operations	7.2%	5.6%	5.4%
7. Laborers (except farm)	3.1%	2.7%	2.7%
8. Service workers	9.8%	8.6%	.6%
9. Private household workers	2.2%	1.0%	.2%

A school-community profile is an invaluable source of reference for school curriculum planners. It provides information about where students may be located and within what peculiar social-economic circumstances. The profile may be helpful in locating resources for the utilization of certain jobs in a career education program. These data, coupled with information from the local and nearby labor market, help determine and define the market in which high school graduates may be looking for jobs. Large communities have more jobs and make it easier to establish training programs. The school cannot change the job market. If students want to go to work they must seek employment within fields for which there are openings. To this extent the curriculum is the victim of general economic policies and conditions within large regions. A high rate of unemployment will have a direct impact upon the success of graduates in finding work for which they have been appropriately trained.

Determining Job Supply and Demand

After the market has been defined with boundaries, the next step is to secure information about available job openings. The school can contact the local Department of Employment. A hypothetical example of how job openings may be determined is as follows in Diagram 7-1. This illustrates one way of developing a preliminary understanding of the need for various types of jobs in the immediate geographic area. The data are for a high school located in a community of 38,000 with surrounding suburbs. The community is fifteen minutes from City A and 45 minutes from City B.

Table 7-6

ANALYSIS OF MALES IN
RIVERDELL BY AGE

Age Range	County	Tract A	Tract B
Under 5	7.9%	7.1%	6.8%
5-9	9.7%	8.1%	10.8%
10-14	10.4%	7.2%	13.9%
15-19	8.5%	7.0%	10.8%
20-24	5.8%	6.2%	3.7%
25-34	11.4%	13.2%	7.0%
35-44	12.8%	9.7%	14.4%
45-54	13.0%	14.7%	14.6%
55-59	5.9%	8.8%	5.6%
60-64	5.1%	6.5%	4.5%
65-74	6.0%	5.7%	4.7%
75+	2.9%	5.3%	2.5%

Table 7-7

ANALYSIS OF FEMALES IN
RIVERDELL BY AGE

Age Range	County	Tract A	Tract B
Under 5	6.9%	5.6%	5.2%
5-9	8.3%	5.6%	9.8%
10-14	8.8%	6.4%	13.8%
15-19	8.1%	6.7%	8.9%
20-24	6.9%	5.9%	4.5%
25-34	11.7%	11.0%	8.2%
35-44	12.6%	10.6%	16.5%
45-54	13.1%	15.8%	15.0%
55-59	6.0%	8.2%	5.3%
60-64	5.1%	5.8%	4.0%
65-74	7.3%	10.6%	5.0%
75+	4.6%	7.2%	3.3%

Table 7-8

POPULATION PYRAMID

Age Range		Percentage of Population
Under 5	580	6.1%
5-9	854	9.0%
10-14	1064	11.2%
15-19	829	8.8%
20-24	464	4.9%
25-34	884	9.4%
35-44	1279	13.5%
45-54	1423	15.0%
55-59	629	6.7%
60-64	478	5.0%
65-74	590	6.2%
75+	405	4.2%

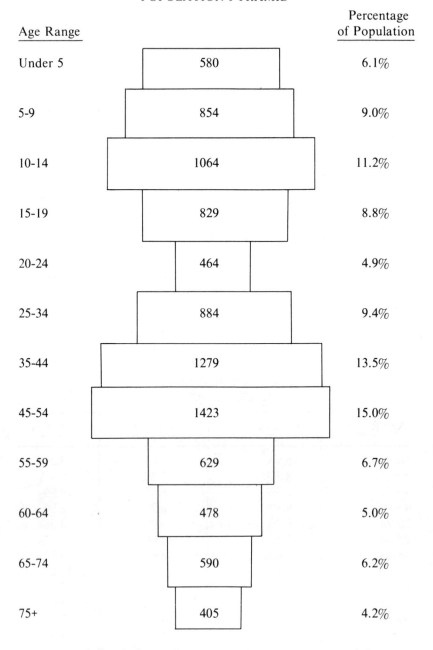

Diagram 7-1

HYPOTHETICAL SURVEY OF JOB OPENINGS
WITHIN THE SPECIFIED JOB MARKET

Legend

S = serious shortage of qualified applicants in area of strong demand
FG = fairly good opportunity for employment, some shortage of qualified applicants
SA = supply of qualified applicants is adequate to take care of demand
LE = limited employment due to over supply of qualified applicants
ND = no demand, serious unemployment in this occupation at this time

Occupation	Immediate Vicinity in Local Community	Extended Community Suburbs	City A	City B
Baker	ND	ND	FG	FG
Barber	ND	FG	ND	ND
Bank Teller	LE	LE	SA	SA
Bellman	ND	ND	SA	SA
Bus Boy	LE	SA	FG	FG
Cosmetologist	LE	SA	FG	FG
Cook	SA	SA	FG	FG
Chef	ND	ND	SA	SA
Cashier	SA	SA	FG	SA
Claim Adjuster	SA	SA	LE	ND
Clerk Typist	SA	FG	FG	FG
Dietitian	LE	SA	SA	SA
Electrician	SA	SA	FG	SA
Fireman	ND	ND	SA	LE
Masseur	ND	ND	LE	LE
Meat Cutter	SA	SA	SA	SA
Mechanic (car)	SA	SA	FG	FG
Mechanic (marine)	SA	S	FG	SA
Mechanic (air condition)	FG	S	FG	FG
Nurse Aid	SA	SA	FG	FG
Nurse (LPN)	SA	SA	FG	SA
Oceanographer	ND	ND	SA	ND
Photographer	ND	ND	SA	SA
Rater (insurance)	SA	SA	SA	SA

Diagram 7-1 (cont)

Secretary	SA	LE	FG	FG
Steward	ND	ND	LE	LE
TV Repairman	SA	FG	FG	SA
Taxi Driver	ND	SA	SA	FG
Waiter/Waitress	SA	SA	FG	FG
Watchman	ND	ND	SA	FG

The data from Diagram 7-1 indicate that serious shortages in the extended community suburbs exist in marine mechanics and air conditioning mechanics. The high school staff was aware that a new marina had been built two years ago and many people had bought condominiums near it. The supply of boats and the demand for maintenance and upkeep exceeded the supply of mechanics. However, they required more information before developing a curriculum and a program. Areas in which there was some shortage of qualified applicants in the local community included air conditioning mechanics, and in the suburbs, barbers, clerk typists, and TV repairmen. In the two cities included in the job market boundaries the following occupations required some qualified applicants:

bakers
bus boys
cosmetologists
cooks
clerk typists
electrician (City A only)
car mechanics

marine mechanic (City A only)
nurses aid
oceanographer (City A only)
secretaries
TV repairmen (City A only)
Waiter-waitresses
watchman (City B only)

Making Curricular Adjustments/ Obtaining More information

After looking over the data the school's curriculum planners decided on the following:

1. To conduct a follow-up survey in the suburbs and City A on marine mechanics;
2. To conduct a follow-up survey on car mechanics, nurses aides, secretaries in Cities A and B;
3. Not to include either cosmetology or oceanography in the curriculum as too expensive;

4. To design a minicourse in baking within home economics;
5. To design several minicourses in cooking within home economics;
6. To include a quarterly elective in skills of being a waiter or waitress within home economics,

The follow-up survey on marine mechanics was sent to thirty firms, and with twenty-eight responding, yielded the data shown in Diagram 7-2.

Diagram 7-2

FOLLOW-UP SURVEY ON MARINE MECHANICS

*An Indication of Areas of Greatest Knowledge
Required in Marine Mechanics*

Scale of Importance	Engine	Steering	Hull	Rigging	Radio
5	27	9	25	12	15
4	1	7	3	7	19
3	0	5	0	3	2
2	0	4	0	3	2
1	0	3	0	3	0

5 = of great importance
1 = of little importance

The school was worried about establishing marine mechanics in the curriculum. While there was a serious shortage in this area the administration and faculty were not sure how stable the market would be once the courses were put into operation. They decided to examine population trends in the marina area. They obtained data from the marina planners which projected an ultimate population of 138,000. These were also verified by city and county planning departments. The current population of the marina was 24,000. Examining the growth rate they determined that there had been a 4-5 percent steady increase each year for the last five years. There was still plenty of beach front property available as well as dock space.

A decision was made that the potential of the job market warranted the investment of equipment and space in the school. School administrators visited existing job sites, contacted suppliers and asked for donations of scrap boats, engines and parts. There was an enthusiastic response. Within two months the school had a miniature boat yard. Two teachers were given special inservice training and were freed over the summer to develop the actual curriculum. Meanwhile a special orientation session was held in various classes in the school explaining to students the types of job opportunities available. The first semester saw thirty-seven students enrolled in three classes of marine mechanics.

The follow-up survey from the managers of 168 firms in Cities A and B on secretarial employees showed some surprising results. When asked what skills secretaries most often lacked which resulted in them being dismissed the managers responded as shown in Diagram 7-3

Diagram 7-3

*SKILLS MOST OFTEN LACKING IN SECRETARIAL
EMPLOYEES DISMISSED*

Skill	Percentage Citing
1. Human relations, inability to deal with unpleasant customers or clients on the telephone or in person on the job;	59%
2. Unwillingness to go beyond the defined work day or task and take an interest in the business or firm;	47%
3. Inconsistent work and frequent absences;	23%
4. Lack of technical training, i.e., shorthand, typing speed, accuracy, spelling, etc.	

After examining the data, the school felt that only moderate adjustments were required in the existing curriculum to accommodate the job market. While the high school business education department taught separately such skills as typing, shorthand, spelling and accuracy, the data indicated that for job applicants to be successful that a curriculum unit in human relations would have to be developed. Typical situations where secretaries came into contact with clients and the public were incorporated into the curriculum. Role playing in various types of job encounters was planned as an appropriate method.

The school decided that oceanography was too complicated an area to develop and the job market too limited. It was thought that by upgrading certain aspects of the electric shop courses most of the skills needed by a TV repairman could be acquired. The school decided not to establish any training for bus boys or watchmen. Students would merely be referred to the job sources.

Other Curricular Activities

The emphasis on career education has an elementary counterpart as well. Elementary students are made more aware of the existence of different jobs and the requirements for them. At the secondary level school libraries should have places where displays and information about jobs are readily available. The secondary guidance department should conduct surveys of students assessing career readiness and interest and hold some student orientation about the world of work. Career days should present opportunities for students to examine and hear what real practitioners have to say about their occupations. Such days should provide for candid exposures to the world of work.

Still other possibilities include tours of large sites where potential employers might be. These may include tourist facilities, factories, mines, manufacturing centers, hotels, or motels. One large school system owns its own hotel where it trains students in all aspects of hotel operation.

The curriculum development sequence for career education or incorporating vocational offerings into the secondary school includes determination of the job market boundaries and market stability, precise information on needed job skills, cost of program and training for the school to make the program operational. If there is no public transportation available the school may find its definition of the job market constrained. All of these considerations should be carefully weighed when developing new curriculum for job training in the secondary school.

Additional Problems with Career Education

While career education hoped to avoid many of the problems of vocational technical education within the secondary school, experience has shown that it may not be possible to avoid some of the failures of vocational education. These are generic problems which confront any kind of training to provide immediate skills for the existing job market.

The Courses Are Considered to Possess Lowered Status

Most secondary schools are marked with social cliques which represent racial, sexual, economic, and ethnic cleavages in the larger community. If one particular facet of the school's curriculum comes to be dominated by one clique as the industrial arts area has for many years, it becomes a place to be avoided by other cliques. If career education is to have a chance it cannot become the "dumping grounds" for the unfit, the unmotivated, and the alienated. Although career education is aimed at bringing more life into the curriculum of the secondary school it cannot afford to be "captured" exclusively by any one segment of the student population. Such status differentials pose very real problems for curriculum developers trying to expand the vitality and scope of the school's program to more effectively deal with all students. The elective system of the secondary school introduces an element into curriculum planning that tends to reflect existing social and academic gaps. Unless career education can find a broad appeal among all students it too will simply become part of the existing course-social class structure of the secondary school.

The Shifting Nature of the Job Market

As the example of marine mechanics clearly showed, a job shortage today may not be a shortage tomorrow. The need for engineers, teachers, and Ph.D.'s in the sixties was quickly met in the seventies. Developing training programs for specific jobs is very risky unless the school curriculum planners can establish some future for a particular kind of work. In order to find work for all those seeking it, the school may be tempted to place or train students for marginal, deadend jobs. Those students who accept such jobs may be unemployed within a decade.

Rising Costs and Technological Obsolescence

While some job skills can be developed within the school's existing curriculum, many will require the acquisition of special equipment which may be costly and due to the rapid turnover of machines in some occupations, be quickly obsolete. This is particularly true in the secretarial area with new electronic machines and word processing systems. Other areas such as printing, electronics and construction have moved faster than the ability of the schools to adequately prepare students to enter a shifting job market and obtain meaningful employment.

Clash with Values Regarding a
Comprehensive Education

What is convenient is not necessarily lasting. What is lasting may not always be immediately transferrable to a job market and employment. The American comprehensive high school has been an ideal for several decades. There are signs that it is fading, at least in the inner city where the demand for integration has led to the development of magnet schools to achieve voluntary integration. Magnet and alternative schools may focus exclusively on one facet of the curriculum such as science or the arts, or in this case vocational—technical or career education. Such singularity of program emphasis moves away from a "balanced" curriculum and forces curriculum developers to relate language and mathematical skills to employability skills. There may not always be a one to one relationship. The idea of the comprehensive secondary school has been to postpone career choices and to allow a period of time for experimentation and some failure before choices were made which turn out to be irrevocable. The curricular "slack time" has allowed some movement across lines of disciplines and postponed some implications of student decision-making. The rise of the community colleges has partially been the result of the need for post secondary school skill training and a place to begin preparation for college. However, the generally explosive nature of pupil indecision has in too many cases fallen upon the poor and the minorities in the high schools of the nation. These students have become lost and have progressively fallen behind in the skill areas of the curriculum. The no-man's land of the general curriculum has been a dead end. In a competitive economy the time to recoup a bad decision or the consequences of no decision about future careers is not without penalties. It is not surprising that some students find the price too high.

Community Rejection

Some communities, especially some minority communities have occasionally rejected the new words *career education* or *vocational preparation* as another method by the establishment to track their children into menial and low paying jobs. Objections have in some cases led to violence or boycotts or simply poor attendance. As Passow notes in his reassessment of secondary education, many business and community agencies have never perceived themselves as extensions of the school. (16) This will require close school-community relationships.

The problems posed by the incorporation of career education as a thrust to the nation's social and economic problems may not be solvable in the schools. There is ample evidence that the schools cannot train students for existing jobs without accepting the existing job structure with all of its inequities. Therefore, the problem which is attempted to be solved by the schools is perpetuated in the schools.

Clash with Traditional Curricular Emphases

At a national conference on career education, the associate director of the Council for Basic Education warned that career education may detract from the goals of basic education and that its emphasis may be antiintellectual. (17) The American Federation of Teachers warned that labor felt that early efforts in career education were defined almost exclusively by management and what was "good" for management. The union listed the caveats which it felt were essential to support the concept:

1. That child labor laws not be relaxed.
2. That minimum wage laws not be sabotaged.
3. That big business, government and labor serve on advisory committees in the schools of the states. (18)

The largest question facing career education is whether or not it can succeed where previous efforts to close the gap between the schools and the world of work have been only partially successful. While the secondary curriculum developer cannot control all of the factors bearing upon an answer, the anticipation of the consequences can prevent a duplication of what was unsuccessful in the past.

CHAPTER REFERENCES

1. Gene I. Maeroff, "Differences Persist on Career Education," *New York Times,* November 11, 1976.

2. W. Norton Grubb and Marvin Lazerson, "Rally 'Round the Workplace: Continuities and Fallacies in Career Education," *Harvard Educational Review* 45, no. 4 (November 1974): 451-74.

3. "Survey Studies 'Job Readiness,'" *NAEP Newsletter* 9, no. 6 (December 1976).

4. Noel Epstein, "Career Education Study Cites Rivalry for Jobs," *Washington Post,* November 9, 1976.

5. Sidney P. Marland, "Career Education—More Than a Name," speech before the annual meeting of the State Directors of Vocational Education, Washington, D.C., May 4, 1971, p. 9. (Mimeograph.)

6. _____ , "Educating for the Real World," speech at the Twelfth Annual Banquet of the Jefferson County Chamber of Commerce, West Virginia, May 26, 1971, p. 5. (Mimeograph.)

7. _____ , *Career Education: A Proposal for Reform* (New York: McGraw-Hill, 1974).

8. These data were cited in *Career Education: The State of the Scene* (Washington, D.C.: Office of Career Education, U.S. Office of Education, November 1974), p. 4.

9. See *Work in America* (Cambridge: M.I.T. Press, 1973).

10. See Recommendation Number 28 of the National Commission on the Reform of Secondary Education in *The Reform of Secondary Education* (New York: McGraw-Hill, 1973), pp. 127-28; 133-37.

11. See Ray C. Rist, "Student Social Class and Teacher Expectations: The Self-Fulfilling Prophecy in Ghetto Education," *Harvard Educational Review* 40, no. 13 (August 1970): 411-51.

12. Christopher Jencks et al., *Inequality: A Reassessment of the Effect of Family and Schooling in America* (New York: Basic Books, 1972).

13. Samuel Bowles and Herbert Gintis, *Schooling in Capitalist America: Educational Reform and the Contradictions of Economic Life* (New York: Basic Books, 1976).

14. Grubb and Lazerson, "Rally 'Round."

15. Data in this section were taken from Fenwick W. English, "Heterogeneity, Randomness and Choice, and the Anthropological Function of the School," Discussion Paper No. 1, Hastings Public Schools, Hastings-on-Hudson, New York, September 1974. (Mimeograph.)

16. A. Harry Passow, "Secondary Education Reform: Retrospect and Prospect," The Julius and Rosa Sachs Memorial Lectures, Teachers College, Columbia University, New York, April 7-8, 1976, pp. 47-48.

17. Maeroff, "Differences Persist."

18. "Labor Plays Active Role in Career Education Meeting," *American Teacher* 61, no. 4 (December 1976): 12.

FOR FURTHER READING

Bailey, Larry J., and Stadt, Ronald. *Career Education: New Approaches to Human Development.* Bloomington, Illinois: McKnight Publishing Co., 1975.

Braden, Paul V., and Paul, Kirshan. *Occupational Analysis of Educational Planning.* Columbus, Ohio: Charles E. Merrill Publishing Co., 1975.

Goldhammer, K., and Taylor, Robert E., eds. *Career Education: Perspective and Promise.* Columbus, Ohio: Charles E. Merrill Publishing Co., 1972.

Hansen, L. S. "Career Development Education: Humanizing Focus for Educators." *The Education Digest* 42, no. 4 (December 1976): 54-56.

Hunter, John A. "Humanities and the World of Work: A Call for Integration." *Peabody Journal of Education* 54, no. 2 (January 1977): 94-96.

Muirhead, Peter P. "Career Education: The First Steps Show Promise." *Phi Delta Kappan* 54, no. 6 (February 1973): 369-72.

Nash, Robert J., and Agne, Russell M. "Career Education: Earning a Living or Living a Life?" *Phi Delta Kappan* 54, no. 6 (February 1973): 373-78.

Nelson, Randolph J. "Providing Career Education through Teachers: Three Related Models." *Peabody Journal of Education* 52, no. 1 (October 1974): 14-17. This entire issue of the *Journal* is given to career education as a national concern.

Ressler, Ralph. *Career Education: The New Frontier.* Worthington, Ohio: Charles A. Jones Publishing Co., 1973.

Smoker, David, ed. *Career Education: A Guide for School Administrators.* Arlington, Virginia: American Association of School Administrators, 1973.

8   Broadening
the Goals

About This Chapter

The unrelated curricular areas grouped for consideration in this chapter were placed here for several reasons, chief among which is that each is a field where a gap exists between social reality and school practice, between what is known and what is done. All are areas where academic goals need to be expanded. None, at present, is central to learning and teaching in the secondary school although a fair case might be made for each in terms of centrality in a curriculum built upon the needs of learners. All are electives. None is being utilized to achieve general social goals to the degree that the traditional academic areas are used or to the extent that recent concepts such as career education are recommended.

Further, each appears to attract more than its share of the controversy that occasionally swirls about all areas of the curriculum. The library, for example, falls heir to censorship in all the subject areas. Conflicting in reading, especially centered on methodology, has been vigorous and continuous since the 1940s. Driver education is perceived by some critics as a *fad;* art and music as *frills.* The controversy surrounding such fields as religion, sex education, and drug education scarcely needs to be underscored.

Beyond this, there is little glue to hold these disparate topics together. Such topics as sex education and drug and alcohol education might well have been treated in chapter five in the discussion of physical education and health as is often done. However, it seemed to the writers that this may not be the best arrangement, either in the organization of a book or in school practice. Similarly, religious studies could have been included with the treatment of the social studies in chapter four. Again, because of the particular problems and prejudices which seem to surface when religious studies are proposed as curricular components, it seemed that the area should be discussed separately. Certainly, also, areas such as art and music, reading, and the library might have been accorded separate chapters except for considerations of length as the book was written. Because of these reasons, this chapter should be thought of as a series of minichapters dealing with unrelated curricular areas.

Keep in mind that the subjects grouped within this chapter are perceived as peripheral by much of the public. Proponents for each are still struggling to make the case for each as part of general education and to set forth the contribution of each to the special needs of large numbers of students. Each reflects considerable effort to broaden the goals of secondary education and to emerge, finally, as acceptable and essential components of the secondary school curriculum.

Sex Education: The
Need and the Reality

The Need

Changing sexual mores have become apparent in the peer group subculture within the schools for both students and teachers. In Texas, a school teacher fought her dismissal because she was pregnant and unwed (1), in New Jersey a teacher attempted to regain her job after a sex change operation (2), and homosexual teachers have formed their own association/union to battle for their rights.(3)

At the student level, North Carolina reports that one-third of the abortions performed in that state were for unmarried teenagers. (4) One out of six teenage girls becomes pregnant out of wedlock in the United States. (5) Venereal disease has risen rapidly at the teenage and young adult levels. The schools have been slow to respond to the problem. Sex education has been roundly attacked in the public schools, (6) and many school officials offer basic sex information in a variety of other curricular offerings such as biology, health, family life education, or home economics. It is generally felt that to offer a course in "sex hygiene" would be to invite a very unfavorable response from the public. (7) Teenagers find that their parents are unwilling or unable to cope with their sexual problems. Some estimates of the percentages of secondary school students who engage in sexual intercourse range for girls about 15 percent at the age of fifteen, 20 percent at sixteen, and 25 percent at seventeen. The percentage of boys is lower because girls tend to engage in sexual relations with older boys. (8) Attitude surveys of teenagers indicate that only one-third were opposed to premarital sex. (9) One school system has organized special learning centers for pregnant girls so that they may finish their education. While schools are prohibited from discriminating against students who are pregnant, few girls want to risk the insults or psychological injury from other students. Without alternatives they simply do not return to school. (10)

The Reality

Changing sexual attitudes have left their imprint on the secondary schools. Few schools or school systems are adequately coping with the problems which, to a great extent, are being ignored. Anything beyond the most basic information about human reproduction is rarely found in the secondary school curriculum. Problems with venereal disease and teenage pregnancy are viewed not as social responsibilities but individual problems. The attitude of too many administrators, parents, and school board members is that whatever pain and ostracism a teenager may suffer it is deserved punishment. This attitude hobbles the ability of the schools to help their students in any meaningful way. Social reality and social response are miles apart.

The data appear to indicate that more secondary school students are engaging in sexual activity at younger ages than ever before. The need for basic information about venereal disease and pregnancy should be a part of every secondary school curriculum. It is even more important to provide opportunities within the formal curriculum to explore attitudes and feelings regarding human sexuality. The questions secondary school students are asking by their behavior will be answered either from street knowledge or within some educational setting. It is apparently not being addressed in the home. If the schools are rendered silent in dealing with this problem as they have been in the past. the statistics stemming from increased sexual activity of students will continue to rise.

Despite the gap between reality and practice in the content of sex education, it should be noted that some schools and school systems have been able to deal directly with problems in this area. Published resources are available and may be adapted for local use to the degree that local social attitudes permit.

One carefully organized source suggests content for each grade level, elementary through high school. (11) Based on a program in Family Life and Sex Education developed in the Anaheim, California School District, the book is a serious effort to present the truth about sexual behavior. Consequently, the volume is introduced with a chapter on human sexuality. In addition, at appropriate grade levels, the content focuses on existing problems and does not avoid controversial issues. For example, suggested content for the seventh grade includes factual information about sexual intercourse and masturbation. That for the ninth grade includes such topics as homosexuality, the levels of premarital sexual involvement and venereal disease, necking and petting, and alcohol.

Another published source includes most of the same topics but is not as rigidly organized by suggested content at each grade level. (12) However, separate chapters are included on such topics as obscenity, illustrative units and lessons in sex education, venereal disease, and the evaluation of programs in sex education. Slightly more than half the volume is oriented to the science content of sex education.

Both books are factual and bridge the gap between social reality and educational practice. Both contain information needed by students in every community. Both contain recommendations that might have to be avoided in some schools and school systems. Obviously, neither is intended to be taken whole but to be used as a point of departure as specific schools and school systems develop new programs or improve existing ones.

An excellent source which summarizes the need for better sex education and which explains the social changes as yet largely unreflected in school practice, is that by Lawrence J. Haims, *Sex Education and the Public Schools.*(13) Finally, such books as that edited by Stewart R. Fraser, (14) a section of which focuses on sex education in foreign countries, include a wide variety of readings on pedagogy, problems, and conflicts in sex education.

Paradoxically, both the need for sex education and the gap illustrated in school practice are rooted in the reality of social beliefs and concerns. Even so, the school cannot avoid its responsibility to try to dispel ignorance in this area as in any other. Such sources as those cited here provide the factual information that is needed.

Academic Study about Religion

Academic study about religion, also identified in such terms as religious studies, religion studies, and the objective study of religion, is not perceived here as it is in chapter nine as an extra curricular force acting upon the school. (see chapter nine, "Religion in the Schools.") Extra curricular religious practices in public schools have been clearly restricted and forbidden by numerous court decisions. By contrast, religion as an academic study is both constitutionally allowable and impossible to avoid.

For example, to ignore religious influences upon the history of humanity would be a distortion of history. Motives leading to the colonization of North America were religious as well as economic and social. Conflicts during that colonization involved religious as well as national interests. Religious themes in literature, art, and music are part of every culture, including the diversity of cultures that collectively constitute the United States. One would have to be an unreasoning antagonist of religion in all its forms to conceive a program of studies that omitted reference to the influence of religion in human affairs. And, any program so conceived would violate fact, misrepresent religion, and distort the curriculum.

Constitutionality

Academic study of or about religion has not been prohibited by the United States Supreme Court. Indeed, although the court found the

New York Regents Prayer to be a violation of the First Amendment in the landmark *Engel v. Vitale* (1962) case, the objection was strictly to the prayer as established by a government agency. (15) The broader question of the study of religion as part of a complete education was perceived clearly by a majority of the Court to be essential. An often-quoted passage from Justice Tom C. Clark's majority opinion in the *Abington v. Schempp* and *Murray v. Curlett* (1963) cases established the position without equivocation.

> one's education is not complete without a study of comparative religion or the history of religion and its relationship to the advancement of civilization. It certainly may be said that the Bible is worthy of study for its literary and historic qualities. Nothing we have said here indicates that such study of the Bible or of religion, when presented objectively as part of a secular program of education, may not be effected consistent with the First Amendment. . . . (16)

Justice Brennan's concurring opinion was equally clear.

> The holding of the Court today plainly does not foreclose teaching about the Holy Scriptures or about the differences between religious sects in classes in literature or history. Indeed, whether or not the Bible is involved, it would be impossible to teach meaningfully many subjects in the social sciences or the humanities without some mention of religion . . . . (17)

Although almost unnoted by the majority of professional educators at the time and ignored for years thereafter, the Court's 1962 and 1963 decisions opened the possibility for ways to deal with religion in the program of studies without fear of violating the First Amendment. Many later Court decisions have been consistent with that cited here (18), and it now seems evident that the future of this subject will rest more with educational decision-making than with legal concerns. (19)

What the public schools may and may not do when teaching about religion was succinctly summarized by James V. Panoch as follows:

1. The school may sponsor the *study* of religion, but may not sponsor the *practice* of religion.
2. The school may *expose* students to all religious views, but may not *impose* any particular view.
3. The school's approach to religion is one of *instruction,* not one of *indoctrination.*

4. The function of the school is to *educate* about all religions, not to *convert* to any one religion.
5. The school's approach to religion is *academic,* not *devotional.*
6. The school should *study* what all people believe, but should not *teach* a pupil what he should believe.
7. The school should strive for student *awareness* of all religions, but should not press for student *acceptance* of any one religion.
8. The school should seek to *inform* the student about various beliefs, but should not seek to *conform* him to any one belief. (20)

Approaches to Religion

Study about religion may either be approached by way of separate courses, such as World Religions, Far Eastern Religions, or Comparative Religion, or through integration with other disciplines, chiefly English and the various social subjects. An impressive amount of curriculum material for both elementary and secondary schools has been produced by funded projects at such widely-separated institutions as the Pennsylvania State University, Florida State University, and Indiana University. Many books, films, filmstrips, and other materials have been published commercially and are generally available. Because religious themes are inherent to understanding in such fields as history, literature, sociology, art and music, the more natural, less controversial, and realistic approach for most schools would appear to rest with the interdisciplinary topic.

Teacher Preparation

A few states, notably California, Indiana, Michigan, Pennsylvania, Florida, and Wisconsin, have led the way in providing opportunity for public school teachers to prepare for working with religious studies on a certified basis. Where certification is possible the most common pattern is to extend licensing to already certified teachers in other subjects following preparation in the methodology and content of religious topics. Thus, for example, Indiana allows certified English teachers to teach Biblical literature. Programs in Pennsylvania, Florida, and other states are similar.

By contrast, at least two states permit certification in religious studies as a separate subject. These states, Michigan and Wisconsin, both require detailed examination and justification of teacher preparation programs prior to state approval. In addition, Michigan's published standards for approval are particularly demanding and specific. (21)

Cautions

The fact that it is constitutionally possible to undertake the academic study of religion in public schools does not deny that such study is sensitive for both school people and for the general public. Only the most casual mention of religion in academic courses will pass unnoted. Serious treatment of any religious viewpoint, theme, or practice will invite reaction. Consequently, the concerns expressed throughout this volume for the involvement of students, parents, community leaders of many viewpoints, and teachers of all appropriate subjects, are particularly applicable to the development of units, courses, or programs where religion is a factor.

Further, an obvious concern is that persons espousing particular religious viewpoints will find their way into schools as teachers. If such people should be unable to maintain objectivity, and unable to balance differing viewpoints with understanding and sensitivity, the most well-planned paper program could collapse in public controversy. To avoid this possibility it is strongly recommended that school leaders be thoroughly acquainted with the official positions and publications of their own professional organizations. (22) Beyond this, school board members, administrators, and curriculum leaders should investigate the recommendations and resources available from such groups as the Public Education Religion Studies Center (PERSC) and the National Council for Religion in Public Education. Both individual and institutional memberships are available in both organizations.

PERSC, established at Wright State University, Dayton, Ohio, in 1972, encourages and facilitates teaching about religion in public schools within constitutional bounds. Through the years it has become a clearinghouse for information, teaching materials, and operational school programs. PERSC also sponsors workshops, seminars, and conferences throughout the nation. One of PERSC's major contributions has been to establish and publish criteria for teacher education programs in religious studies and, by way of a nationally organized committee of readers, to evaluate curriculum materials for school use.

The National Council, presently located at Ball State University, Muncie, Indiana, is a coalition of approximately forty member organizations including churches, colleges and universities, societies, committees, and foundations. Its major purpose is to serve the members of the coalition by sharing information in order to create public and professional awareness and support for objectively organized religious studies. The Council's bulletins, special reports, and reports of meetings are an important source of authoritative information.

Finally, such publications as the *Religious Education Journal* provide opportunities for current issues in the field to appear in print. (23)

No one should enter into an academic program centering on religious topics without thorough understanding of the legal basis for such study, without certain knowledge of what can and cannot be done, without mastering the curricular content to be covered, and without investigating the characteristics of successful, field-tested programs.

Art and Music

The case for the fine arts has been made by many writers, and the argument, however expressed, narrows to the self-evident fact that art and music are necessary for a complete education. A fundamental need for self-expression through art and music seems to be basic to human nature. Considering the centrality of the arts in human experience one finds it hard to disagree with the author who wonders "how any instructional operation that does not include the arts can be called a school." (24) Aesthetic experience is simply central to civilized life, a point that has been made by many eminent scholars both in the arts and in education. (25)

Art Content (26)

Much secondary school art content has come into programs indirectly through related work in other subjects rather than by direct art experience. Sculpture and architectural forms are illustrated and discussed in history. Art in the home is found in homemaking units. Poster design is studied in advertising. The industrial arts, in particular, have opened opportunities for practical artistic experience. Jewelry making, wood carving, ceramics, plastics, linoleum block and silk screen process printing are among a large number of worthwhile art forms adopted by industrial arts. Laudable though these correlations may be, they still operate so as to make art an incidental part of the school program. Many students receive little or no art experience.

Part of the problem is posed by the conventional attitude that art courses are for the talented only. Art is perceived to be strictly for the creative student. And, of course, many do create and create well, both in school and beyond school. However, for each person who creates, there are dozens who do not. The substantial majority of citizens are not makers of art. They are consumers, and they need opportunity in school to learn to appreciate and understand that which they buy and use in the name of art. Thus, a major task for art educators is to expand the goals set for art to include outcomes centering on art consumption and appreciation. The case for art in general education can only be made in terms of such expanded goals. Art, as well as any other subject, can help the student develop good judgment, gain a greater appreciation for life, and obtain satisfaction from worthwhile achievement. (27)

Music Content

Secondary school music programs have tended to emphasize large group activities such as band, orchestral, and choral groups. Although these activities entertain the public and gratify parents, they meet the needs of only about one-fifth of the students. Music as part of general education for all students has been pushed into a subordinate position.

In part, this situation is a result of history. Prior to 1900 music in the secondary school was largely vocal. Singing during assembly programs was the most common activity. No effort was directed toward providing systematic courses in music. Nor were musical activities given academic credit toward graduation. Instrumental music appeared during the late 1800s in the form of volunteer instrumental groups of one type or another in scattered schools. After 1900, supported by the effort of professional music and education associations, instrumental music gained general acceptance. Vocal offerings steadily increased in variety and quality. General music or music appreciation became accepted courses in junior high schools.

Currently, work in music is counted for one or two credits toward high school graduation. Nearly all secondary schools sponsor the large group music activities mentioned above. Some schools encourage smaller instrumental ensembles and smaller vocal groups such as quartets. Even for those pupils who do not enroll in a music course, some experience with music comes through assembly programs and projects in other courses. Nearly all music activities, both vocal and instrumental, continue to be either elective or extracurricular. They are scheduled throughout the school day as well as outside school hours.

As with art, where exhibition is the major criterion for judging the effectiveness of the music program, school people as well as the general public are at fault. If uniforms for the marching band become the major item in the music budget, the faculty in music is partly to blame. Where the band exists for no purpose other than to add color to athletic contests, the values of the school and community are open to question. Goals set for music need to be expanded to include emphasis on understanding music and its role in society and on using music. Playing music, important as it may be, is too limited as a base for building music into general education. (28) A wider range of alternatives is needed, such as even greater emphasis on small group and individual opportunities in music and the development of music programs designed especially for the handicapped. (29)

The Single Issue

The single key issue in both art and music is that, while the fine arts are basic to human nature and central to civilization and to liberal education, both art and music continue to be peripheral to the formal school program of studies. They are among the first programs to be reduced or abandoned during times of budget cuts, ranking with and below athletics in this regard. Largely elective and/or extracurricular, neither art nor music has yet earned its rightful place as a requirement in school programs designed to meet the needs of all students.

Elements of Safety Education: Driver Education and Drug and Alcohol Education

Safety education is a phrase coined to describe all aspects of safety, including accidents and their prevention, at home, on the highway, at work, and during recreational activity. Applied to school, it has been pointed out that a school system with as many as 10,000 students and employees poses a wider range of safety problems than a similarly sized factory. (30) Yet, the typical industrial plant employs safety engineers and medical personnel to a far greater degree than do most schools.

Safety education has been used as an umbrella beneath which are subsumed such diverse programs as those in driver education, drug and alcohol education, and closely related programs in health and sex education. Books on school health include chapters on school safety. Those on safety education include topics on physical education, health, and athletics. Volumes dealing with physical education may deal with all of these topics, including both driver education and drug and alcohol education.

Ultimately, all of these topics will have to be understood and approached as interdisciplinary in nature, requiring all the resources of the school if they are to be dealt with adequately. Until then, the approach of every school will necessarily be fragmented and disorganized. The efforts of isolated departments and individual teachers can never identify the goals and meet the priorities of students in these areas. This assessment fairly describes the situation in both driver education and drug and alcohol education.

Driver Education

Driver education entered the high school program during the 1940s and 1950s as a response to the rising toll of injuries and fatalities on the nation's highways. Traditionally left to parents or private agencies, responsibility was urged upon the schools by a combination of forces including automobile manufacturers, major oil companies, police and traffic authorities, and insurance companies. Lower insurance rates for those who completed driver training, the availability of dual-control cars at low cost through local automobile dealers, and a general public demand to do something to reduce the number of accidents, eventually led to acceptance of driver education as a school responsibility.

Typically, the course was assigned to a male physical education, industrial arts, or social studies teacher who was willing to assume the task for extra pay, and who was also willing to take the workshop, course, or other summer session training to insure his preparation. Courses were organized as a combination of behind-the-wheel experience and classroom work given to such topics as buying an automobile, buying automobile insurance, traffic laws, emotions and driving, alcohol and driving, night vision, and, in later years, the values of seat belts and other safety equipment.

Plainly, driver education did not act to curb the accident rate. Injuries and fatalities continued to climb steadily year by year until the federal government imposed maximum highway speeds as an energy-saving measure. Even so, the programs are now well entrenched and appear worthwhile, if only to achieve the more realistic goal of preparing citizens who are more skillful and who demonstrate better attitudes than their predecessors on the road.

Currently, programs range from the now traditional elective course taught at odd hours on local streets by an available teacher, to elaborate facilities which may include private roads for behind-the-wheel instruction. One such driving range is described as a 40-acre facility complete with a driver education building and a control tower for observing driving areas. These include a gravel road, a city street, a complicated intersection, an expressway driving straightaway, driveways, and winding roads. The facility is used also for training school bus drivers and truck drivers. (31)

Classroom work currently is planned to develop positive attitudes, a goal generally conceded to be of greater importance than the development of driving skill. (32) Currently, also, efforts continue to develop minimum statewide standards for driver education in all states, available to all students, and taught by fully certified instructors. (33)

Drug and Alcohol Education

Laws dating back to the 1870s are in effect in most of the states mandating that the subject of alcohol be covered in the schools. Motivated by temperance advocates, the early laws stressed abstinence as a goal and assumed that teaching would focus on the evils of drinking. (34) These laws were largely ignored or forgotten following the repeal of Prohibition although some of the earlier style programs continued into the 1940s and 1950s, and elements of the fear approach may still be practiced in some schools.

Up-to-date reports suggest that current programs should be centered on student needs. Realistically, the responsible use of alcohol is condoned in this society. Hence, although alcohol abuse is not acceptable, abstinence as a goal is unrealistic. Prevention of abuse rather than total abstinence at least is achievable. (35) (36)

Further, the use of fear tactics and lack of objectivity do more harm than good. To moralize about the evils of drinking, to expect abstinence until legal age, or to try to create fear, are unworkable and self-defeating approaches. (37) At least 80 percent of youth age seventeen to eighteen use alcohol, and most do so in a responsible manner. (38) Thus, the responsible use of alcohol rather than its abolition is perceived as a reasonable posture of the school in dealing with the subject.

These comments in no way suggest that the improper use of alcohol is not a serious problem in the United States. On the contrary, there is no doubt that alcohol is the number one drug problem in the country, affecting large numbers of both youth and adults. The age of use is steadily decreasing as might have been expected when the legal age of adulthood was reduced to eighteen. Even when adulthood was recognized at twenty-one, youth drank publicly at ages sixteen to seventeen or whatever age passed in dimly-lit taverns and bars. Now, it is not uncommon for children of fourteen to sixteen to attempt to pass themselves off as adults in order to buy alcoholic beverages. Drinking at even younger ages is widely reported.

The problem is a serious one and is limited neither to the United States nor to this century. After all, the use of beer and wine predates the Christian calendar by thousands of years. Physical, mental, and emotional problems directly traceable to alcohol abuse have afflicted people through the ages and continue as afflictions in modern nations.

This is why the subject needs to be approached in a responsible manner and why schools need to recognize alcohol education as a total curricular concept and not as an isolated course or unit taught by the physical education teacher. This is the curricular thrust recommended by most writers. (39) (40)

The same points are emphasized for what now passes as drug education in American schools. The misuse and abuse of drugs other than alcohol, both legal and illegal, is a nationwide problem affecting both youth and adults. Yet we approach this national problem by setting aside a unit in physical education, science, or some other subject. Existing programs are shot through with errors and inaccuracies. They illustrate lack of planning because most came about as the result of local pressure rather than because of rational thought. Moralizing and fear tactics are common. The goal of avoiding all drugs, impossible in this society, is adopted instead of realistic objectives relating to proper use and control. (41) Far from acting to prevent drug abuse, many current programs present students with information on how to use drugs, romanticize the drug user, and probably contribute to the increasing use of drugs. (42)

Short of scrapping the existing enterprise, it is suggested that drug education be incorporated into comprehensive health education programs and that effort to modify basic attitudes and values be built into the courses. (43) (44) The present writers heartily agree. In addition, school books, audiovisual materials, and curriculum texts dealing with the subject might cease to anchor themselves with detailed lists of illegal drugs and their descriptions, methods of use, and effects on the body, thus providing students with ready-made references for home and street use.

The School Library

The school library is both a place to be studied and a place in which to study and work. In the first sense, use of the library is taught, or should be taught in all academic classes and also by special presentations involving the library staff. As a place in which important work may be done, the library is perceived increasingly as a place for doing, making, listening, viewing, sharing, and working together. It is no longer merely a location for quiet reading and research in printed materials. The school library as an instructional materials center is not a new concept (45), but it is a concept not implemented widely until recent years.

As an instructional materials or instructional media center (IMC) the library is more than a repository for books and journals. Its holdings also include audiovisual materials such as films, filmstrips, tapes, recordings, and photographs. Materials are not only borrowed from and used in the library. Such items as graphic materials, slides, and audio tapes are created in the library. This concept of the library has resulted in physical as well as staff changes.

Physically, the library as an IMC can no longer consist of a single large room, given to rows of tables for reading and studying. Rather, several rooms may be needed for the differing tasks of viewing, listening, and creating. Even the large, traditional library area may include individual study carrels and locations where audiovisual materials may be used.

This concept of the library has resulted in considerable added responsibility for the library staff. As IMC personnel, librarians may be called upon to teach students in the use of technical materials. Library holdings of all types, audiovisual as well as printed, must be closely integrated with the existing programs of study. Thus, increasingly, library staff members are expected to work with teachers to develop curriculum materials and to develop instructional programs. The librarian as curriculum developer may help teachers prepare instructional materials and may help students learn how to use such materials. He or she serves an important role in the ongoing work of teachers, administrators, and guidance staff. With so much to know and so much to do, the work of the modern secondary school library demands several kinds of support personnel in addition to the librarian. As a minimum these include: (a) Clerical employees such as graphic artists, processing clerks, typists, and acquisitions clerks; (b) Paraprofessionals such as audiovisual and library technicians; and (c) Associate librarians where the operation is large, to include research specialists, media specialists, and subject matter specialists. (46)

Censorship

The problem of censorship is discussed in detail in chapter nine and need not be repeated here. (See "Book Banning," chapter nine.) However, it might be noted that school officials at both local and state levels have adopted guidelines based on freedom of choice. Controversial materials cannot be avoided. (47)

However, the censorship problem is more complex than many school people are willing to admit. Too often the defense of academic or intellectual freedom is automatic without regard for the educational value of the items under consideration or for the values of the community that maintains the library. In many instances the librarian treads a fine line as he or she strives to satisfy critics of sexism or racism and, at the same time, placate the defenders of academic freedom. (48) For example, because of vastly changed social conditions, works of fiction written thirty or forty years ago and which, at the time, were entirely acceptable may be quite unacceptable today because of blatant sexist or racist themes, vocabulary, or stereotyping. Thus, the librarian is obliged to exercise a degree of selectivity in purchasing or retaining library materials, even to the point of opposing some academic expectations.

If a school librarian sincerely believes that a work may violate standards of morality, integrity, and responsibility set as curriculum goals for a school, he or she should say so and, if necessary, refuse to endorse the work for the school library. School librarians cannot be expected to defend everything. (49)

The nationally publicized Kanawha County, West Virginia, protests in 1974 is a case in point. Among the more harmless titles protested were Melville's *Moby Dick*, Plato's *Republic*, and Orwell's *Animal Farm*, and it is hard to understand or to defend mentalities that would ban such books from school libraries. Even so, at least one thoughtful school librarian wrote to sugest that perhaps the right of a community to share in determining educational input for its children is at least as important as the question of opposing censorship on principle. (50)

Where differing groups present differing notions of their rights and responsibilities in the republic, conflict is to be expected prior to consensus. No one in school work should condemn the process or expect to win all the decisions. This is simply the way that democracy works.

Reading in the Secondary School

As much as some people might want it otherwise, students do not enter into secondary education reading at exactly the same rate of speed and with the same degree of comprehension. Because of many valid reasons some fall behind and some pull ahead until, by the ninth grade, some have not progressed beyond average third or fourth grade levels. (or lower) and some have reached to college sophomore levels (or beyond). Some of the valid reasons for this situation include differences in mental

The section on *Reading in the Secondary School* was adapted from a paper prepared for one of the writers' classes by Mr. Albert J. Shannon, reading resource teacher, Milwaukee Public Schools. The authors are grateful to Mr. Shannon for the organization of this section and for the writing that he contributed to it. Permission to include his materials is appreciated.

capacity, physical illnesses, emotional or mental problems, sight, hearing, or speech problems, foreign language background, differing opportunity for home experience in reading, and the mobility of the American population which forces many pupils to move from school to school throughout the elementary years. Under the circumstances, it does no good to blame teachers at earlier school levels nor to condemn the entire school system. Differences in reading ability and in interests and tastes with regard to reading are to be expected. The important goal is that secondary school teachers do something about the reading problems that all must expect to confront.

The nature of the reading process has been defined and redefined over the years to include the elements of decoding, comprehension, interpretation, appreciation, and application of the written word. The nature of the reading act itself will be under continued debate by linguists, psychologists, and educators for years to come. Let the reader, then, not be lost in the semantic labyrinth of the theorists, but simply approach reading with the understanding that it is an essential skill for learning in all subjects. All teachers share the responsibility for teaching that which must be learned about reading in their particular subjects. This is just a way of saying that, if a teacher uses maps, charts, and graphs, students must be helped to understand the terms used on them. If a teacher uses a laboratory manual, students must be helped to understand the directions for experiments and projects. In essence, every teacher who uses reading, and this means all teachers, shares the responsibility for teaching those reading or study skills needed in the given area of curricular concern. To the extent that a teacher uses reading to convey information, he shares in the responsibility of conveying the process as well as the content. (51) The era of edging out the processes needed for information gathering and assimilation at the expense of covering the subject is dead. Subject area teachers, with the support of the reading professional, are the keys to using reading in the secondary school.

Reading plays a significant part in the curriculum of the American secondary school. (52) (53) A general examination of the various roles that reading plays in secondary schools today must include the *Developmental Role,* the *Supplemental Role,* the *Remedial Role,* and the *Resource Role.*

The Developmental Role. The role of reading instruction from a developmental viewpoint is one founded on the use of a scope and sequence of skills in the reading program. The developmental aspects of the program may include class level instruction in vocabulary, comprehension, and study skills. All students at specified grade levels participate in sequenced reading instruction intended to develop specifically identified skills in ordered progression.

The Supplemental Role. Reading instruction in the high school is often offered through an elective program to complement the academic program of studies. Courses in speed reading, advanced reading skills, and college vocabulary are typical of supplemental type course offerings. Students are often screened for admission to such courses and are given elective credit through the English or Reading Departments.

The Remedial Role. There is a continuing need for all levels of remedial instruction on the high school level. Students classified as remedial are often at least two to three grade levels behind in reading achievement. The essence of remediation at the secondary school level is individualized diagnosis followed by small class instruction.

The Resource Role. The resource role that reading plays in the total secondary school program is vital. The role is personified in the reading resource teacher whose task it is to integrate reading and study skills into the subject areas of the curriculum. The reading resource teacher, in cooperation with the subject area teacher, synthesizes the content of the various subjects with the reading processes needed to learn the information. The resource teacher is, in essence, a master teacher schooled in methodology and reading, who can demonstrate precisely what it means to teach the use of reading in different subject fields.

A final component of the resource role is the involvement of the supportive services staff and the administration in the total school reading program. The reading resource teacher must involve personnel from the top down in what H. Alan Robinson calls "not a subject" but the key "process used for learning." (54)

The Status and the Future of Reading

It is obvious that the above roles of reading depict the ideal balance and position of reading in the secondary school. The ideal is not the real in far too many instances today. The gap is evidenced by the following list of common shortcomings in current secondary school reading programs:

1. The use of untrained and often unwilling teachers, especially English instructors, to teach reading courses;
2. The lack of adequate state certification requirements for reading teachers and reading resource teachers;
3. Overemphasis on the remedial role and little or no concentration on a school-wide effort in reading;

4. The hurried adoption of a reading program without clearly defined long-range goals, without total school involvement in planning, without administrative support, and without adequate budgeting;
5. The over-reliance on kit materials and the faddish programmed reading technology of the moment.

All reading programs in secondary schools must go through growing pains and eventually settle into the structure that best meets the needs of the particular school. No one program is best for all schools; no one method is best for all students. There is a need for schools of education, teachers' associations, professional associations of reading teachers, administrators, and school board members, to work more closely in the development of reading programs to meet the specialized needs of particular schools and school districts.

The future of reading, however, is most dependent on the classroom subject teacher. The teacher is the key. Nicholas P. Criscuolo was encouraging when he optimistically reported in 1976 that, despite differences in subject matter, secondary teachers "are now demonstrating a healthy commitment to the development of comprehensive reading programs." (55)

The commitment must be held and redoubled as we travel through the 1980s. The success of reading in the secondary schools and the consequent success of students is dependent on the knowledge, attitudes, and actions of subject area teachers.

Others

This chapter has not attempted an exhaustive treatment of all emerging curricular areas and areas where the gap between social reality and school practice is subject to question. The program of the school always will be subject to the pressures and demands of the society which created it. Programs come and go in response to the demands of state legislatures, the tensions of international relationships, advancing technology, new discoveries, social changes, economic crises, and a host of other influences. Established courses and programs come into conflict with those designed to meet current needs because the school day and the school year have maximum time limits. Within the demands set by time, the task is to find the time to try out promising proposals while not being forced to abandon tested practices.

Within this context, such an area as consumer education still struggles for reconition even as the topic is taught in home economics and business education classes. So presented, of course, consumer education reaches less than half the students because fewer than half of American students enroll in home economics and business courses combined. Environmental education, truly a crucial study at all levels, reaches some students in social studies classes and others by way of science but, in the process, misses many who do not take the particular courses where the topic is included. The same comment might be made about conservation education, surely an area which poses some of the most critical and difficult problems facing the nation.

All of these areas, as well as those treated in more detail in this chapter, along with others identified as interdisciplinary in other chapters, can never be covered in more than an isolated and fragmented manner unless the school organizes for dealing with interdisciplinary problems. Hopefully, the reader will perceive merit in some of the ideas and proposals set forth in Part 4 of this book, where educational decision-making for today and tomorrow is brought into focus.

CHAPTER REFERENCES

1. "Court Rejects Job Bias Charge of an Unwed Pregnant Teacher," *New York Times*, January 21, 1975.
2. Gene I. Maeroff, "Teachers Now May Act Just Like People," *New York Times*, July 4, 1976.
3. Joel Fishman, "Teachers Seeking Homosexual Rights," *Yonkers Herald-Statesman*, July 22, 1976.
4. Leslie Wayne, "Abortions Little Affected by Law but Customer Interest Laging," *The News and Observer*, June 15, 1972.
5. Nick Taylor, "School Officials Tread Tightrope on Quantity of Sex Education," *Atlanta Journal and Constitution*, September 10, 1972, 2-A.
6. For a review of the sex education controversy in the public schools see Mary Breasted, *Oh! Sex Education!* (New York: Signet Books, 1971).
7. A view supported by most school administrators. See Taylor, "School Officials Tread Tightrope."
8. The data cited here are from an article reprinted from *Newsday* by David Behrens which appeared in the *Sarasota Herald-Tribune*, "In Regard to Sex, Teenager Says Parents Are Ostriches," July 29, 1973.
9. A survey conducted by *Seventeen Magazine*, as cited in Behrens, "In Regard to Sex."
10. Milly Ivins, "Schools for Pregnant Girls to Close; Teachers Foresee Harm to Students," *New York Times*, September 25, 1976.
11. Esther D. Schulz and Sally R. Williams, *Family Life and Sex Education: Curriculum and Instruction* (New York: Harcourt, Brace, and World, 1969).

12. H. Frederick Kilander, *Sex Education in the Schools* (Toronto: The Macmillan Co., 1970).

13. Lawrence J. Haims, *Sex Education and the Public Schools* Lexington, Massachusetts: D. C. Heath and Co., 1973).

14. Stewart R. Fraser, ed., *Sex, Schools, and Society: International Perspectives* Nashville, Tennessee: Peabody International Center, George Peabody College for Teachers, 1972).

15. *Engel v. Vitale,* 370 U.S. 421 (1962).

16. *School District of Abington Township v. Schempp; Murray v. Curlett,* 374 U.S. 203 (1963), p. 225.

17. 374 U.S., p. 300.

18. For detailed examination of Court decisions, see Peter Bracher et al., eds. *Religion Studies in the Curriculum: Retrospect and Prospect, 1963-1983* (Dayton, Ohio: Public Education Religion Studies Center, 1974). See especially, Charles M. Whelan, "The Decisions of the Court," pp. 22-31.

19. Whelan, "The Decisions of the Court," p. 28.

20. James V. Panoch, "The Relationships between Religion and Public Education," A PERSC Reprint (Dayton, Ohio: Public Education Religion Studies Center, undated). Cited in Peter Bracher et al., *Public Education Religion Studies: Questions and Answers* (Dayton, Ohio: PERSC, 1974), p. 2.

21. See Frank L. Steeves, "State-Approved Curricula in Religious Studies," A PERSC Reprint (Dayton, Ohio: Public Education Religion Studies Center, 1973), 12 pp.

22. See, for example, *Religion in the Public Schools,* a report by the Commission on Religion in the Public Schools (Washington, D.C.: American Association of School Administrators, 1964).

23. *Religious Education Journal,* published by the Religious Education Association, 409 Prospect Street, New Haven, Connecticut 06510.

24. Kenneth A. Bartosz, "Why Music? Why Arts? Why Now?" *The School Musician* 48 no. 1 (August-September 1976), pp. 58-59.

25. For example, see Harry S. Broudy, "Quality Education and Aesthetic Education," a paper reprinted by George Pappas in *Concepts in Art and Education* (Toronto: The Macmillan Co., 1970), pp. 280-90.

26. Some of the writing in this section on content in art and the following section on content in music first appeared in print in Frank L. Steeves, *Fundamentals of Teaching in Secondary Schools* (New York: The Odyssey Press, 1962), pp. 305-08. Updated and revised for inclusion here.

27. Michael F. Andrews, "Accent on Art," *Arts and Activities* 77 no. 4 (May 1975): 24, 45-46, 48.

28. See Jack E. Schaeffer, "More Music for More Students: Broadening the Base of Involvement," *NASSP Bulletin* 59 no. 393 (October 1975): 18-22.

29. See "Music Education—Its Place in Secondary Schools," a series of six articles, NASSP Bulletin 59, no. 393 (October 1975): 1-36.

30. Kenneth F. Licht, "School Liability and Safety Education," *The Education Digest* 36, no. 3 (November 1970): 22-24.

31. See "On the Drawing Board," *Nation's Schools* 90, no. 5 (November 1972): 46.

32. Alfred R. Stone, *Caution: Driving Ahead* (Austin, Texas: Steck-Vaughn Co., 1974).

33. See "Washington Report," *The American School Board Journal* 159, no. 13 (July 1972): 15.

34. See Gail Gleason Milgram, "Current Status and Problems of Alcohol Education in the Schools," *The Journal of School Health* 46, no. 6 (June 1976): 317-19.

35. Morris E. Chafetz, "The New Attack on Alcoholism," *Compact* 8, no. 3 (May-June 1974): 5-6.

36. Lee N. Hames, "The Case for Having the Public School Teach Our Youngsters How to Drink," *The American School Board Journal* 163, no. 3 (March 1976): 38-41.

37. Lena M. DiCicco and Hilma Unterberger, "Does Alcohol Follow Drugs?" *NASSP Bulletin* 57, no. 372 (April 1973): 85-91.

38. Milgram, "Current Status ," p. 319.

39. Lee N. Hames, "Why Alcohol Education Is Such a Tough Task for the Schools," *The American School Board Journal* 163, no. 3 (March 1976): 43.

40. Chafetz, "The New Attack."

41. Bernard Bard, "The Failure of Our Drug Abuse Programs," *Phi Delta Kappan* 57, no. 4 (December 1975): 251-55.

42. Bard, *ibid.*

43. Aria C. Rosner, "How We Do It," *The Journal of School Health* 45, no. 8 (October 1975): 468-69.

44. Harold J. Cornacchia, David J. Bental, and David E. Smith, *Drugs in the Classroom: A Conceptual Model for School Programs* (St. Louis: The C. V. Mosby Co., 1973).

45. Richard L. Darling, "The School Library as an Instructional Materials Center," *Education Age* 2 (May-June 1966): 45-46.

46. James W. Brown, Ruth H. Aubrey, and Elizabeth S. Noel, eds. *Multi-Media and the Changing School Library* (Sacramento, California: California State Department of Education, 1969).

47. See, for example, SLJ News, "Selection Policies Guidelines Adopted by N.Y. State Regents," *School Library Journal* 23, no. 4 (December 1976): 9.

48. Betsy Rush, "Weeding vs. Censorship: Treading a Fine Line," *School Library Journal* 21, no. 3 (November 1974): 42-43.

49. Mary F. Poole, *"The Upstairs Room,* Room for Controversy?" *School Library Journal* 20, no. 4 (December 1973): 67-68. See also, "Expletives Deleted," Readers' reactions to Ms. Poole's article, *School Library Journal* 21, no. 1 (September, 1974): 48-49.

50. Shirley A. Smith, "Crisis in Kanawha County," *School Library Journal* 21, no. 5 (January 1975): pp. 34-35.

51. Harold Herber, *Teaching Reading in Content Areas* (Englewood Cliffs, N.J.: Prentice-Hall, 1970), p. 6.

52.-53. For extensive treatment of secondary school reading methods, see: Lou E. Burmeister, *Reading Strategies for Secondary SVMTOL Teachers* (Reading, Massachusetts: Addison Wesley Publishing Co., 1974), and David L.

Sheperd, *Comprehensive High School Reading Methods* (Columbus, Ohio: Charles E. Merrill Publishing Co., 1973).

54. H. Alan Robinson, *Teaching Reading and Study Strategies: The Content Areas* (Boston: Allyn and Bacon, 1975), p. 20

55. Nicholas P. Criscuolo, "An Interdisciplinary Approach to Reading," *Journal of Reading* 19, no. 6 (March 1976): 488.

PROLOGUE:

Toward a
Total
Curriculum

III Beyond
the
Subject
Areas

Efforts to define the curriculum inevitably lead to the conclusion that it includes all that is done in a school—all the content of the formal courses, all that occurs as a result of school services, all that happens in the extracurricular program, and all change of behavior that results from the school environment whether officially sponsored by the school or unofficially organized by students. Definition of the curriculum centers on what teachers include as the content of courses of study but, broadly conceived, encompasses that which takes place in all other school programs, activities, and services. Carried to a logical conclusion, the curriculum for each individual student becomes the sum total of change in behavior as a result of school experiences. It includes what is known or understood that was not known or understood prior to the experience, that which can be done that could not be done earlier, and that which is believed or appreciated as a result of what happens in school.

This sweeping viewpoint toward the curriculum in no way diminishes the basic role of the secondary school as an academic institution. Neither does this inclusive conception of curriculum deny fundamental purposes of secondary education which, as emphasized earlier in this volume, should lead students to careers, to further education, or to both. The definition merely recognizes that the total curriculum of a school involves more than formal courses of study and that legitimate objectives for the adolescent years include more than career choices and/or plans for further education.

Even if more limited objectives were perceived for secondary education, much of that now in schools outside the program of studies would still remain. The school library, for example, would stay intact because most of what is found in school libraries relates to educational and occupational endeavors. Guidance services would still be necessary and would continue to deal with formidable problems because of the complexity of career choices in modern American society and because of the bewildering variety of one-to-eight year programs for education beyond and apart from high school.

However, as the American high school developed during the latter part of the nineteenth century and throughout the present century, it became a uniquely comprehensive institution. Its student body is heterogeneous rather than selective. It exists to serve all youth and not those chosen for a particular concept of what secondary education should be. This is quite unlike schools for adolescents in other nations which are primarily single purpose and selective, and which prepare students for the university *or* for vocation. The single purpose pattern of secondary education has never appealed to the mass of Americans. Few strictly college-preparatory public high schools have been established, chiefly in urban locations. There are a larger number of solely vocational high schools, again largely in the cities, although in some midwestern and western states, area vocational high schools are to be found. Of course, many high schools under independent control continue only to prepare students for college. However, even private schools have added commercial and other programs to the traditional college-preparatory work, and most of these schools provide a full range of services and extracurricular activities. The typical American high school, public or private, is seen as a comprehensive institution by its constituents, doing all that is possible to meet the needs of a relatively heterogeneous student body.

Thus, as noted in chapter three, the goals accepted for secondary education in this country have become increasingly broad and diverse. New national problems and concerns have simply resulted in the addition of new goals to an existing array of earlier commitments. Programs to implement the extended goals have been created and add to the diversity of courses, services, and activities that characterize the total curriculum of the typical American junior and senior high school. Every school, of course, includes some courses and activities which linger on largely because of tradition and inertia. However, by and large, most of what transpires in today's secondary schools is there because the people want it to be there. In fact, programs and activities outside the program of studies may provide the learning environment and motivation needed by some in order to achieve success in the more formal curriculum.

Athletics, to illustrate, has received its share of criticism including overemphasis, the need for large amounts of space and equipment, expense, the physical danger in some sports, and the almost total dedication that some athletes are expected to give to their sport during the season of play. Yet, let any school board threaten to eliminate interscholastic athletics from the school program and the public outcry is immediate and loud. The people, both those who attend the schools and those who pay for them, associate athletic teams with their schools and perceive values in athletics that enrich the traditional educational program. Each year, thousands of athletes enroll in colleges only because of the opportunity provided by their success in athletic competition. Other thousands—nobody knows how many—remain in high school because of the chance to compete in athletics. Other athletes, and the reports are numerous, achieve success in business and other careers because of publicity due to athletics and perhaps, also, because of attitudes and skills derived from such competition.

It is safe to conclude that the comprehensive character of American secondary education is here to stay, provided that each school fulfills its fundamental academic purposes. It is not so clear that every high school must continue to duplicate the academic programs of every other high school in the name of comprehensiveness. Communities large enough to support several high schools may well distinguish academic emphases or specialties among schools. Even so, major programs apart from the subject areas are needed in every school. Therefore, chapters nine through eleven bear upon some of the issues and conflicts in major programs beyond the subject areas. The importance of these programs to the lives of students and to the unity of each school as an institution should not be underestimated.

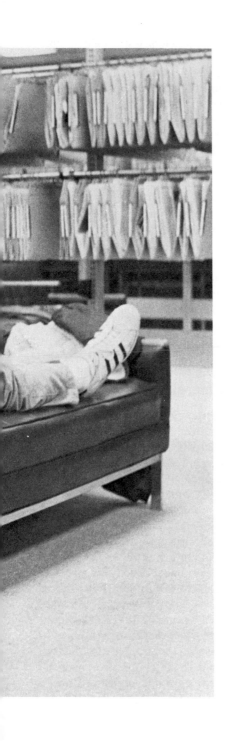

9 The
Cocurriculum
and
the "Extra"
Curriculum

Probably no area of the secondary school has changed as much as the cocurriculum. The cocurriculum represents a direct extension of the educational program (the interaction between the school and the students via rules and regulations) and is heavily influenced by peer group norms and broader social problems. To the extent that peer group norms and wider social problems disrupt the formal curriculum of the school or alter it, they become part of that curriculum, i.e., the "extra" curriculum. The extra curriculum was not created by educators nor can it be abolished by them. The extra curriculum is thus a set of patterns which involve the school, its students, and the community in the larger society. Often the impact of the extra curriculum is decidedly negative. In 1975 American school children committed 100 murders, 12,000 armed robberies, 9,000 rapes, and 204,000 aggravated assaults against teachers and other students. (1) The extra curriculum involved instances of book banning, attacks by political groups upon specific educational practices or concepts, and included severe disruptions due to teacher strikes and racial disturbances or riots. The secondary school does not and cannot stand alone and isolated from larger societal ills. In many cases the schools are simply mirrors of a larger malaise.

The Traditional versus the Emerging Cocurriculum

The most traditional definition of the cocurriculum takes the form of the student press, student government, student dress, and school conduct as well as school clubs, dances, and other activities. In the past students had little to say about how these activities were conducted. However, in a series of landmark decisions by the United States Supreme Court, highlighted by the *Tinker v. Des Moines Independent Community School District* (1969) (2), students in the public schools were recognized as equal to adults in being guaranteed First Amendment protection. The case involved the efforts of the school administration to suspend students who wore black arm bands to protest the Vietnam War. The Court majority ruled that as such, armbands were almost "pure speech" and that as such students were protected by the Constitution. (3)

The shift in the legal status of secondary school students has ushered forth a new era in developing the school's cocurriculum. Rules and regulations of the school must be reasonable, and they must conform to nondiscrimination on the basis of sex, age, religion, or race. Secondary school students have a right to wear their hair and clothes in a manner they deem appropriate. Such personal factors are not subject to school regulation unless they actually interfere with the learning process. (4) Students facing suspension or expulsion have a right to due process, may be represented by legal counsel, and must have access to information which may be used as evidence against them. Many secondary school students can vote for Board of Education members and school budgets as the result of the passage of the Twenty-Sixth Amendment to the Constitution which lowered the voting age to eighteen years. Secondary educators should take careful note of these legal decisions and their implications when planning the cocurriculum of the secondary school.

Student Clubs

Student clubs have traditionally formed an important and exciting kind of activity for secondary school students. Usually clubs incorporate both academic and social interests, though some are exclusively one or the other. Clubs which have normally occupied an important place in secondary schools may include some or all of the following:

chess club	chemistry club	key club
student ushers	debate society	physics club
drama club	photography club	French Club
National Honor Society	stage crew	varsity club
leader's club	current affairs club	literary magazine
audiovisual crew	library club	

Clubs can be a vibrant aspect of a secondary school offering students a multifaceted approach to capturing their interest in a variety of possible applications of their formal curriculum experience. Clubs can render important school services and provide students with many responsibilities and opportunities for peer group acceptance. Clubs can be discriminatory as well and isolate certain students or groups, particularly if they base entrance upon illegal sex, racial, ethnic, or religious qualifications. Secret clubs such as high school sororities and fraternities have all but disappeared and have been ruled illegal in most states. More ubiquitous are car or motorcycle clubs which may meet off campus, and which on occasion, can become the source of friction and possibly violence with gang rivalries.

Important guidelines for the formation of student clubs on the campus of the secondary school are that such organizations have a faculty sponsor, a written set of rules and procedures, and that membership be open to interested students without regard to race, sex, ethnic, or religious qualifications.

Student Dances

Student dances have encountered difficulties in recent times. The widespread problems with teenage drinking and the use of marijuana and drugs has disrupted many secondary school dances and led to physical abuse of chaperones and general disorder. Teenage rock bands have raised the price of hosting dances considerably, often drink while playing and increase incidences of gate crashing by nonsecondary school students.

Some schools have reported problems in soliciting teachers to supervise such dances, even when they are paid. Hiring increased numbers of off-duty police, issuing school I.D. cards, maintaining accurate guest lists, limiting access to entry, and patrolling restrooms on a regular basis have helped alleviate some problems. In general large groups of students inadequately supervised with access to alcohol and/or marijuana and drugs lead to vandalism and violence. Some secondary schools have refused to offer dances because of their inability to control the situation and have referred them to community recreation departments

Assemblies and Speakers

Student assemblies can be a place where students plan entertainment, solicit help for various projects, make speeches, put on skits, plays and talent shows. These activities have traditionally enjoyed great success in the past. However, many secondary schools are reporting increasing student rowdiness and discourteous behavior in assemblies, even when they are student planned and where the student government pays for the speakers on topics of high interest.

Assembly behavior can be improved with structuring in some cases. Increased structure can be obtained by publishing seating charts by class, being sure classes are accompanied by the teachers, the absence of total darkness and screening performers so that dull subjects or speakers are excluded. Secondary school students, who have been reared on television with highly paid performers, may be extremely harsh on blossoming talent or outright mediocrity. Also, speakers who are unaccustomed to appearing before younger audiences may have to be counseled about pacing, humor, or tone which may lead to rowdiness.

Students have a right to express their opinions and to invite speakers to the school to express opinions on a variety of subjects in assemblies planned by them. Restrictions on speakers should be limited to actions or advocacy which may lead to violence or endanger the health and safety of students, faculty, or be disruptive of the school's educational program. (5) These guidelines may present some problems in areas of controversial issues in the secondary school such as abortion, gay liberation, racial problems or controversial political actions taken by the government on a variety of issues.

A letter to a governor of one state protesting a college professor's explanation of a new political party at a high school assembly led to an investigation by the State Superintendent of Public Instruction, an attack upon the high school curriculum as conflicting with community values, a board recall election, charges that left-wing literature was on the student required reading list, and allegations that a secret library existed of anti-American literature in the school. (6)

Student Government

A student government, under the thumb of the school administration, soon becomes a "ghost" and a meaningless exercise in learning the mock procedures of the democratic process; process without substance. Secondary school student government too often reflects regulations developed by the administration which strip students of legal, fiscal, and major legislative powers. Votes are merely a procedural exercise, campaigns shaped around harmless issues and personalities of the candidates, and the outcomes matter little except to the immediate students involved.

Student government should function within a written constitution or set of bylaws which are developed by students. They should be set within state law and board policy. Within this framework student government activities should not be the subject of adult veto powers. (7)

Many secondary schools attempt to provide their students with as much practice in the electoral process as possible, even to the point of renting voting machines and insisting that students register within political parties. If students are apathetic about their own student government, the cause usually lies with the administration and the faculty who have over the years shorn it of any power or important decision-making functions. Few students are impressed with the appearance of importance. If student government deals with important issues which are genuine, students will become actively involved. In New York State a student may appeal any decision made by the school administration or board of education directly to the Commissioner of Education. (8) Students also serve with teachers on a student grievance committee which is indedendent of the administration. In some school systems boards of education have added a student member to their membership underscoring the importance of student input in the decision-making process at that level. (9)

The Student Press

The student press, consisting of the newspaper and yearbook and perhaps a literary magazine, has historically been closely supervised and tightly controlled. The development of a significant underground press in the sixties often undermined the viability of the established student press and led to more freedom of expression and broader topics being included in the traditional press.

Recently the budget pinch of many districts has forced cutbacks in the number of such publications, and the student press has moved away from traditional topics such as football games, gossip, and general announcements to discussions of broader social issues and areas of immediate student concern. Some student newspapers have even featured teacher union statements regarding strikes or job actions and students have taken positions on such matters.

Guidelines for the student press are those which would normally apply to a regular press such as libel and obscenity laws. Within these guidelines student newspapers should be free to address issues which are of immediate concern to pupils, school related and social issues, and events happening in the community. Changes in the student press have probably been more far reaching within the last decade than those in the student government. This has become characteristic of the real world press as well. Topics which were not considered appropriate for home reader circulation are now routinely addressed in the community press.

Athletics

Athletics have always been one of the most visible and powerful cocurricular activities of the secondary school. Many schools find that the athletic program is one of the major ways a community identifies with the public school program. The recent emphasis on Title IX has served to expand the scope of secondary school athletic programs. The controversies and problems with big time high school athletics are reviewed in chapter ten.

Middle school athletics are recommended to be intramural rather than interscholastic in order to avoid the problems encountered by the junior high schools. The junior high school has become in too many cases a developmental program for high school varsity athletics, something the middle school hoped to avoid.

Intramurals have been one response to the emphasis upon competition and physical skill demanded by interscholastic athletics. The purpose of intramural activities is to provide a channel for healthful and controlled team sport for students who do not want to engage in intensive preparation and training. Well-developed intramural programs can provide an instructional activity for secondary schools which are both enjoyable and educational. The key to a good intramural program is good organization and planning by a highly motivated physical education department and the recognition and support by school officials. Intramurals are not a program frill, or a "sop" to students who cannot make interscholastic teams, but a full-blown educational program in its own right.

The Emerging Extra Curriculum

The adolescent and young adult peer group culture brings to the secondary school values which often conflict with the rules and regulations of the school and its formal curriculum, as well as those of the larger adult society. The school, by being isolated from the larger society on the basis of age grouping of clientele, helps to preserve and foster counteradult culture values and practices. The inculcation of these values creates a distinctive impact upon the overall secondary school atmosphere, as much or more than the formal school curriculum.

Peer group culture is a curriculum in itself, to which few adults in the school have total access or understand completely. The most visible impact of the peer group upon secondary school life has been negative. Such problems as the increasing utilization of alcohol, drugs, and sexual promiscuity result in higher rates of vandalism, violence, venereal disease, and teenage pregnancy. Educators must be aware of both the scope of the problem and its impact upon the school and the curriculum.

Student Dress Codes

Perhaps no area of the extra curriculum has been so heavily and impassionately challenged by students and their parents as school rules which relate to dress and hair length. Issues of hair length have been so important to students and their parents that cases have been argued in the federal courts. (9) In general, the courts have felt that regulations on pupil hair length have little to do with health, safety, or the educational program, and the only problem arises when school authorities attempt to enforce them. (10) The courts have ruled that regulations on hair length are not important enough to apply to fundamental liberties under the U.S. Constitution.

Dress codes which once specified in detail what students could wear and not wear, from shoes to formal and informal attire, have largely been erased. Where once girls were suspended from school for wearing granny dresses, culottes, and other "avant-garde" attire, such restrictions are recognized today as a matter of individual taste. Dress codes must depend upon clear evidence that attire is disruptive to the educational program, constitutes a clear danger to the student involved, or is demonstratively obscene (in which case it would also be disruptive). (11) As various clothing and hair styles run the cycle of teenage fads, school administrators and teachers should wisely refrain from becoming involved unless such fads are actually disruptive. Most secondary schools dealt effectively with the fad of "streaking" under this approach. Recently some of these changes in the extra curriculum have come under attack from minority group leaders as unnecessarily distracting to the learning process and the school program. (12)

Smoking

Smoking by students in secondary schools has always been a problem. Federal estimates indicate that between 30-40 percent of the high school student population are smokers. (13) The American Cancer Society estimates that there are 4.5 million teenage smokers in the United States. (14) With the inclusion of marijuana on the school grounds the smell of smoke often permeates the restrooms and hallways. Few states have attempted to lower the age for buying or using cigarettes. Many law enforcement agencies refuse to enforce the laws against minors purchasing cigarettes.

Probably the most critical problem with smoking is in secondary schools which actively enforce antismoking regulations. Restrooms become thick with smoke. Harassments, fights, extortion, and other disruptions are common. Many students report fear in using the restrooms in secondary schools. Fires may be common as students throw butts into stage scenery, custodian's closets, or in other flammable areas.

Some secondary schools have quietly designated a smoking area for students and insist that students who smoke use it. This frees the restrooms from smokers and gangs. (15) While many would argue that the school should attempt to cope with the problem by stressing the information between smoking and assorted attendant disease, such attempts are rather feeble when compared to the millions of dollars spent on advertising for smoking which zeroes in on younger age smokers. Smoking is often a sign of peer group acceptance and secondary school students may find the prospect of dying at a tender age incompatible with peer group demands. Many secondary schools have serious problems regulating and coping with the smoking problem. Unless the value system of the peer group is also part of the formal health curriculum, informational campaigns about the evils of smoking will not be able to stem the tide of the problem in the schools.

Cheating

Estimates on cheating in secondary schools are difficult to secure. Some research on the subject has indicated that at least half of the student population cheats at some time or another. (16) The discovery of student infiltration of statewide tests in New York prompted the cancellation and invalidation of the Regents in several subject areas. (17) Students had reprinted the answers which they sold for profit. Reasons for cheating extend from heavy academic pressures to outright pupil laziness. Excessive competition creates unreasonable demands upon students to be successful, often surpassing their actual abilities. Also, certain peer groups within the student subculture may countenance cheating as a legitimate response to perceived unreasonable school demands or "establishment oneupmanship."

Drugs and Alcoholism

Peer group values regarding the use of drugs and alcohol have brought many social values and conflicts into the nation's secondary schools. The drug flow within the schools has risen prolifically. The use of marijuana is fairly open in many secondary schools. It is smoked in the restrooms and around the school premises. In one high school, approximately 11 percent had drug arrest records. (18) Reports by students about drugs in the schools have led to proposed or real crackdowns, (19) principally in the form of school security guards or police in the schools. The presence of such personnel often become issues with the minority community.

The use of alcohol by secondary school students has also risen dramatically. One survey of the freshmen and sophomore class of a New York high school in the suburbs indicated that 60 percent of the students admitted to drinking and 24 percent of those drank more than once a week. Of that group, 4 percent admitted to drinking in school. In addition, 46 percent of the students indicated that they had had their first drink before the seventh grade. When asked why they drank, 57 percent agreed that young people drink to get the approval and acceptance of their peers. (20) Schools are not the only places where there has been a reported increase in teenage drinking. Dozens of towns and cities are finding public drinking a problem between the ages of twelve to eighteen and have moved to adopt ordinances prohibiting drinking in public places. (21)

The relationship between drug use and crime in the schools is not clear, but the evidence indicates that they are not totally separate phenomena. Robberies and theft have skyrocketed. Over a two-year period in the New York City Schools assaults increased 44 percent, robberies increased 35 percent and there was a 195 percent increase in disorderly conduct. (22) School vandalism is estimated to cost the public a half billion dollars per year. (23) Some school systems have mounted extensive public relations campaigns showing the costs for each pupil of vandalism in the schools. Others have installed a variety of advanced electronic equipment such as laser beam systems, sound-sensing devices and old-fashioned burglar alarms. Such systems only protect the schools at nights and on weekends. Much vandalism occurs during the school day.

Changing Sexual Mores

By 1973 one of every five births in the United States was to a teenager. A third of these births were to unmarried girls. 76 percent of first births by girls in age ranges fifteen to nineteen were conceived before marriage. (24) The Planned Parenthood Federation of American stated that more than one million American teenagers—one in ten—become pregnant each year, though at least two-thirds did not want to become pregnant. (25) Data such as those cited indicate the swift change occurring in society of teenage sexual agressiveness and its profound and often tragic impact upon the lives of many young Americans.

Cyclical Curricular Issues as Larger Social Ills

The secondary school has responded in a variety of ways to problems of the extra curriculum and those of even a larger social context. The secondary school has attempted to incorporate some features of the extra curriculum into the formal curriculum by making them the subjects of study. Courses such as health education or family education have included such subjects as smoking, drugs, and alcohol, and recently, information about reproduction and sex. The secondary school has also responded with the utilization of school sanctions.

Despite protests by civil rights groups that the use of sanctions against students fall disproportionately upon minority students, secondary schools continue to employ corporal punishment, suspension, and expulsion as a response to problems created by the extra curriculum. A study in Florida by the Governor's Task Force on Disruptive Youth showed that 44 percent of the students suspended or expelled from school were black when only 23 percent of the high school population was black. (26) Some racial disturbances at secondary schools have begun when minority groups have protested the unequal treatment of school sanctions upon their group. (27) Many large school systems have abandoned the official use of corporal punishment, only to find that school personnel, administrators and teachers continue to use it in defiance of official policy.

Secondary schools with high rates of corporal punishment, suspension or expulsion should examine their curriculum, school policies and regulations. In too many cases such sanctions are used for very minor offenses: smoking, truancy (This is a contradiction, but true), class cutting, chewing gum in class, etc. The lack of viable curricular alternatives, overcrowding, poor teaching and deplorable physical facilities are some of the reasons students may try to opt out of school. Truancy, absenteeism, and class-cutting are not only damaging ways students attempt to leave school, but they are expensive as well. (28) If efforts were made to retain the students in school through the use of curricular, staffing, and organizational alternatives, most systems could pay for the cost with monies recouped from higher pupil attendance figures. It has been estimated in the New York City schools that more high school students drop out of school than graduate and the blame has been laid to the lack of adequate staffing and school alternatives as one source of the problem. (29) In addition, some secondary schools are resorting to stricter procedures to cut class absence rates such as lowering pupil grades for a given number of such infractions.

School Violence

A United States Senate Subcommittee on Juvenile Delinquence reported that from its survey of 757 school districts in the United States that 70,000 teachers were victims of serious assaults in 1975. The same report indicated that from 1970 to 1973, assaults on teachers rose by 77.4 percent. (30) In a Hollywood, Florida school a bomb placed in a student's locker blew out a classroom wall, (31) and in Texas a bomb placed on a cafeteria conveyor belt maimed a school custodian trying to remove it. (32)

In White Plains, New York, the aftermath of a high school football game saw fistfights develop in the stands and on the field. Cheerleaders were chased to a car where the windows were smashed with rocks and the terrified girls cut with the glass. (33) In Chicago, a high school quarrel between two students over twenty-five cents, ended with one shooting and killing the other in the school's assembly hall. (34)

A special grand jury investigation of school discipline in St. Petersburg, Florida indicated the lack of appropriate curricular alternatives for students and the failure on the part of school administrators to report school discipline problems for fear of being considered weak principals, added to the problem. (35) Accurate data on school violence is one of the strongest recommendations of the National Commission on the Reform of Secondary Education. (36) Some of the individual states have passed new laws on school safety in response to the crisis.

As these incidents have increased in secondary schools, the simple response has been to hire police to patrol the schools. The fact that student values, mores, and larger social issues may be causative agents of school violence and therefore should be addressed in the formal curriculum of the school is usually ignored. In some cases it is the lack of reform in the traditional secondary school curriculum which may partially account for the pervasive feelings of boredom, tension, and containment by students. The line between the formal curriculum, its studies and emphasis, and the extra curriculum is actually nonexistent. What influences student behavior and school life must be addressed by the school, if not in the classrooms directly, then in the hallways, restrooms, playgrounds, and lunch/recreation areas. If problems in the school are not addressed with students as they have not been with sex education and racial conflict, they must be addressed administratively. The degree to which the unresolved problems consume vast amounts of administrative time is a reflection of the fact that the formal curriculum is silent on the same issues. Pupil problems must be resolved with pupils participating. In order to do this, the real problems of students must become part of the formal curriculum.

The secondary school curriculum has been the subject of a variety of attacks of a political nature. Such attacks represent the extra curriculum as sociopolitical extensions into the school. Some are direct attacks upon a particular curriculum, and others are attacks upon secondary school organization or student body composition. The attacks as representative of the extension of the extra curriculum have far reaching implications for the formal curriculum and academic freedom in the secondary school.

Book Banning

Books deemed offensive in secondary school libraries and classrooms still draw the ire and fire of school boards, administrators, and irate parents. In Drake, North Dakota, the Board of Education ordered all thirty-two copies of Kurt Vonnegut's *Slaughterhouse Five* burned. The book had been selected by a high school English teacher. (37) In Island Trees, Long Island, New York, the Board of Education ordered eleven books taken from the school library book shelves, among them *The Fixer* by Bernard Malamud, *Why I Am Not a Christian* by Bertrand Russell, *Black Boy* by Richard Wright and *The Naked Ape* by Desmond Morris. (38) This brought a countersuit filed by five students and joined by Kurt Vonnegut, Jr. and the New York Civil Liberties Union. (39)

The Board of Education of Pasadena, California barred quotations from folksinger Joan Baez and black comedian Dick Gregory as "breaking down respect for authority." (40) The protests were led by a self-taught fundamentalist minister who viewed the materials as contrary to fundamentalist teachings he derived from the Bible. (41) Columnists attack textbooks, particularly those which portray the "Founding Fathers" as anything other than heroes. (42) Textbooks in Mississippi draw the protests of black groups who object to the demeaning of their people in the adopted text and point out a superior text is available. (43)

The selection of books for classrooms and libraries is still a volatile one in America. Texts and books which expose a side of life or that of the nation which does not conform to various viewpoints, religious or otherwise, are most often the subject of attack. The American Civil Liberties Union believes that books should be selected on the basis of a public "open list," and that professionals should have wide choice. Books should be chosen on criteria of accuracy and scholarship, the degree to which they match the curricular objectives, and be free from "unfounded or prejudiced opinions on racial, cultural, religious, or political matters." (44) In a recent federal court case, the Court of Appeals ruled that school officials could not arbitrarily go through a school library and remove books they found offensive. (45)

Book banning and book burning are contrary to the responsibility of the professional teacher to select materials appropriate to the curriculum, and the responsibility of the board of education to help young adults deal with all matters in decision making on controversial issues. Boards should adopt criteria for textbook selection and staff members with parental input should be free to select the materials based upon those criteria. Textbooks should be openly viewed and discussed prior to adoption. Board subcommittees may hold hearings on both the criteria and books to be selected. Secondary school curriculum developers must be continually alert to the intrusion of a partisan viewpoint in dealing with matters related to book selection, utilization and regulation.

Religion in the Schools

In their evolutionary history in the United States, the public schools have openly espoused religion and proffered a distinctly Protestant version of morality upon public school children. Catholics found such viewpoints so offensive that they withdrew their children and founded their own school system. (46) The United States Supreme Court found the practice of Bible reading as a school exercise unconstitutional and a violation of the First Amendment. (47) Later the Supreme Court found the New York Regents Prayer below unconstitutional.

> Almighty God, we acknowledge our dependence upon Thee, and we beg Thy blessings upon us, our parents, our teachers and our country.

The Court majority found that the Regents prayer was established by a governmental agency as part of a governmental program to foster religious activities in the public schools. As such it violated the Establishment Clause. (48) Since these two decisions, Bible reading and prayer in the schools have been perennial topics of controversy. Various states have attempted to instill prayer in the nation's classrooms in a variety of guises and formats. One after another they have all been struck down.

The emerging trend is to seriously question the advisability of promoting or endorsing religious services in the public schools. The display of religious symbols such as a creche (Nativity Scene) have caused considerable controversy and led to recommendations to ban them from the school's curriculum. (49) A study conducted by the Anti-Defamation League of B'nai B'rith of 103 communities in 31 states and the District of Columbia indicated that 91.5 percent of the respondents admitted to conducting school activities such as concerts, plays, etc. with a religious content. More than half of the respondents found the practices objectionable. (50) Undoubtedly these practices and customs will be the subject of controversy and possible litigation in the future.

The National Conference of Christians and Jews believes that the study of religion is an important aspect of the school's curriculum. But they differentiate between *studying* and *practicing* religion. They are careful to distinguish between indoctrination and instruction. The approach of the school in developing a study of religion is that such studies are academic and not devotional, and that they should strive for awareness and not acceptance. (51) Such curricular offerings in the schools as using the Bible as a source of literature study are often found in secondary schools. The practice of devotional Christmas or Easter celebrations are clearly contrary to the guidelines of the National Conference. In particular, the secularization of Christmas has produced many problems for secondary school educators, particularly in attempting to distinguish between secular and religious symbols and studies.

Direct Attacks upon Specific Curricula

Occasionally members of a community subgroup will directly attack a particular curriculum of the secondary school. This has been the case with sex education for example. It has also occurred on a nationwide basis in the social studies. Deviations from the straight narrative chronological approaches to teaching the social studies have come under fire. Edward Fenton's social studies books and inquiry-based curricula have been the subject of some attack. The criticism of the Fenton based approach in U.S. history is that it does not indoctrinate to a particular point of view and that certain subjects are given more page space than others. One critic of Fenton's books refused to adopt it in Georgia because it allocated more space to the Vietnam War than the American Revolution. (52)

Another social studies curriculum which has been the subject of a Congressional inquiry is MACOS (Man: a Course of Study). MACOS was developed at Harvard University under a grant from the National Science Foundation. MACOS is an interdisciplinary approach to the teaching of the social studies which uses the primitive culture of the Eskimos to examine different social and economic values of the family. (53) MACOS has been the subject of violent attacks which decry it as promoting cannibalism, infanticide, genocide, and senilicide. (53) interdisciplinary, inquiry-based approaches in the social sciences have come under strong attack from conservative educational quarters in the United States. It appears to be the feeling of some conservative groups that any kind of inquiry-based, value-laden approach to the teaching of social studies represent threats upon the nation's solidarity.

Attacks upon Organizational and Curricular Alternatives

Modular flexible scheduling, an innovation which changed the traditional secondary school schedule from five equal periods per day to varying blocks of time per week, has also been the subject of severe criticism from educational conservatives. The most controversial feature of flexible scheduling has been the concept of unscheduled or unstructured time for students. This means that within the school day students had a choice about their educational activities. This could include going to a small group room, a lab, a resource center, the student lounge, or sitting outside the school on the lawn. However, in many communities, this sharply ran aground on citizen perceptions that a "good" school was one where students were behind desks all day long. Finding students not in class on a five period day caused a number of communities, parents and citizens to become very upset.

The President of the Parents' Auxiliary of a Florida high school criticized modular flexible scheduling for allowing, "kids everywhere but in the classroom—in the bathrooms smoking, loitering in the parking lot and in the woods making love." (55) Another father of a student on modular scheduling sued the board of education for a loss of instructional time and alleged that the new plan failed to meet minimum standards set by the state. (56) In New York a new superintendent cracked down on students who were not able to handle the unscheduled time with the result of sustaining an organized student protest, (57) and in Chicago a dispute with the teachers union over alleged mishandling of flexible scheduling led to it being abandoned in the district. (58)

The idea behind the unscheduled time and varying units of time was to try and break up the traditional lock step secondary school schedule. The rationale behind it was almost irrefutable, that is, that there is no need for every student to have the same subjects for the same periods of time. Any analysis of student needs will demonstrate the fallacy of equal scheduling of subjects. Furthermore, the move to less formal structuring and the impetus to train students to handle the idea of choice in the curriculum is excellent preparation for college decision-making. However, the failure of secondary school staffs and administators to plan for alternatives when students did not assume responsibility for decision-making ultimately led to a demand to close down the scheduling plan. Given a choice between lock step scheduling and boredom, or chaos and choice, most communities and boards do not appear to be overly troubled with making a decision.

Catastrophic Interruptions of School Life

There are several kinds of catastrophic interruptions of life in secondary schools today. These would be prolonged teacher strikes and/or job actions, racial disturbances or riots, and the loss of adequate funds to support the schools resulting in their suspending all operations.

Teacher Strikes and Job Actions

A teachers' strike represents a severe disruption of the school's education program. Depending upon strike conditions, the time and length of the strike, the damage to the educational program can be extensive. During a strike students can become involved and take sides. (59) Lack of student supervision can lead to vandalism and destruction of school materials. Prolonged strikes present difficulties for seniors who may be depending upon scholarships based upon final tests or grades. They may also cause serious problems in student-teacher interrelationships.

Job actions or "work to rule" strikes may also have a damaging impact upon a secondary school's curriculum. These types of teacher union responses encountered in job actions have had great negative impact upon students:

1. Teachers refusing to grade pupil tests or conference with pupils before or after school;
2. Teachers refusing to assume coaching, club, or other extra pay responsibilities;
3. Prolonged delays in returning student homework assignments;
4. Teachers refusing to attend "Back to School Nights," or participate in school or school system professional committee work;
5. Teachers calling in "sick" or overloading certain district services, such as films, checking out student files, etc.

Job actions have also been common in other public agencies such as air traffic controllers and governmental agencies such as the Internal Revenue Service. In some cases they are more damaging to a school's program than an actual strike. If a school's program is closed due to a strike, the students are less likely to become involved. The tension, friction, and disharmony of a job action are serious losses for a school's curriculum and directly affect the extra curriculum of the secondary school.

Racial Disturbances and Riots

With the increasingly mandatory, court-ordered integration of the nation's secondary schools, racial fights and disruptions have occurred in many parts of the nation. Some of the disturbances involve active intervention of the police. Many have led to serious injury of students and faculty. In Danbury, Connecticut, racial fighting erupted and in-

jured twelve students and resulted in the loss of several days of instruction. (60) In Pensacola, Florida, Escambia High School became an
armed battleground when the student body voted to retain the team
name, "The Rebels," and fly the confederate flag. (61) Dixie Hollins
High School suffered similar riots and violence over flying the confederate flag. A school district in Denver, Colorado experienced several
violent incidents and closed four schools as Chicanos and other members of the student body considered a message on a T-shirt provocative.
(62) More incidents in a cafeteria of a high school in the Washington,
D.C. area between blacks and whites led to fighting and even the
disruption of a parent's meeting. (63) In Detroit a high school principal
was allegedly tarred and feathered for trying to improve race relations at
his school. (64) Perhaps the most tragic and violent school disruption in
recent years occurred in Boston when South Boston High School was
integrated by a Federal Court Order. (65)

Racial conflicts in the nation's secondary schools have not been
isolated to one section of the country. School personnel have been afraid
to deal with interpersonal issues in the classroom and within the formal
curriculum of the secondary school. Topics which might lead to an
airing of the issues are avoided until there is an explosion in a cafeteria
or hallway. (66) Racial violence does not happen overnight. Prolonged
periods of frustration and pent up emotion usually build over an extended period of time. Finally, a symbol such as a confederate flag, an
insensitive remark, or slogan on a T-shirt ignites violence.

Racial violence can often be avoided if the issues which cause the
conflict can be aired. Biracial committees, and human relations training
have worked if implemented at the first signs of trouble. When the
violence occurs it wipes away much of the formal curriculum. To continue to look at the problem as "outside" that curriculum is part of the
problem. In most cases while a community wide decision has led to
integration, the school must deal with the problems by making the
results of integration part of its formal curriculum. In this way, human
explosions can be avoided. The fact of the matter is that the "extra"
curriculum is not really extra at all. When it is recognized as essential the
first conceptual step will have been taken to reforming, improving, and
expanding the formal curriculum.

School Closings Due to Taxpayer Resistance

Another catastrophic interruption of school life has been the complete
shutdown of schools due to taxpayer resistance to approving funding
measures. The 56,000 pupil Toledo, Ohio school system was shut down

for five weeks due to the fact voters would not approve the necessary tax measure to keep the schools open. (66) Teachers had to suffer five weeks without any salary and 70,000 other students were forced to leave their schools in seven other Ohio school districts for the same reasons. (67) The same pattern was followed in Oregon where the schools were closed, partially due to increasing suspicion that such secondary school courses as macrame, horticulture and "fishing for English," were frills and should be abandoned. (68)

The increasing financial strain on the local property tax to support secondary education has reached its limits of public support in these states and there is evidence that similar situations are on the verse of happening elsewhere. Clearly the inequities of supporting public secondary education are widespread. These states provide vivid examples of what can happen when the public loses confidence in its schools.

The extra curriculum as larger societal ills will not be ameliorated with rhetoric and slogans. One possible response is to embrace one or more measures of accountability discussed in chapter twelve as a method to restoring public confidence in the efficiency of the schools. It will take more than public relations, it will take results, and while results are conceptually simple to imagine, they are tremendously complex to provide. When the schools are closed or disrupted, the curriculum becomes what is necessary to reopen them. The cocurriculum and the extra curriculum are misnomers. There is only one curriculum and it is inclusive.

CHAPTER REFERENCES

1. The statistics were compiled by the National Education Association as cited in a United Press International story, "U.S. Sets Program to Fight Violence in the Schools," *Washington Star,* November 9, 1976.

2. Tinker v. Des Moines Independent Community School District, 393 U.S. 503 (1969).

3. For a thorough review of court decisions in this area, see Richard Gyory, "The Constitutional Rights of Public School Pupils," *Fordham Law Review* (New York: Fordham University Press, December 1971), pp. 201-62.

4. See American Civil Liberties Union, "Academic Freedom in the Secondary Schools," (New York City, New York, September 1968).

5. Ibid., pp. 10-12.

6. This letter was sent to Governor Ronald Reagan of California from a parent in the Poway Unified School District on January 4, 1968. It resulted in an investigation by State Superintendent Max Rafferty. Later the charges were

dropped, and the State cancelled its investigation after a series of stormy meetings with school officials and parents. The investigation occurred between January and June of 1968. See also Harold Keen, "Anti-Americanism Charges Will Be Probed," *Los Angeles Times,* June 11, 1968, Part 1.

7. Robert L. Ackerly, *The Reasonable Exercise of Authority* (Washington, D.C.: National Association of Secondary School Principals, 1969), p. 16.

8. State Education Department, "Guidelines for Students' Rights and Responsibilities," Albany, New York, 1974.

9. Karr v. Schmidt, United States Court of Appeals, Fifth Circuit, April 28, 1972. The case involved a high school boy in the El Paso, Texas, school district.

10. As cited in the testimony in Karr v. Schmidt. See also Beau Cutts, "Fulton School Hair Rules Appealed by Parents, Teens," *Atlanta Constitution,* October 4, 1972.

11. See Eldon G. Scriven and Alton Harrison, Jr., "Student Dress Codes," *The Education Digest* 36, no. 6 (February 1971): 291-92.

12. Paul Delaney, "Jesse Jackson Begins a Model Program in Chicago to Improve the Moral Atmosphere in Black Schools," *New York Times,* June 8, 1976, p. 17.

13. Julia Malone, "On High School Smoking Rules," *Christian Science Monitor,* January 16, 1973.

14. As cited in Paul Delaney, "St. Louis Youths Are Going to Class to Try to Fight the Smoking Habit," *New York Times,* December 8, 1976.

15. The National Commission on the Reform of Secondary Education discussed the often intolerable conditions prevalent in secondary school restrooms. The Commission urged the repeal of laws against smoking by adolescents and urged secondary schools to designate smoking areas. See "The Crises in School Security," Chapter 10 in *The Reform of Secondary Education* (New York: McGraw-Hill, 1973), pp. 115-25.

16. Gene I. Maeroff, "West Point Cheaters Have a Lot of Company," *New York Times,* June 20, 1976.

17. Lee Dembart, "4 Regents Tests Cancelled after Discovery of Thefts," *New York Times,* June 15, 1975.

18. Michael Medved and David Wallechinsky, *What Really Happened to the Class of '65?* (New York: Random House, 1976).

19. Peter Sleeper, "Drug Use in Schools Hot Issue," *Montgomery County* (Maryland) *Sentinel,* April 26, 1973.

20. Fenwick W. English, "Preliminary Review of Student Survey on Attitudes and Practices in Regard to Alcoholic Beverages," Hastings Public Schools, Hastings-on-Hudson, New York, October 15, 1975. (Xeroxed.)

21. Anson Smith, "Suburbs Turning to Ordinances to Combat Public Teenage Drinking," *Boston Globe,* August 26, 1976, p. 3.

22. "Violence Called a Long-Term Problem," *New York Times,* December 17, 1975, p. 50.

23. Figures cited in a Senate subcommittee on juvenile delinquency in a 1975 study, "U.S. Sets Program," *Washington Star.*

24. Marilyn Brant Chandler, "Alternatives to Abortion," *New York Times,* October 23, 1976.

25. "Pregnant Teens: Too Many, Little Aid," *Chicago Tribune,* December 12, 1976, p. 44.

26. Associated Press, "Poor Black Males Lead Suspension," *Sarasota Herald Tribune,* December 16, 1973.

27. Over a hundred persons were arrested in Anniston, Alabama, in a protest over the expulsion of a black student. United Press International, "140 Arrested in Alabama School Issue," *Arizona Republic,* October 28, 1971.

28. One school system estimated that losses to absenteeism of state aid was approximately 13 percent of its income. Wally Page, "Hendry Schools Forfeiting $178,000 in Absenteeism," *Fort Myers News Press,* March 25, 1973.

29. David Vidal, "Rise in Dropouts in New York City Shocks Regents," *New York Times,* October 11, 1976.

30. "U.S. Sets Program," *Washington Star.*

31. United Press International, "Blast in Florida School," *New York Times,* February 4, 1975.

32. "Conroe Custodian Maimed by School Cafeteria Bomb," *Houston Chronicle,* January 15, 1975.

33. Charles Lachman and Robert Thompson, "Violence Prompts Security Evaluation, *Herald-Statesman,* Yonkers, New York, November 2, 1976.

34. Jack Slater, "Death of a High School," *Phi Delta Kappan* (December 1974): 251-56.

35. Sheila Mullane, "Mensh Stresses Need to Change Schools," *St. Petersburg Independent,* November 28, 1973, 3-A.

36. In recommendation number twenty-two, the National Commission stated that the laws should require school principals to file detailed reports on all serious assaults within the schools. *Reform of Secondary Education,* pp. 115-22.

37. Kay Bartlett, "Town That Burned Its Sophomores' Books," story of the Associated Press of December 16, 1973, which appeared in the *Sarasota Herald Tribune,* Sarasota, Florida.

38. "Long Island School Board Is Facing Fight on Banning of Books," *New York Times,* March 31, 1976.

39. "L.I. Students File Suit to Overturn School Book Ban," *New York Times,* January 9, 1977.

40. "Pasadena to Vote on School Unit Recall," *New York Times,* March 3, 1975, C-19.

41. James T. Wooten, "Bomb Indictments Latest Battle in Textbook War," *New York Times,* January 27, 1975.

42. Patrick J. Buchanan, "New History Makes Mockery of America's Great Heroes," *Philadelphia Bulletin,* June 8, 1975, A-17.

43. Jason Barry, "Teaching Mississippi History," *New York Times,* October 10, 1975.

44. American Civil Liberties Union, "Academic Freedom."

45. Associated Press story, "School Officials Barred from Removing Library Books," *Boston Globe,* August 31, 1976. The Sixth United States Circuit

312 COCURRICULUM/"EXTRA" CURRICULUM

Court of Appeals ruling on action in Strongsville, a Cleveland suburb in which Kurt Vonneut's *Cat's Cradle* and Joseph Heller's *Catch 22* were banned by the board of education.

46. David B. Tyack, *The One Best System* (Cambridge: Harvard University Press, 1974), pp. 84-85.

47. *Abington School District v. Schempp* (1963) U.S. 203. See William O. Douglas, *The Bible and the Schools* (Boston: Little, Brown, 1966).

48. Paul Blanshard, *Religion and the Schools* (Boston: Beacon Press, 1963), pp. 27-50.

49. Mary Sullivan, "Religious Observances in Schools Opposed," *Boston Record-American*, July 19, 1972.

50. Irving Spiegel, "First Amendment Violation Seen in Schools' Religious Practices," *New York Times*, May 30, 1976.

51. The guidelines are extrapolated from James Panoch, "What Public Schools May and May Not Do under the Schempp Decision," in Francis S. Harmon, *Religious Freedom in America* (New York: The Interchurch Center, 1976), p. 31.

52. Tom Linthicum, "Fenton Says Teaching Issue Is Board's Main Criticism," *Atlanta Constitution*, December 20, 1971.

53. See Peter B. Dow, "MACOS: The Study of Human Behavior As One Road to Survival," *Phi Delta Kappan* 57, no. 2 (October 1975): 79-81.

54. The conservative Phoenix-based press, *Weekly American News*, roundly attacked MACOS. "MACOS, Social? Study?" 8, no. 33 (September 1, 1971).

55. "Rickards Parents' Group Hits Flexible Scheduling," *Tallahassee Democrat*, February 23, 1972.

56. Sheila Mullane, "Northeast's Mod Plan Sought," *Evening Independent*; St. Petersburg, Florida, November 28, 1973.

57. "Students Protest Teaching Method," *New York Times*, February 29, 1976.

58. "Modular Plan Dies As Charges Fly," *Chicago Tribune*, April 16, 1970.

59. For an example, see Roy R. Silver, "Teachers in Farmingdale Go on Strike," *New York Times*, May 7, 1976.

60. Michael Knight, "12 Hurt As Racial Brawls Shut Danbury High School," *New York Times*, October 2, 1975.

61. Wayne King, "Racial Animosity Turns to Violence in Pensacola, Florida, on Issue of Calling High School Teams, 'Rebels,'" *New York Times*, March 7, 1976, p. 33.

62. Ted Carey, "Power Balance Tips in School Racial Violence," *Rocky Mountain News*, March 18, 1974.

63. Lance Gay, "Hyattsville School Shut after Stormy Meeting," *Washington Evening Star*, April 14, 1972, Section B.

64. United Press International, "Klansmen Accused of Tarring Principal," *Atlanta Constitution*, June 23, 1972, 28-A.

65. John Kifner, "Tensions and Violence in Boston Schools Are Rooted in Traditions of White Ethnic Neighborhoods," *New York Times,* May 18, 1975, p. 48.

66. William K. Stevens, "56,000 Pupil School System Shut As Toledo Voters Bar Tax Rise," *New York Times,* December 11, 1976.

67. "Toledo Schools Close; Teachers Get Five Week Payless Furlough," *American Teacher* 61, no. 4 (December 1976): 3.

68. "Closed Schools in Oregon District Pose Dilemma for the Taxpayers," *New York Times,* November 8, 1976, p. 18.

10   Interscholastic
Athletics

The Unique Role of Athletics in
American Schools and Society

Although interschool athletic competition is by no means unknown
outside the United States, in no other nation has the interscholastic
athletic program grown to dimensions that are readily observable in the
American pattern. In the United States, and only in the United States,
athletic competition among educational institutions at all levels, elementary school through the university, is a continuous fixture of school
life, from the opening of the school year in the fall to its closing in the
spring. At least thirty-one major and minor sports are recognized.
Millions of students participate, and many millions of dollars are needed
annually to keep the enterprise going. The welding of interschool athletic competition into the educational system is a uniquely American
phenomenon.

In other countries much of the competition that Americans assume
matter-of-factly should be school-related is scheduled under entirely
different sorts of sponsorship. Teams may be organized on the basis of
governmental units, local and regional. Or, teams may represent various
occupational groups, military units, or other segments of the organized
society. Under such conditions the "national" teams that represent many
nations in international competition, the Olympic Games for example,
are, in fact, truly national organizations. The participants scale a ladder
of increasingly difficult competitive levels and ultimately are selected for
the pinnacle of international competition on the basis of individual
achievement.

By contrast, the athletes who represent the United States in such
events are typically volunteers. They represent college and university
athletic departments or are members of strictly amateur local athletic
clubs and associations. There are no government subsidies. The money
for American participation in international athletics is donated by the
people during the perennial drives for funds that precede the events.

Along with these observations, consider that the most highly skilled
level of athletic competition in the United States is entirely professional
in all the major sports. This, also, is unlike the pattern for athletics in
other countries. Again, this is not because professional athletic competition is unknown in other nations; indeed, such examples as hockey and

---

*This chapter follows an outline prepared by Dr. Floyd Boschee, chairman, Department
of Education, Sioux Falls College, Sioux Falls, South Dakota. Dr. Boschee also contributed many of the ideas and much of the writing having to do with the evolution of
interscholastic athletics and the values in these programs. Those portions of the chapter
written by Dr. Boschee are included with his permission.

football in Canada, soccer in western Europe and South America, and baseball in Japan, come readily to mind. However, only in the United States is the scope of professional sport so highly organized, so all-encompassing, and so much a part of the life of the people. One sports season overlaps another throughout the entire twelve months of each year. Newspaper, magazine, and television coverage of sports events, both professional and school, is extensive and detailed. As each season wears on toward the point where championships are decided, media coverage intensifies. Rivalries are sharply drawn and clearly pictured for readers and viewers. Individual accomplishments are set forth and glorified. The football or other brand of hero is a very real person in the lives of both the young and of the adults who follow his career. Both professional and school sports permeate the lives of the people.

This peculiarly American hierarchy of school sports at all levels combined with professional sports at the apex of the system has resulted in a natural but not altogether desirable situation. Schools at lower levels have become athletic feeder schools for those at higher levels. Sports reporters and coaches involved with high school teams watch the progress of junior high or even elementary school performers. Colleges vie for the services of outstanding high school athletes. And, in the end, professional teams under complex sets of rules, agreements, and legal decisions covering each sport, bid for the college players, who, it is felt, can do most to maintain the professional club's winning—and profit making—record. Thus, whether the schools wanted such a role or not, they have become training institutions for the nation's professional sports organizations as well as for each other in athletics at each level of schooling.

Some aspects of this situation are certainly undesirable as, for example, when professional sports organizations attempt to go below the college level to draft or buy athletes. However, by and large, the system is well bounded by a host of regulations both voluntary and legal. And, on analysis, what pertains in athletics is not so different from what exists in all other areas of school life. Schools advance athletes to other schools, but athletes are also students. Both athletes and students who are not athletes move from school level to school level as a natural consequence of success at one level leading to entrance into another. This is educational progress and not a peculiarity of the athletic system. And if, finally, schools prepare for professional sports participation so, in like manner, do they prepare for entrance into other occupations. Thus, the purpose of this discussion is not to criticize the status of interscholastic athletics in American education but only to point out that the prominent role of athletics in American schools is unlike that of the school system of any other nation. Nor is the intention here to suggest that practices in athletics in other countries are "better" or "worse" than practices in this nation. The intention here is to describe what exists, and no more.

However, because of the prominence given to interschool competition in athletics, this competition has become the most highly visible cocurricular activity. The only contact that many citizens have with the local high school is via the sports program. In school systems both large and small an outstanding team competing toward a regional or state championship can bring all other school activities, including academic endeavors, to a virtual halt until the issue is decided. Because this is so, and because the conduct of athletics brought its own set of issues and problems to the surface of an already turbulent educational stream, interscholastic athletics as an aspect of the secondary school extraclass program is treated separately in the present chapter.

Evolution of Interscholastic Athletics

Although the development of interschool sports contests chronologically paralleled the development of physical education programs in the United States, the two topics, athletics and physical education, are not precisely the same. As set forth in chapter five of this volume, physical education is a general requirement in the program of studies. Its curricular continuity is built into the earliest grades of the elementary school and continues through high school. Physical education may or may not include athletic competition with other students. In either case, physical education is not limited to such competition. By contrast, the emphasis in athletic participation, either individual or by teams, is set on the competition itself. Interscholastic competition among schools is voluntary, governed by agreed-upon regulations rather than by state expectations, and, far from being a general requirement, participation is limited to the most able students.

This does not suggest that athletic participation in interschool events lacks educational value. On the contrary, if the case could not be made for such competition on the basis of educational value there would be little point in continued school sponsorship.

Interscholastic athletics came into being during the latter part of the nineteenth century as a student-initiated, student controlled, and student-scheduled operation. Along with other extraclass activities in music, speech, and art, athletics at first was ignored by administrators and faculty members. Out-of-class or "play" time was considered to be in conflict with the strictly academic purposes of the school. As long as athletic and other student activities did not interfere with the academic program they were considered to be student business and no responsibility of the school.

This attitude left students to administer their own extraclass undertakings and during the early years of the twentieth century a wide variety of student-sponsored activities came into being. These included special interest clubs, secret societies, publications, hobby groups, and various forms of student government. Interscholastic athletic contests continued to increase in number with few, if any, rules or regulations. It was not uncommon for individuals who were not enrolled in a school to play as members of a team. Intensified intrusion on study time and academic matters became evident, not alone by athletics but by the entire extraclass movement.

Obviously, school people could not ignore the movement. Hence, the next step was to oppose and attempt to restrain extraclass activity by students. Advisors from the faculty or community were appointed to guide and direct various student groups, including athletic teams. Unfortunately, the mere presence of adult advisors did not resolve the problems. Many advisors worked actively to perpetuate such undesirable developments as the exclusive secret society. For those advisors concerned with athletics, winning became the essential emphasis in order to attract spectators and contributions. Unethical practices continued, such as nonstudent participation and recruitment of students for athletic abilities. The traditions that were established and the precedents set during this time still haunt interscholastic athletics.

By 1925, however, several forces had combined to bring all elements of the extraclass program firmly under the control of the school. First, the impact of the Progressive Movement gradually changed the secondary curriculum from a sequence of courses dominated by college entrance requirements to a curriculum with considerably broadened emphases. (1) Also, the influence of such statements as the 1918 publication of the Seven Cardinal Principles (2) stressing such goals as health and worthy use of leisure time, resulted in increased recognition of the value of all extraclass activities, including interscholastic athletics. For the past fifty years, extraclass activities have been controlled and utilized as part of the planned program of the school.

In athletics early efforts toward control came in the form of state level associations, organized to formulate rules to govern high school athletic contests. State associations were created as early as 1895 in Wisconsin and Michigan and in Illinois in 1898. During the same years, local public school athletic leagues came into being in many major cities. (3) The purpose of a league or conference was, and is today, to determine procedures and standards for athletic activities.

The number of state associations and local leagues increased rapidly until, in 1922, the National Federation of State High School Athletic Associations was organized. In 1970 the word *athletic* was removed from the name of the national organization to reflect the expanding responsibilities of the National Federation in nonathletic activities.

The National Federation now includes membership from all fifty states and the District of Columbia, with affiliates from eight interscholastic organizations in the Canadian Provinces. In brief, the major purposes of the Federation are to coordinate the efforts of the state associations, to participate in the formulation of rules, to provide a national voice, and to gather information. (4) The work of the Federation is bolstered by hundreds of local and regional leagues and conferences spread throughout the nation, representing both public and independent schools.

It is doubtful that all school people accept all the rules of their state athletic associations. However, educators are privileged to change and enforce the rules for interscholastic athletics in their respective states. To continue this privilege it is imperative that teachers and administrators support their state associations and proceed through appropriate channels to modify rules they dislike. Once given to the courts or to state legislatures, the privilege of making and enforcing the rules may be lost.

Values of Interscholastic Athletics

Given the responsibility to lead and direct school programs, boards of education, administrators, and teachers must believe that the multiple purposes of secondary education are not capricious contemplations. As with any other aspect of the school's program, interschool athletics came into being, despite opposition, because it met needs that were not even recognized as needs at the time. Since all experience is part of education, it is evident that a well-organized, carefully-planned, well-taught sport experience can be educationally valuable. Therefore, "for the athletically active students, sports are not merely a casual pastime." (5) They are, rather, a fulfillment of life, adding social, moral, ethical, and physical contributions to the secondary student's present condition and to his continuing and ultimate condition.

Testimony for the virtues of athletic competition has come from national leaders in the professions, business, and politics. (6) Summed up, such testimony may be categorized under headings which pertain to qualities of character and citizenship, elusive personal traits such as determination and self-control, which, it is claimed, are naturally and inevitably developed during the athletic confrontation.

The same sort of testimony is provided when former high school athletes reflect on their experiences and identify the influence of high school sports in developing values. In a study conducted with seventy-four athletes who had graduated from high school over a ten-year period preceding the research, 94 percent said it helped to "develop cooperation and teamwork;" 92 percent indicated that their athletic participation had helped them establish "real friendships;" 89 percent of those questioned thought that athletics had helped them to develop and maintain physical fitness; 88 percent indicated that it helped "develop calmness and poise under pressure;" 84 percent said that it helped to "develop courage and self confidence;" 77 percent implied that it helped them "develop leadership;" and 65 percent considered that better habits of eating, sleeping, and exercising had carried over into their present living. (7)

Some adults seem to believe there is a lessening of intensity of interest in athletics, perhaps because a substantial number of young people have rejected winning as the major reason for athletic participation. Definite attitudes toward athletics emerged from a survey of 1,000 delegates who attended a national conference of the Fellowship of Christian Athletes. (8) Numerous sports and virtually every section of the country were represented. One of the leading questions asked of the student athletes was, "Why do you compete?" A substantial majority replied that they participated primarily because they enjoyed athletics.

Asked, "Is winning overemphasized or deemphasized in our society?" the responses were revealing. Nearly half, 48 percent, replied that winning is overemphasized. Only 21 percent believed that winning is deemphasized. A tiny 4 percent felt that the present emphasis on winning is about right. Small percentages took "don't know," "neither," or "winning is everything" positions. (9)

The same students, asked the important question, "What emphasis do *you* place on winning?" responded by a large majority that winning is important. However, they were quick to add, "as long as you don't cheat," "sportsmanship comes first," and "it's important to be a good loser." (10)

The last comment leads one to give thought to the question, "How can losing be of value to a young athlete?" As adults, we realize from everyday experience that we lose and win a little each day. We must be able to take setbacks and live with them. When young people lose in an athletic contest, they lose only on the scoreboard. They perceive assets in losing as well as in winning. Perhaps this message is as important as any that athletic or any other form of competition has to impart. If youth today are not solely interested in winning for its own sake, it may be because they are more interested in improving and developing themselves as individuals. The message in terms of education is clear. Whatever their divergent philosophies, youth today are seeking to establish values in society. Educators cannot ignore the effort.

Primarily, as Justice Byron R. White maintained (11), athletic games exist because they are fun for the participants. The experience is enjoyable for those who compete. Playing, practicing, planning strategy, supporting and following the team are defensible ways of channeling energy into an approved program and away from other, perhaps less desirable, activities.

In addition, for selected participants, athletics offers direct entry into higher education and careers that, for many, would be denied. For others, athletic participation in school is central to the educative experience, a major reason for remaining in school.

Issues and Criticisms in Athletics

That the previous section presented arguments pointing toward the values of interscholastic athletics should not be taken to imply that the area lacks its detractors and critics. Quite the contrary, interschool competition has been criticized on a number of grounds, including long-standing and persistent observations as well as more recent issues. Commonly expressed negative sentiments include the following.

Athletic Competition Is Overemphasized. Almost taken as a cliche when mentioned during any discussion of athletics, overemphasis should, nonetheless, be taken seriously. Although stated as a singular word, as though it were a single thing, overemphasis may be manifested in many ways. It may mean a single-minded devotion to winning with a consequent plunge in morale, community and school spirit, and a sense of individual failure when the inevitable loss or losses occur. Incidentally, no rational competitive schedule can permit a particular athletic team to win all of its contests year after year to amass some astronomical school total, usually widely publicized and applauded. It is equally true that no proper schedule permits consecutive losses over a period of years, assuming at least average coaching capability and facilities in both instances. Under either of these circumstances consideration should be given to realignment of league, conference, or other schedules.

Overemphasis may mean the offensive sight of a boorish coach yelling obscenities at referees or at his own players during a tense contest. Adult leaders who lack the self-control and self-discipline to set examples for the young men and women they are supposed to teach do not belong in the profession.

Overemphasis is indicated when young people are called upon for physical tasks beyond their capabilities, e.g., before they are physically, emotionally, or psychologically ready for the strain and/or contact of interschool competition.

Overemphasis is indicated whenever grades or other records are altered for the benefit of athletes or when eligibility rules such as residency are bypassed.

And, finally, to taxpayers, overemphasis frequently is related to the cost of maintaining athletic facilities and supporting competitive events among schools.

Athletic Activities Cost Too Much. One of the most persistently voiced criticisms of athletic programs is that they cost too much. "Too much" is not readily defined but, in times of general taxpayer resentment, it would be hard to argue that any aspect of the school's program should be above financial scrutiny. The fact is that school systems throughout the country, including widely reported examples such as San Francisco, Seattle, Rockford, Illinois, and Philadelphia, have curtailed or eliminated athletic competition during recent years. Usually, however, athletics is not singled out for such treatment. Other extraclass activities and in some instances, elements of formal academic programs have also been reduced.

One way to illustrate the cost of athletics or any other school program is to express the cost of the program as a percentage of the cost of total school operation. If so expressed, programs that seem expensive when given in total dollars are perceived as considerably less costly. Thus, the large figure of $1,300,000, given as the amount budgeted for athletics by a large metropolitan school system for one fiscal year, might appear to be a vulnerable budget item for cost-conscious critics. However, this figure is less than 1 percent of the total cost of school operations (12), a percentage that is consistent with athletic expenditures in other large cities. The expenditure, considered in terms of the numbers of students served, the values accruing to participants, and the contribution to student body and community identity may be defended as far from excessive. It might be noted that, in this example, total income from ticket sales, donations, and other sources totals about $75,000 per year, only about 6 percent of the amount needed to carry on the many programs. Again, this is the sort of evidence necessary to enlighten those who may argue that athletics should be able to survive on gate receipts.

Particular sports, and football is seemingly vulnerable, may be identified as being especially costly. The basic cost of completely equipping one varsity football player, in safety, is estimated at from $230-

$250. Multiply this by the number of players, the salaries of coaches, cost of supplies, travel, insurance, and other factors known to the general public, and one does not need to add the cost of football fields and grandstands to perceive football as an expensive operation. And, expressed in total dollars, it is. However, when illustrated in terms of the cost per participant, the cost of football is seen to rank on a par with soccer, tennis, and baseball. It is more expensive than track or wrestling. Per participant, football is considerably less costly than basketball, gymnastics, and golf. Table 10-1 illustrates the actual budget for interscholastic sports for boys and girls in a metropolitan school system for 1976-1977. (13) As the data in Table 10-1 illustrate, salaries account for more than half of the total budget, a typical expectation for any school activity. Also, it might be noted, girls' basketball in this particular instance is the most expensive sport per participant. This cost may be

Table 10-1

PER PUPIL COST BY SPORT: MILWAUKEE PUBLIC
SCHOOLS, 1976-1977

Boys' Sports	Total Budget	Estimated 1976-77 Participants	Est. Expend. Per Participant	Number of Coaches	Coaches' Salaries
Football	$237,105	1,770	$133.96	66	$ 92,581
Soccer	33,626	265	126.89	11	14,975
Basketball	158,242	770	205.51	44	56,494
Gymnastics	18,720	120	156.00	5	9,271
Swimming	46,932	470	99.86	16	23,679
Wrestling	73,840	680	108.59	24	30,815
Baseball	79,982	635	125.96	28	36,519
Golf	29,144	165	176.63	15	19,259
Tennis	36,462	280	130.22	15	21,111
Track	117,472	1,285	91.42	43	61,617
Cross Country	33,565	355	94.55	17	21,827
Girls' Sports					
Swimming	36,979	315	117.39	13	17,259
Tennis	30,821	180	171.23	15	19,259
Volleyball	58,365	370	157.74	30	38,519
Basketball	89,889	420	214.02	30	38,519
Gymnastics	27,169	220	123.50	8	10,840
Track	81,594	880	92.72	27	38,938
Cross Country	29,348	255	115.09	15	19,259
Softball	38,433	270	142.34	15	19,259
Total	$1,257,688	9,705	$129.59 av.	437	$590,000

expected to diminish as the number of girls participating in basketball increases.

The recommendation to express athletic costs in terms of the total costs of school operation and in terms of the cost per participant per sport is not intended as a recommendation to mislead the public. Rather, these are the sorts of data that every school system should be able to assemble by way of indicating the true cost of athletic programs.

That cost is a major factor in current curtailment of some athletic programs is highlighted in a study undertaken for the National Sporting Goods Association. (14) During any period of financial strain the taxpayer may be expected to seek relief. Hence, complete and open explanation of costs combined with efforts to substantiate the value of school sports will, in the long run, be the best course for the schools.

The Objectives and Values Claimed for Interschool Athletics Could Be Realized by Way of Club or Intraschool Competition. To a degree, this is true, e.g., some of the values of interschool athletics could be attained through in-school arrangements. Other values would be lost. For example, whatever all school support and identity is engendered by athletics would disappear. Publicity for the school would decline. Top athletes would be denied the media exposure which many need for further educational opportunity. And, the crux of the matter is that the best athletes, denied the chance to compete against peers or to play with peers on the same team, would compete as members of amateur athletic organizations apart from the school. In the end, it seems likely that we would turn full circle and, once again, nearby natural rivals would schedule their own contests, uncontrolled by the school and unfettered by rules and regulations.

As was pointed out in the opening section of this chapter, interscholastic athletics occupies a unique place in American schools and society. As long as this condition prevails, it would be very difficult for particular schools and particular individuals to withdraw from the established tradition.

Athletic Injuries Are Both Numerous and Unnecessary. All injuries are unfortunate and athletic injuries are no exception. However, the desire to compete at games seems to be basic to the human spirit. Whether it is a ten-year-old who gets hurt on the playground, a seventy-year-old man who wrenches his back on the golf course, a seventeen-year-old boy who injures his knee at football, or a forty-year-old woman who breaks her leg skiing, the principle is the same. People of all ages and both sexes enjoy competition, either against each other or against a standard set for themselves.

During these competitions accidental injuries occur. Injuries also occur when driving automobiles, working, walking down stairs, traversing icy sidewalks, climbing out of bathtubs, and paddling canoes. Injuries in school may occur on the basketball court, in the chemistry laboratory, in the homemaking class, in the industrial arts shop, or in any other location where pupils are active and using equipment, whether or not they are engaged in competition. The fact that injuries happen is not a sound reason for abandoning any human enterprise, including athletic competition.

The writers suggest that the key word in this discussion is *accidental*. The criticism may become a serious issue if any injury should have been preventable. For this reason only superior equipment should be used, strict physical examinations required, proper conditioning demanded, defensive skills taught, equitable competition scheduled, the rules enforced, and all competitions held with approved officials in charge and medical personnel in attendance. Injuries that happen outside these conditions are preventable. (15)

Interscholastic Athletics Benefit a Few and Neglect the Vast Majority. All forms of interschool competition, debate, for example, science fairs, for another, are subject to the same criticism. Stkenykudged as the most capable in each school become the representatives of the school. As representatives they must, by necessity, be a small minority. Hopefully, no school is so bereft of opportunity that the issue has to become an either-or choice. That only a few can represent the school as debaters ought not to deny others from engaging in debate. Opportunities exist in clubs, student councils, and in all extra class decision-making groups where discussion and argument have a place. Debate techniques are taught in some classes and implemented in others. The opportunity for each student to compete at his level of skill usually is available. Similarly, that only a dozen or so players can be members of the varsity squad should not deny others the chance to play basketball. The sport is taught and played in physical education classes. Junior varsity teams are available as are class teams, and teams lossely or formally organized on a club basis. Here, also, the aim should be to allow those who want to participate to do so at their appropriate skill levels.

Schools Have Not Provided Equal Opportunity for Male and Female Participation. Historically, athletic programs in secondary education evolved for males. Boys initiated the first contests, scheduled them, and participated in them. Until the 1950s, interscholastic athletics remained largely a male domain. This situation was supported by tradition as well as by a large majority of women physical educators who, throughout the

1930s and 1940s, convinced colleagues and the public that the so-called evils of competition should be avoided for girls and women. This Victorian philosophy permeated girls' participation in athletics as well as in many other endeavors until well into the 1960s.

As a working philosophy, of course, the viewpoint that girls are less daring or competitive than boys is pure myth. It is based on social custom and history rather than on biological or psychological fact. Human beings, by nature, are competitive. That men and women compete at different levels in contact sports or in contests based upon strength is beside the point. On the average, men are larger and heavier than women. This does not mean, therefore, that women should be excluded from competition. Girls as well as boys should have the opportunity to relate to each other in terms of their ability, an achieved status. By contrast, most girls relate to each other in terms of their ascribed status, a social position. For high school girls, "the opportunity in athletics to relate to each other in terms of achieved status is a new experience." (16) Athletics can allow girls to achieve beyond their initial expectations and ultimately set higher goals for themselves.

According to Resick and Erickson, the real beginning of expansion for girls' sports occurred in 1958. It was in that year that the Girls' and Women's Sport Section of the American Association for Health, Physical Education, and Recreation gained division status. (17) Throughout the 1960s the women's liberation movement, as part of the larger struggle for civil rights, culminated in the Education Amendments to the Civil Rights Act in 1972 (Title IX). Put simply, Title IX is an absolute prohibition of discrimination on the basis of sex by any educational institution receiving federal benefits. Although the media focused on athletics because of the public visibility of athletics, the law covers many other areas of school work including counseling, academic courses, health and insurance benefits, admissions, financial aids, marital or parental status, and extraclass activities other than athletics. This sweeping legislation includes all educational levels, elementary school through graduate school.

Applied to athletics Title IX permits teams composed of one sex where bodily contact or competitive skills are factors. However, the institution must make affirmative effort to provide equal opportunities for the other sex to participate. The use of equipment and supplies must be equally available to teams of both sexes. The same general eligibility rules must apply. The law does not demand equal aggregate expenditures nor equal per capita expenditures for male and female teams. The focus is clearly upon equality of opportunity. The intention is to assure that no member of either sex is excluded from the chance to participate in athletic competition.

Despite whatever difficulties the law may have caused by way of increased expenditures, scheduling, use of facilities, and so on, it must be concluded that the goal of expanding and improving girls' athletic programs is both desirable and attainable. This should not come about solely because of federal law but because it is the right thing to do.

Extent of Participation

More than four million boys and nearly two million girls are currently involved in interscholastic athletics. During the period 1971-1976 girls' participation increased 459 percent, reflecting the impact of Title IX. Boys' participation increased 12 percent. More than thirty separate sports are recognized by the National Federation of State High School Associations. In terms of the number of participants the top six sports for boys are: Football, with slightly more than a million; Basketball, approaching three-quarters of a million; Outdoor Track and Field, nearly 650,000; Baseball, approximately 400,000; Wrestling, more than 300,000; and Cross Country, approaching 205,000. In addition, from 125,000-150,000 boys participate in interscholastic golf, tennis, and swimming. (18)

In terms of the number of participants, the top interscholastic sports for girls are, in order: outdoor track and field, basketball, volleyball, softball, tennis, swimming, gymnastics, and field hockey. Specific figures for girls' participation would be misleading because of the spectacular increases recorded since 1971. However, it might be noted that more than 395,000 girls participated in outdoor track and field and more than 387,000 in basketball in 1976, figures that may be expected to accelerate until 1980 or thereafter.

Because of the smaller number of players needed on a squad, basketball claims the largest number of schools sponsoring this sport for both boys and girls, followed by outdoor track and field for both sexes. Then, for boys, follow football, baseball, cross country, golf, and wrestling. And, for girls, volleyball, tennis, softball, and gymnastics.

The purpose here is not to get mired in specific figures, but rather to show that interschool sports activity is broadly based and strongly supported for both sexes. Clearly, interscholastic athletics is here to stay.

Quality of Leadership

If interscholastic athletics is to develop the lasting values that have been claimed, it cannot be handled in a perfunctory or haphazard manner. Values derived from athletic participation are not automatic as a result of interacting with a ball or implement used in a game. Rather, the athletic coach is the architect of interaction between and among the participants and the game, and in many instances between and among the participants themselves. If the results of this interaction are increased maturity, learning, and understanding, along with beneficial transfer to daily living, they come about because of conscious effort and hard work on the part of both coaches and participants. The coach is central to educational outcomes as, indeed, all teachers are in their respective courses of study. It is the coach who is directly involved with the lives of youth and, in many instances, their future educational and career choices. The coach is responsible for controlling and channeling the anxieties, aggressions, and fears of young human beings. He or she is involved in the success and failure of activities that young people take very seriously. Responsibility for recognizing and developing physical attributes is accompanied by responsibility for recognizing and dealing with a wide spectrum of attitudinal, motivational, and psychological traits. These are obligations that cannot be taken lightly and cannot be taken for granted. Optimal benefits from participation in athletics can only result from quality leadership. (19)

Quality leadership is predicated upon the concept of prepared leadership. Consequently, such organizations as the National Federation of High School Associations, the National Council of State High School Coaches, and the Division of Men's Athletics of the American Alliance for Health, Physical Education, and Recreation, have endorsed recommendations for the certification of coaches. These recommendations emphasize educational values and safety as well as competition and excellence. To date, more than twenty states have established certification standards for coaches. These standards, in general, require college work in the principles, academic foundations, and medical aspects of coaching. They are a step in the right direction toward uniform, quality leadership in the coaching ranks. (20) (21)

The Future of Interscholastic Athletics

Interscholastic athletics is firmly rooted in American secondary education, and athletics in general is a prominent feature of American society.

More young people are competing in sports than at any previous time. Secondary schools have increased the number of sports and the number of teams within each sport. Additionally, youth are saying that they enjoy competitive athletics. Adults who participated in their youth support the endeavor. Most people agree that the *potential* for developing positive values through competitive athletics does exist.

However, for an assured future, athletics in the secondary school cannot become solely an amusement for the public nor a diversion for participants. Rather, the interscholastic athletic program needs to be perceived as an integral part of the total school program, a part through which young men and women can satisfy fundamental human needs for success and excellence. It is this perception of athletics that ultimately justifies optimism about its future.

CHAPTER REFERENCES

1. For a more detailed discussion of the impact of the Progressive Movement, see Elmer Harrison Wilds and Kenneth V. Lottich, *The Foundations of Modern Education* (Chicago: Holt, Rinehart and Winston, 1970).

2. National Education Association, The Cardinal Principles, 1918. See Chapter 3, this volume.

3. Chalmer G. Hixson, *The Administration of Interscholastic Athletics* (New York: J. Lowell Pratt and Company, 1967), p. 6.

4. National Federation of State High School Associations, *Official Handbook: 1974-75* (Elgin, Illinois, 1974), pp. 6-49.

5. National Association of Secondary School Principals, *The Mood of American Youth* (Reston, Virginia, 1974), p. 24.

6. For example, see Justice Byron R. White, "Athletics: ' . . . Unquenchable the Same' ?" *School Activities* 37 (November 1965): 11-14.

7. Leona Holbrook, "Human Values in Sports Education and Their Relationship to Social Ends," *Development of Human Values through Sports* (Washington, D.C.: American Alliance for Health, Physical Education and Recreation, 1974), p. 25.

8. Skip Stogsdill, "Anatomy of a High School Athlete," *The Christian Athlete* 16, no. 11 (November 1972): 17.

9. Ibid., p. 19.

10. Ibid.

11. Justice Byron R. White, "Athletics . . . " See "Why Have Athletics?"

12. Budget figures provided by courtesy of the Milwaukee Public Schools, Milwaukee, Wisconsin. Cited with permission.

13. Data for Table 10-1 and all other figures used in this discussion were provided by courtesy of the Milwaukee Public Schools. Reprinted by permission

of Mr. Jack Takerian, Co-Commissioner in Charge of the Interscholastic Athletic Program, Milwaukee Public Schools.

14. Lawrence L. Steinmetz and David H. Bowen, *Sports in Schools: Jeopardy and Uncertainty* (Chicago: National Sporting Goods Association, 1971).

15. For a comprehensive discussion of athletic injuries with emphasis on prevention, see Carl E. Klafs and Daniel D. Arnheim, *Modern Principles of Athletic Training* (St. Louis: The C. V. Mosby Co., 1969). See, especially, Chapter 5, "Physical Conditioning for the Prevention of Athletic Injuries," and Chapter 9, "Recognition, Evaluation, and General Care of Athletic Injuries."

16. Elizabeth East, "Experiences and Observations of a Student Athlete," *Development of Human Values through Sports* (Washington, D.C.: American Alliance for Health, Physical Education, and Recreation, 1974), p. 67.

17. Matthew C. Resick and Carl E. Erickson, *Intercollegiate and Interscholastic Athletics for Men and Women* (Reading, Mass.: Addison-Wesley, 1975), p. 17.

18. National Federation of State High School Associations, *1976 Sports Participation Survey* (Elgin, Illinois: The National Federation, 1976). All figures and other facts about sports participation included in this section are based on data in the 1976 and other surveys.

19. "Professional Preparation of Future Coaches in a Modern Society," a paper presented to the American Association of Health and Physical Education National Conference, Detroit, Michigan, April 1971, by John L. Dayries, University of Montana, Missoula, Montana.

20.-21. For more detailed information about standards for the certification of coaches, see: National Federation of State High School Associations, *National Federation Notebook: Physical Education and Coaching Certification* (Elgin, Illinois: The National Federation, February 1975); and Matthew G. Maetozo, ed., *Certification of High School Coaches* (Washington, D.C.: American Association for Health, Physical Education, and Recreation, 1971).

11   Guidance and
Psychological
Services

Organized guidance and psychological services in the secondary school stand in a unique position as "gatekeeper" for curriculum improvement. The function of *gatekeeping* in human dynamics is to regulate the flow of communication and ensure that all parties contribute to the dialogue. As such the gatekeeping function is one of balancing a number of forces and variables and anticipating the impact of each upon the individuals and groups within the school.

No other department in the secondary school deals with such a broad slice of the student body at one time, or faces the variety and severity of student problems which run a gamut of interpersonal relations to academic problems, and is confronted with such a large data base for determining and regulating the effectiveness of the school program. The hub of the modern secondary school is the guidance office with its staff of qualified counselors and specialists. Psychologists, social workers, psychiatrists, nurses and physicians as well as special education and learning disabilitiy teachers occupy an important place under the guidance umbrella.

Secondary school curricular and organizational departmentalization have introduced increasing subject skill specialization at the cost of often losing sight of and responsibility for the development of the whole student. The disappearance or diminution of the homeroom as a viable concept in many secondary schools (1) has made it mandatory that some segment of school personnel concentrate upon the student's overall adjustment, his or her attitudes about self and life, vocational and college preparation, and often blatantly hostile attitudes towards other students of different backgrounds or races. Increasing student-teacher friction over grades, homework, tests and classroom methodology often propel the guidance staff into the middle of a stormy exchange in which they must be student advocates walking a narrow line between representing legitimate student grievances, but still responsible to colleague norms which act to shield the faculty and administration from adverse outside opinion. Some guidance personnel find this "buffer" role fraught with role conflict, uncertainty and guilt. They are torn between school standards that may seem unreasonable and the responsibility to bring about student acceptance of such standards in order to maintain order and discipline. They must act to reduce pressure from the administration or faculty for harsher responses to deviant pupil behavior. This "never-never" land makes it difficult to propose specific objectives for secondary school guidance departments. Many researchers find the lack of objectives a major problem in improving guidance services. (2)

The guidance department has both overt and covert goals within the secondary school. Some are known and accepted and others are masked. Overt and legitimized goals of guidance serving as a clearing house for testing and test data, coordinating medical and welfare services to needy students and their families. Still overt in nature may be the resolution of conflict between individual teachers and students, or between parents, students, and teachers. The covert functions of guidance represent those areas of decision-making in which value judgments may be made about the future or actual potential of students as it relates to "realistic" advice about studies or jobs. It is the guidance department which performs the socially sensitive function of sorting pupils. Sometimes this is objectively accomplished with the utilization of test data, and other times more subjectively with subtle kinds of pressures in group or individual counseling sessions. This function is usually kept well hidden and insulated and has been the sore spot in classifying schools as racially or sexist oriented. (3)(4)(5)(6)

Another covert function of guidance in the secondary school is that of coopting or absorbing student protest or unrest about aspects of the school's curriculum or rules. It is often the guidance department which first uncovers curricular "deadwood" or the incompetent teacher and which can reduce the pressure from parents and pupils by providing a legitimized place to let off steam or by changing teachers or courses to reduce pressures on the administration for needed curricular or personnel changes. Guidance data can be the subject of administrative or system manipulation. If the administration desires to make certain curricular or personnel changes, evidence can be compiled from student requests for class changes or other information given to the guidance staff in individual or group counseling sessions. Still additional data can be made available from colleges receiving the school's graduates and their evaluations of the degree of student preparation and competencies. Test scores released to the public or to central office can also be powerful levers for subsequent demands for action or change in the school's curriculum. For these reasons there are strong pressures on secondary school guidance departments from parents, pupils, faculty and administration. The pivotal place of guidance in the school and the data and information which filters through and is shaped by the guidance department can develop strong advocates and enemies. Some guidance departments respond by developing guidelines of strict neutrality desiring to offend no one and feeling that to become the captive of any particular camp will impair the overall functioning of guidance services. Still others feel that the ideal role of the guidance department is a mediating or intervening one and that properly accomplished, program and curricular improvement can be developed only if guidance plays an active role in the secondary school.

As a component of the school social system the guidance department functions with certain organizational boundaries and constraints. As long as the guidance component stays within these boundaries it is in a state of equilibrium within the larger system. However, if it creates too much tension and threatens the existence (and thus the equilibrium) of the larger system, the school will take steps to curtail, close down or expel it from its boundaries. These organizational norms mean that the guidance department must be careful in performing its gatekeeping functions within the secondary school.

Guidance data can be divided into two types for feedback in decision-making at three levels within the secondary school. These two types of data are produced with qualitative or quantitative procedures. Qualitative data are most often secured from unstructured situations such as case studies or anecdotal descriptions of student groups or individuals, classroom situations or the general school milieau. (7) Quantitative data refer to precoded or prestructured procedures or instruments which produce data which can be subjected to either parametric or nonparametric statistical inference. Such data most often are represented in frequency charts and graphs showing percentages with categories of response. (8)

Diagram 11-1 indicates a breakdown of the decision-making levels within the school in which the two types of data secured within the guidance denartment can be utilized to intervene in the operation of the secondary school or school subsystem. All of the data can be related to various types of secondary school program goals. Much can be related to specific curricular offerings. A brief review of the types of data generated or collected by the secondary school guidance staff with its curricular implications may be helpful in determining the power of that department to influence the development of secondary curriculum.

Data Produced for Individual Assessment

Qualitative assessment of students in the secondary school include case conferences and case studies of specific pupils, data produced from nonstructured interviews, conferences, medical examinations, or home visitations. Consider this description developed by a secondary school social worker after a home visitation.

The Granger Home Visitation

We had difficulty finding the Granger's house. The house itself was shielded from the view of the road and we passed it several times in the car. Finally we spotted a mailbox in an overgrown shrub and turned into a dirt road. Behind the larger bushes was the house. It was supported on large concrete blocks and bricks and was a bungalow type. There were what looked like bathroom carpets in varying oval shapes along the path leading to the front steps and door. The screen door had large holes in it and on the top step was a large brown dog napping. On the front of the house we could see tar paper through places where slabs of side board had been removed or ripped off.

A small lady opened the door and welcomed us. The dog began barking but did not growl. It went inside as we got closer to the house. We went up the stairs exchanging greetings and entered what was the living room-kitchen. There were several round shaped rugs which did not cover the dust on the old wooden floors. Light appeared through several of the slits in the floor. I noticed the hairs all over the furniture

---

Diagram 11-1

TYPES OF FEEDBACK PROVIDED BY THE GUIDANCE
DEPARTMENT IN A SECONDARY SCHOOL

Context for Decision-Making	Qualitative Procedures	Quantitative Procedures
Individual (one to one)	-case conferences -case studies -nonstructured inter- view -anecdotal observation -medical observation -home observation	-individual scores from norm-referenced tests -individual scores from projective or interest inventories/tests -semi or structured interviews -analysis of grades or GPA -longitudinal sampling or comparisons -critical incident survey
Group(s) classes, classroom, grade level, ad-hoc vertical groups	-analyzed dialogue -anecdotal descriptions -group case studies	-time series analysis -norm-referenced data -group surveys -class climate survey
School	-follow-up studies of graduates -case study of school -educational audit -participant observer format (analysis)	-accreditation study -college placement records -school climate surveys -grade trend analysis -parent surveys -curricular scope analysis -National Merit Finalists

but managed to sit down on a rather well worn sofa chair. The arm rests were ragged and the stuffing was gone in several places. The only couch was drapped with a faded blue blanket.

Mrs. Granger introduced herself and her daughter Helen who she said was not at high school because she hadn't felt well that morning. Right behind my chair was a small kitchen table, a stove and a rusty refrigerator which elicited various kinds of sounds and squeaks during the time we were there. Beyond the refrigerator and to the right was an open door to a bathroom. One single light bulb hung by the wires only from the top of the ceiling. To my left was an open door which was Stephen's room according to his mother. Mrs. Granger, who revealed that she was not Stephen's real mother, said that Stephen had to sleep in the same room with Helen because he was afraid to stay on the couch at night by himself. Her husband had not come home on Monday from work (It was Wednesday morning). She said that she didn't worry too much unless several days went by and he was not reporting to work. He often stayed out with friends and "bunked" with them at their houses. Since he was on road construction this pattern was evidently part of the job in traveling far distances to and from work. She did not appear worried.

Stephen had gotten into trouble at school because he refused to stay for after school detention. He had "cut" several classes and was assigned the detention as punishment and to make up the missed work. Mrs. Granger said she had told Stephen not to stay for detention because he would miss his bus home and the distance was hard for a boy with frequent asthma attacks. She said that she knew Stephen had disobeyed his teacher for not reporting but felt that the school should be able to take care of their problems with her son without resorting to after school detention. She said she worried a great deal if the weather was bad and Stephen had to walk home. She estimated the walk to be between 45 minutes and one hour.

We asked if Stephen talked to her about his school work or problems. She said he didn't talk too much about school, but she knew he had few friends and was very shy. To the side of the room a large black and white TV set was going with the volume turned down. Occasionally Mrs. Granger or Helen would glance at the program (a quiz show) and smile and return their attention to the conversation. Mrs. Granger said that Stephen really had no place to study at home. Since his sister was not feeling well she often went to bed early and he couldn't study in his bedroom. Since she and her husband watched TV a lot, (they couldn't afford to go out much she indicated) Stephen sometimes started his homework, only to be caught up in the show they were watching. She said he even tried doing his homework in the bathroom but had given up when it got too cold.

We indicated our concern for Stephen's frequent absences, his refusal to stay after school, participate in class, or turn in completed assignments which had led his teachers to request a home visitation. Mrs. Granger offered us some coffee but we indicated that we had just had one at school. We asked her if she could come to school for a conference with some of Stephen's teachers. She said she would try but that she was not sure of transportation and it would have to be on a day when both Helen and Stephen were at school. She said they had only one car and her husband usually took it with him. She also said she was afraid to leave their house as it had no locks on the doors and it was a fairly "rough" neighborhood. We thanked her for her courtesy and the opportunity to come to their home. We indicated that we would call and perhaps send a car out to her house for her. She said that would be "nice." As we left the brown dog restationed himself on the front step.

The narrative filed by the social workers together with medical data on Stephen's allergies and past health problems prompted the guidance staff to develop some specific learning prescriptions for him. First, the social worker and assigned counselor met with Stephen's teachers in a group case conference. They reviewed his medical and school records. They indicated the conditions of the home and the attitudes of the mother. They cautioned the teachers not to keep him after school and to try to provide time within the school day to allow him to complete his homework. Stephen was scheduled into a study hall and each teacher agreed to watch his work and ask him to meet with them during this time if possible. The teachers were genuinely shocked at the revelations of Stephen's home conditions, his lack of proper rest, and study opportunities. The social worker commented that Stephen's father was a drifter, possessed a history of problems with drinking and according to his employer, Ace Construction Company, had been fired once and was a marginal employee. The social worker was trying to secure family counseling at a Family Counseling Clinic in the community. Stephen's I.Q. was 110 on a group based test, and even though he was in the tenth grade his reading level was only 5.8, and math level 6.2. He had never shown any great motivation for school work. He was shy and unassuming. His counselor indicated that he was an isolate and totally withdrawn from his peers. His social emotional growth in any meaningful heterosexual development was negligible. He preferred to play with sixth or seventh graders. He appeared somewhat fragile and anemic looking. Sometimes he refused to sit near certain girls and he had failed physical education for not dressing for gym class. When he did dress he refused to take a shower with the rest of the boys. Sometimes he had been involved with incidents with older boys, but most often as the subject of ridicule or bullying.

The guidance staff expressed outrage at the inability of the school to effectively deal with Stephen Granger. The only road open to them was tracking. They felt while his past academic performance did not merit placement in highly motivated, college-bound classes, neither did it warrant placement in the bottom tracks where Stephen was sure to find failure from bullying of older students with a history of school related problems. There was no middle curricular or instructional ground for Stephen. He was either "college prep" or "vocational." For Stephen Granger both worlds presented real rejection and failure. The only alternative appeared to lie in the guidance staff scheduling Stephen in the future with teachers who had known histories of being sympathetic and flexible in their classroom approaches.

The school psychologist examined Stephen's norm-referenced test data file and teacher anecdotal comments. She decided that Stephen had made the best academic progress in a highly structured situation with an open and warm teacher. Class assignments which demanded an inquiry approach and a lot of inferential structuring by students seemed to frustrate him. He was unaware of himself and needed constant reinforcement. She therefore drafted for each teacher a description of the type of classroom environment in which Stephen would be assured of maximum academic success for him and gave it to each of his teachers at a subsequent conference.

The guidance staff also decided to make a presentation to the school's faculty curriculum committee. They would ask for an investigation of some "middle ground" curricular alternatives. While they knew the word "alternatives" was a dirty word with some of the older faculty members they felt they had no choice but to broach the topic and stress the need. The support of the principal in this matter would be crucial.

The case of Stephen Granger utilized both qualitative and quantitative data. The guidance staff was perplexed and troubled by the lack of appropriate curricular offerings for Stephen. While they could have counseled Stephen out of the school by presenting to him and his mother the picture of an inflexible but sympathetic school, they chose to challenge the lack of curricular offerings as the school's problems rather than the client's. In too many secondary schools the curriculum consists of only two basic tracks with no alternatives; college prep or vocational. Students like Stephen who have some ability but deplorable home conditions and no parental support for school work, are placed by default into learning conditions which produce failure. Individual case studies or descriptions can provide in-depth background information for school related performance and a powerful lever for introducing school wide changes. The problem sometimes is that the school blames the client and assumes little or no responsibility for creating the maximum climate for student learning success.

Data Produced for Group Assessment

Probably the most common type of data produced in the secondary school is group based, that is, some group comprises the frame of reference. I.Q., achievement and aptitude tests are the most commonly administered by class, i.e., grade level. One popular method of assigning guidance staff is by grade levels. Groups comprise a significant base for guidance functions in the secondary school. Such groups may be individual classes or ad-hoc groups called for the purpose of improving pupil self-image or academic achievement. (9) With the tendency to cut back on guidance staff as a method for trimming budgets, particularly in large urban school systems, the guidance-pupil ratio has been increased significantly from Conant's recommendation of 250: 1. (10) Group counseling appears a partial solution to the overloading of guidance services, and perhaps one of the few ways any kind of preventative work in guidance can be economically done in the future. (11)

One example of how a particular class can become the focus of the guidance activities on a qualitative data base is the following anecdotal description of a junior high school English class. The counselor originally went into the class to observe a particular pupil as a part of a detailed case study for a conference with teachers and colleagues. It soon became apparent that the teacher and the class were experiencing major difficulties.

Anecdotal Description

Teacher: Ms. Judy Gannon
Pupil To Be Observed: Richard Gage
Class: Seventh Grade English
Date: October 11, 19XX

Time	Event
1:30 pm	Ms. Gannon reviewed the English assignment. She wrote on the board, "pp. 121-123-*Better English For Junior High School.*" The class was divided into two group. She began to work with one group. During this time Richard Gage shot paper wads through a straw with another boy (later identified as Frank Pierce.) At one point several paper wads were shot

into the pupil group Ms.Gannon was directing. There appeared to be twenty-one students in the room. At various times several students either shouted or screamed. Sometimes there were no words, just a scream.

1:39 pm   Two students left the room without asking permission. Richard chased another boy around the room shooting paper wads at him. Four students left the room.

1:42 pm   Ms. Gannon asked Frank for the straw. He would not give it to her. Instead he argued he would not use it any more. She followed him into the corner but was not able to get the straw from him.

1:45 pm   Of the fifteen students in the room only nine appeared to be working on the assignment. The rest were talking with each other or engaged in some game. Richard Gage sat at his desk paying with the straw. He then got up and went to the door and opened it and closed it. Two boys left the room. After a few seconds Richard disappeared.

1:50 pm   Richard returned with a teacher from another class who appeared to be upset. She motioned to him to sit down. She apparently knew where his desk was as she pointed to it. Richard then went over to the corner where Frank was sitting and the two boys wrestled each other to the floor. The teacher asked them to go outside (Ms. Gannon). They ignored her but after a few glances from her they went outside.

1:57 pm   Two boys (other than Richard and Frank) engaged in a Kung Fu match in the center of the room. One boy said "Take two shots," whereupon the other boy kicked him in the upper leg. They then wrestled each other to the floor. During this time Richard observed and the teacher worked with several individual pupils.

2:00 pm   Several objects (such as gloves or gym socks) were thrown across the room. Richard then went over to Frank's desk and the two boys played "bulldozer" shoving each other around the room into desks and against the walls of the room.

2:04 pm   There were only fifteen students in the room.

2:07 pm   Four students returned to the room.

Two students left the room
One student returned
Another student returned
Two students left

2:11 pm   A loud scream came from somewhere in the room. one male student kicked open the door. Ms. Gannon called "freeze," and looked around the room. The students ignored her and went on with what they were doing. Richard Gage was still blowing spitwads through his straw at several girls.

2:13 pm   Ms. Gannon said aloud, "OK, class, it is spelling time. Take out your lists and let's get to work." There was no immediate or apparent impact upon any student of this command. A chair was knocked over. Another scream from somewhere in the room. One student was drawing on the board. Several students entered the room.

2:14 pm   Ms. Gannon said, "Ok, finish the spelling lists for homework. Now get ready to go. The class got up and left. Richard Gage put the straw inside his notebook and left the room. After moments had passed the bell rang. Ms. Gannon refused to look my way. She straightened her desk and I left.

The development of the anecdotal record presented several problems for the guidance staff. First, the contract with the teachers union prohibited anyone but the school principal from engaging in an evaluation of a teacher. Secondly, the guidance staff had developed a good working relationship with the faculty. If the record were turned over to the school's administration it could be possibly used in a dismissal proceeding in which case it would become public knowledge that a guidance counselor had been involved. After some discussion the guidance staff felt that this would jeopardize their working relationships with the faculty and the teachers union. The data would remain confidential or be destroyed. It would be rewritten with emphasis only upon Richard's behavior and work. However, a realistic view of Richard was impossible in this situation without describing the situation itself. The Director of Guidance scheduled a conference with the school principal and merely informed him that there were conditions in Ms. Gannon's class which appeared to require administrative leadership. No mention was made of the record. The principal asked how this came to be known and the fact that the counselor was observing a pupil was mentioned.

The guidance staff also decided to confer with Ms. Gannon and inform her of their view of not only Richard but the unwholesome learning conditions in the room. When she was informed that they were in no way responsible for formal evaluation she admitted to them that she had a problem with this class and was unable to know what to do. They made suggestions as follows:

1. Meet with the counselor of each pupil and review the cumulative folder and family history of each student who had learning problems in the class;
2. Schedule conferences with the parents of students with certain problems;
3. Develop a class profile of achievement by using norm-referenced test data. What was the class mean I.Q., score on the Stanford Achievement Test in language development, punctuation, reading, etc.? How did this compare to her other classes? From the data available from these quantitative instruments, find the items within the tests that a majority of her pupils had missed before. From this item analysis key these "gaps" into her selection of texts and development of lessons for the class;
4. For key students, work with them during their free time at school on an individually prescriptive basis and check their work closely.

The guidance staff further offered help to the teacher in gathering the data and analyzing it. The use of the I.Q. in this context deserves some attention. The purpose of the calculation of the class I.Q. was not to lower or raise the teacher's expectation for the class, thus creating a self-fulfilling prophecy. (12)(13) Rather it was to prod the teacher to look for data which might be helpful in finding differences that could be keyed into her instructional program. The fact that much of the I.Q. is cultural is fairly well accepted within the profession. Even this knowledge would be helpful in ascertaining pupil differences and finding ways to develop missing skills and knowledges in classroom lessons. If I.Q. data are handled diagnostically (i.e., as a way to develop prescriptive learning activities rather than a label) such information can be useful in differentiating the school curriculum and individualizing the instructional program.

Data Produced for School Assessment

As the movement towards accountability accelerates in the nation, more and more secondary schools are having to produce data about the effectiveness of their programs. Traditional measures like accreditation are not enough since they most often assess the quality of a secondary school to *input criteria,* rather than *output criteria.* Input criteria are indices such as pupil-teacher ratio, books per student, adequacy of facilities, existence of course descriptions, etc. Output criteria relate to measures of pupil learning. The apparent paradox of rising educational costs and lower pupil achievement in the nation's secondary school students on national tests (14) have raised profound skepticism among citizens about paying any more for lowered educational effectiveness.

Traditional kinds of guidance data which can be useful in assessing the characteristics of a secondary school beyond accreditation standards, but which are still largely input criteria are comparisons of curricular offerings with other schools, parent surveys, and to some extent follow-up studies of school graduates. Some follow-up studies can be related to output standards. Common types of data which can be gathered by secondary school guidance departments are illustrated in the following examples.

Curricular Comparisons

Citizens, board members, administrators and students are interested in knowing the degree to which a given secondary curriculum is comprehensive. One measure is to calculate the number of courses offered within the secondary school and compare it to similar sized schools. Diversity of program is a perennial problem for small high schools, particularly in areas with a declining enrollment and rising costs. Diagram 11-2 shows a comparison of four small high schools in terms of course offerings. Such data can be gathered from the guidance or administrative offices of the schools.

Data about course offerings as shown here can be valuable in asking certain questions about the viability of course offerings. Other questions can be raised regarding the strength of the teaching staff, the procedures by which electives are developed and or selected, and the reasons why students may be lacking certain key educational skills when they are offered (or not offered) certain courses. Another aspect which can be questioned is the existence of a complete sequence of courses within certain areas, for example from beginning to advanced courses in science. While the data are almost totally quantitative in nature it can lead to certain qualitative questions. Some of these can be answered in pupil surveys or follow-up studies.

Student Follow-up Studies

Most high school guidance departments attempt to survey their graduates. Follow-up studies can be a relatively simple tabulation of college

Diagram 11-2

COMPARISON OF CURRICULAR OFFERINGS
BETWEEN FOUR HIGH SCHOOLS

(n = 1000 students)

Courses	John Jay	Benjamin Franklin	John Adams	Abraham Lincoln
English	11.5	9.5	14.5	8.0
Social Studies	8.5	8.0	9.5	5.5
Mathematics	12.0	12.5	13.5	12.5
Science	12.5	8.0	13.5	6.0
Foreign Language	16.0	11.0	10.0	15.0
Business Education	10.5	6.0	7.0	12.0
Art	4.5	1.0	9.0	3.0
Industrial Arts	8.0	2.5	10.5	3.0
Home Economics	3.5	—	2.0	2.0
Music	6.0	1.0	7.0	4.5
P.E./D.E. and Health	4.5	5.0	5.0	4.5
Totals	97.50	64.5	101.5	76.0

choice for each class as shown in Diagram 11-3, or a more sophisticated type of follow-up as shown in Diagram 11-4.

This follow-up study of graduates provides some evidence of differences in post secondary school status by race and sex. If only the last column of figures were reported the school could say something to the effect that 69 percent of its graduates matriculated to higher education,

Diagram 11-3

SAMPLE FOLLOW-UP SURVEY OF
HIGH SCHOOL GRADUATES

Status	Boys White/Black		Girls White/Black		Total
Attending four-year colleges/ universities	73%	23%	50%	38%	46%
Attending two-year colleges	16%	31%	18%	28%	23%
Attending other educational institutions (secretarial/ business school, etc.)	3%	14%	11%	20%	12%
Serving in the Armed Forces	2%	18%	1%	4%	6%
Employed	5%	4%	16%	4%	7%
Unemployed	1%	10%	4%	6%	6%
Other (in jail, etc.)	—	—	—	—	

Diagram 11-4

FOLLOW-UP STUDY OF REASONS WHY
GRADUATES VIEW THEIR CURRICULAR
OFFERINGS AS INADEQUATE

Subject	Poor Teaching	Courses Lacked Important Skills	Not Enough Courses	Other (Program conflict, lack of interest, etc.)
Art	4%	12%	43%	41%
English	48%	20%	13%	19%
Vocational/Technical	2%	11%	31%	56%
Science	23%	18%	14%	44%
Mathematics	64%	15%	17%	4%
Home Economics	7%	9%	34%	50%
Social Studies	21%	38%	24%	17%
Foreign Language	18%	19%	16%	47%
Business Education	9%	23%	41%	27%
Physical Education	6%	37%	32%	25%
Music	10%	9%	31%	50%

12% to some other type of training, 6% went into the armed forces, 7% directly into the world of work and 6% were unable to find employment. On the surface these figures may be misleading. When analyzed by race and sex the study shows that 89% of the white males matriculated to higher education as compared to 54% of the black males, 68% white females and 66% of the black females. More blacks than whites were attending other educational institutions, serving in the armed forces, or were unemployed. Data shown in the diagram should raise questions within the faculty and administration about the "hidden" curriculum, i.e., that curriculum which is racist or sexist in nature. What practices, methods, expectations led to these results? How can the school's official curriculum be redesigned to offer greater opportunities to minorities, compensate for the effects of home environments which do not reinforce essential school related skills and which in turn lead to dead end jobs or unemployment?

Diagram 11-4 shows a break down by curricular area and indicates the response by high school graduates of why they felt their education to be inadequate. The required areas of the curriculum such as English and mathematics received the most critical review of poor teaching by the students, followed by science and social studies. Social studies was indicated as the greatest curricular area lacking important skills by the graduates. The response indicated that the curriculum was too shallow in art, business education, home economics, vocational technical, physical education and music. What could a school do with these kind of data to improve its curriculum and teaching? Find below a dialogue between the following characters at Paul Jones High School as an example of translating follow-up data into curriculum.

Principal---Dr. Leland Walker
Director of Guidance---Mr. Seymour Lafinder
Senior Counselor---Mrs. Alice Rosen
Math Department Chairperson---Mr. Henry Tobin

Dr. Walker: I called you together this afternoon to review the data from the follow-up study which the guidance department recently completed and which I asked to be distributed to the staff. I wanted Henry here with us to interact and offer his viewpoint as to what the data says specifically about the math department.

Mr. Tobin: Well, I can tell you that the math department is shocked and angry at this report. We feel that we have a sound, solid program and that our students have traditionally done well in math at college. We simply don't understand this response. We feel that the questions were slanted and that the graduates didn't really understand what they were responding to.

Mr. Lafinder: Come on, Henry, this is the same format we've used for the last two years. The only reason the math department is upset is that Dr. Walker, made the results known to the staff. The results have been just about as bad for the math department the last two years.

Mrs. Rosen: Henry, we're not going to get anywhere trying to defend the results of the math department. I'm not terribly concerned about finding scapegoats but as a counselor I'm very concerned about the increasing volume of complaints I'm receiving from parents about math courses. They are different than the type of complaints we receive except for English perhaps.

Mr. Tobin: How are the complaints different?

Mrs. Rosen: Well, for example, the students say that two teachers in particular are just devastating. First they find them rigid and sarcastic. Old Hal Hanratty regularly reduces the girls to tears. He makes them feel like dummies, even the gifted college-bound seniors. They despise him.

Mr. Tobin: Yes, Old Hal isn't going to change much these days.

Mrs. Rosen: And Marie Gordon, she just plods, plods, plods. I don't think she would get excited if the building burned down. She is so dull that kids go crazy in there. They won't take it like they used to. And the courses, Henry, there isn't a practical course in math in your department. It's still Algebra I and II, and Geometry I and II and trigonometry for the math majors. You've got Hal and Marie teaching the required courses to most of the kids and then they drop off like flies. Compared to English, Henry, most of our complaints are in the more advanced courses and in composition requirements. But English has branched out and the department has found ways to reach students that math hasn't.

Mr. Lafinder: Henry, we've discussed this over time. I think we've got to seriously look at who's teaching what and try to create a little more life in the math department.

Dr. Walker: I would ditto that, Seymour. It seems to me that we should be able to more effectively differentiate the math curriculum for our math students. Our graduates are saying they lack practical skills like computing their income tax, interest rates and mortages. Perhaps if we put you and Brian Godshell at the lower levels where most of the students come into contact with math, our advanced courses would reflect better enrollments.

Mr. Tobin: Look, I've worked a long time to teach the advanced sections. That's my baby. These kids are the ones who need the kind of specialization that I've had in industry. I know what they need and I'm not saying that either Hal or Marie can't do it, but I don't think they will get the same kind of work I give them.

Dr. Walker: Well, stopping short of involuntary transfer, Henry, what is best for the good of the deartment? We can't run away from this data. The kids are calling it as I see it and the guidance staffs sees it. What would you suggest?

Mr. Tobin: There's more to this than just a popularity contest and that's all this is. The math department has been proud of its standards over the years. We feel we make the kids work and today with television and other distractions kids want what is easy. Math is simply not easy stuff. It's sequential and it builds upon prior knowledge. Other subjects don't have to worry about sequence the way we do.

Dr. Walker: None of us want to lower standards, Henry, That's not the point of this discussion at all. I think you've confused several things here. First, these kids have no axes to grind. They're not in school anymore. They're reflecting on their school experience from college and the world of work. If academic rigor were required in their current jobs and studies I'm sure that it would be reflected in retrospect. The real world has a way of sobering one up to what was meaningful about school and what wasn't. We've all had kids come back to us and say they didn't like something at the time but still found in life that it was really important to them and urged us to continue with our convictions. I think we have to redefine what standards really mean. Standards for whom? Even our college math majors, at least those we could identify, were critical of the math department. Now that's the select group you really cater to, Henry, and all is not peaches and cream with them either. It seems to me we have both a curricular problem and a problem with certain personalities in your department. How long has it been since Hal has taught anything else in the department?

Mr. Tobin: Hal's taught Algebra I for eighteen years.

Dr. Walker: And he's still using the same book and lecture notes too.

Mr. Tobin: Now wait a minute Dr. Walker, Hal is using the new State Text . . .

Mrs. Rosen: That may be true, Henry, but I run into Hal a lot at the xerox machine, and he's copying pages from that old Algebra text to pass out to his classes. The book may have changed but Hal hasn't.

Dr. Walker: And, Henry, when was the last time you spent one full period with Marie Gordon? Have you really been in her room? I was there last Friday and one student finally turned to me and said, 'How can you take this?'

Mr. Tobin: Ok, ok, there aren't any Mr. or Mrs. Chips in the math department, but I'm only the department chairman. I can't lean into these people too hard. They were here in this school doing a good job long before I ever arrived on the scene. I feel funny talking to them about this. I feel as though they think I'm too young and they really know what it is all about.

Mr. Lafinder: They were that way with the last department chair person, Henry, and she was older than both of them.

Mr. Tobin: Ok, ok, what should I do? I'm not just going to go down there and start screaming my head off.

Dr. Walker: Nobody is asking you to, Henry, I think we have a problem, as a school, our curriculum in math requires some adjusting and I believe it is time to consider some changes in assignment as well. I know you feel that you have to defend the math department but nobody really is attacking it.

Mr. Tobin: I guess I know that, Dr. Walker, you've been pretty patient over these last two years and I guess I haven't been as hard on my own people as it now appears I should have. But I certainly don't relish going in alone.

Dr. Walker: Henry, this isn't just your problem, it's our problem. I would suggest that we all meet with your department to review the follow-up data. When it becomes clear that we are not on a witch hunt maybe we can relax and do some positive introspection about what this is telling us.

Mr. Tobin: Thank you. I think a meeting with the department would be productive proceeding in the way you've just described. But I would like to talk one on one with Hal and Marie before the meeting. There are some things that I would like to get off my chest just personally with them. After all, I've defended them too and I can't do it anymore. But they should know that prior to our meeting.

Dr. Walker: That's fine, Henry, but please reassure them that we are not meeting to find scapegoats. I sure wouldn't want to feel like we are having an inquisition over this. I'm perfectly willing to look at other data as well. Our math scores have slipped too you know.

Mr. Tobin: I know. I really don't know why. We've worked hard to maintain them.

Dr. Walker: It's a complex question, Henry, I think there are lot's of reasons but let's look at that within the context of the larger curricular picture. That can come out anywhere we feel it's appropriate. I'll call the next meeting.

In retrospect several things are important to emphasize in this transition from data to real departmental action. First, the attitude of the administration was positive. While the guidance department had collated the data, the meeting was called by the administration. The publishing of the data to the entire staff created pressure to act upon the information. While the initial reaction was negative, within the context of the conference positive beginnings were made to examine the overall problem, consider alternatives, and seek additional data. Intervention in the school's curriculum was sparked by a guidance activity. The decision to apply the information was administrative in the last analysis.

Another type of schoolwide data which can be productive is an analysis of grades. Many secondary schools have developed the capacity to grade report cards by computer. This means that the retrieval of important information about grades can be used upon relatively short notice without a lot of laborious compilation involved. Comparisons between quarters or semesters over several years can be developed. Diagram 11-5 indicates the percentages of students receiving failing grades by subject for one quarter. The data from this diagram compiled in the school's guidance office should raise serious questions about

Diagram 11-5

PERCENTAGES OF HIGH SCHOOL STUDENTS
RECEIVING FAILING GRADES 1ST QUARTER

Subject	Percentage
Tenth-grade social studies	57%
Ninth-grade math	27%
Ninth-grade English	23%
Spanish I	13%
Tenth-grade English	9%
Ninth-grade social studies	8%
Tenth-grade math	6%
American History (11th grade)	3%

requirements and methods at the lower grades of this high school. Over half of the tenth grade has failed social studies. Over one-quarter of the ninth graders are failing mathematics. Questions which should be raised about the school's curriculum should also be extended to the lower schools and the adequacy of their programs as well.

Still another use of grades is made when they are compared to the hypothetical "normal distribution."(15) Assuming that a school's population were normal for statistical purposes the percentage of "A's" might be 7%, "B's" 24%, "C's" 38%, "D's" 24% and "F's" 7%. The degree to which the school deviates from this assumed normality can be examined by department and grading period as shown in Diagram 11-6.

Diagram 11-6

GRADE DISTINCTION BY DEPARTMENT
FOR FIRST SEMESTER

Department	A's	B's	C's	D's	F's
Normal distribution	7%	24%	38%	24%	7%
English	6.8%	36.5%	33.3%	15.3%	2.5%
Social Studies	14.1%	39.9%	25.0%	12.2%	3.8%
Mathematics	13.9%	33.1%	28.0%	11.9%	5.6%
Foreign Language	19.6%	36.0%	28.4%	9.3%	3.4%
Business Education	21.3%	37.2%	27.0%	8.6%	1.6%
Vocational Subjects	23.5%	35.2%	23.5%	5.8%	5.8%
Science	16.5%	37.0%	27.7%	12.2%	2.3%
Physical Education	38.5%	48.0%	9.8%	2.5%	1.0%
Applied Arts (Music, art, etc.)	44.1%	30.7%	6.3%	2.7%	.65%
Total	22.02%	37.42%	22.53%	9.46%	2.63%

Scanning the grades received by students it is clear that they are "skewed" towards more "A's" and "B's" than perhaps warranted by assumptions of a normal distribution. Several tentative conclusions may be developed. They range from the observation that the students are well prepared and therefore doing better. Hence the distribution is not "normal." Another may be that the teachers are grading easier and standards have slipped. The latter explanation has occurred at the college level and has been called *grade inflation.* (16) One way to ascertain if the factor of grade inflation is at work is to obtain data five or ten years earlier in terms of the grade breakdown by subject areas. A hypothetical analysis might look something like that shown in Diagram 11-7.

Diagram 11-7

COMPARISON OF GRADES IN
TENTH GRADE ENGLISH

Year	Number	A's	B's	C's	D's	F's
1956	352	4%	14%	36%	30%	16%
1966	435	9%	12%	46%	28%	5%
1976	487	13%	15%	35%	34%	3%
1986	301	24%	38%	24%	12%	2%

A preliminary analysis shows that in 1956 the grade curve was "skewed" towards the "D" and "F" side of the scale but that by 1986 the trend had been reversed. It is possible to hypothesize again many reasons for this change. Such normal curves rarely exist in reality and as the elective subjects are introduced in the curriculum they cease to have much meaning. Most students in the advanced choir or orchestra represent anything but a normal distribution. The fact that most grades will be "A-B" is well accepted in most situations for that reason. However, the imposition of the normal curve against the existing or past grading curves can raise important questions which should be attempted to be answered by the faculty, administration and guidance staffs of the secondary school. Some of these may be:

1. To what extent do deviations from either a normal curve or past grading curves represent a shift in grading standards or changes in the student population or some combination of both?
2. To what extent are deviations, current grading criteria, or standards understood by the faculty?
3. Should grades continue to be given to pupils in their present format?
4. Should alternative procedures for determining and assigning grades be considered?

5. Are grades assigned capable of being translated into specific pupil behavior patterns and/or instructions to the student and his or her parents besides, "He must try harder," or "She is not working up to her potential"? How would a student in advanced art behave differently to be graded an "A" instead of a "B?"
6. Is the grading an effective motivator for pupil learning?
7. Do grades really communicate effectively to parents what a student has learned?

The area of grades and grading is one of the perennial controversial subjects in secondary schools. However, the existence and use of grades as indicators of pupil progress can be an important source of infor-

Diagram 11-8

RESULTS OF A PARENT CURRICULUM SURVEY
OF A MIDDLE SCHOOL

Item	% of Parents Who Expressed Opinion	Rating of Parents			
		Program Inferior	Program Adequate	Program Superior	Don't Know
1. Teaching of basic language skills	94%	48%	20%	18%	14%
2. Teaching of map skills and concepts in geography	91%	27%	49%	14%	10%
3. Teaching of basic math skills in computation	90%	36%	46%	7%	11%
4. Teaching self-responsibility for learning	89%	12%	47%	20%	29%
5. Teaching of library skills	87%	14%	21%	5%	60%
6. Teaching of inter-personal skills	75%	9%	50%	13%	28%
7. Teaching of skills in art and music	73%	20%	43%	29%	8%
8. Teaching of conservation and ecology principles	69%	27%	32%	11%	30%
9. Teaching of physical fitness skills	66%	19%	50%	21%	9%
10. Teaching of skills in family life	52%	8%	84%	3%	5%

mation to a school faculty and administration as they examine the curriculum and related methodology. The compilation and publication of grade trends can be an excellent beginning to reexamine the function of grading in the secondary school as well.

Another type of structured, quantitative feedback which can be gathered by the guidance department in the secondary school is that of parental opinion about the school's curriculum. There can be little question that increasing parental involvement has become a dominant trend in shaping the public schools. Parents want and are demanding a voice in school policies, procedures and curriculum. Diagram 11-8 shows the results of a parent survey of a middle school community.

The results of the parent survey were puzzling to the faculty and administration. The perceptions of parents regarding program adequacy and strength did not match their own. By any objective measure, the school's basic skills program was strong. The school's test scores were consistently in the top quartile in the state. The actual school time allocated to the teaching of the skills was well above all the other curricular areas. The staff wanted to know on what data or information parental opinion was based? Therefore they surveyed the parents again and asked them to indicate the sources of information upon which they formed their perceptions of the school's program. The response received was as follows: (Diagram 11-9)

Diagram 11-9
SOURCES OF INFORMATION UPON
WHICH PARENTS FORM OPINIONS
OF THE SCHOOL PROGRAM

Source of Data	Percentage of Parents Who Indicated It As A Data Source
The student published newspaper	13%
The local community weekly newspaper	43%
From other parents	63%
Radio or television programs	18%
National news magazines (*Time, Newsweek*, etc.)	29%
From my own children	84%
From children I know who attend the school or who have attended the school	53%
Impressions from driving by the school	18%
Reports of school problems by the opinion polls	24%
School Board Meetings	3%
Parent-Teacher Association Meetings	9%
Parent-Teacher Conferences	11%

The response indicated that a key data source for most parents about program adequacy was how their own children perceived and reacted to the school's curriculum. The faculty pondered the situation and felt that perhaps the skills were too well "hidden" in the program. The staff implemented a simple approach by reiterating with the students at the end of the day what they had learned. Further polls indicated that this technique, along with more information to the local newspapers, helped bring parental opinion closer to what the objective analysis of the program had indicated.

Assessment of School Climate

Perhaps the most difficult type of schoolwide assessment for the guidance department is that of determining the school's working climate for professionals. Climate represents the overall atmosphere or tone of the school. Climate has behavioral consequences and effects. The key person in establishing the school's climate is the school principal. Principals who desire to run a "tight ship" will find a higher anxiety factor among the staff, greater faculty dependence upon rules and procedures. Students will find the school rigid and harsh. By contrast, principals who behave differently, who are less personally anxious about rules and regulations and who exhibit a high degree of personal "thrust" will motivate teachers more positively in establishing the school's overall tone.

It should be obvious that a principal who is fearful of revealing his true support or lack of support from the staff may resist allowing any type of climate assessment to take place. For this reason guidance departments should consider carefully the role of the principal at their school and the possible uses of the data once gathered prior to undertaking a climate study. (17)

Other types of data which can be gathered for the school as a decision-making unit are the participant observer procedure used by anthropologists. Stuart B. Palonsky, a college professor, became a high school participant observer for four months. He moved freely between various student groups such as the "hempies," or pot smokers, Black Jocks, College-Bound Boys, Black Academics. He found that the high school he observed did nothing to alleviate student conflict. (18)

The educational audit has been advanced by Leon Lessinger as an approach to school evaluation by an outside group of specialists who examine how well the school has done to reach identified objectives. The group then files a public report on the school's progress, similar to accreditation but based upon different criteria. (19)

Barriers to Effective Guidance Intervention in Secondary School Curriculum Development

Overloading of the Guidance Staff

Guidance staffs cannot function very well if their counselor/pupil load is excessive. Counselors bogged down in paper work are not effective with pupils and have little time to gather data, collate, analyze or use it to improve the secondary curriculum. For this reason every effort should be made to reduce the total guidance/pupil ratio to not more than 200 students per counselor or less if possible.

Lack of Guidance Department Work Differentiation

Secondary school guidance and psychological services are still too insensitive to school and pupil requirements. The tradition of assigning counselors and psychologists by grade levels or vertically across grade levels by alphabetical order of student is not effective. Instead some counselors may specialize in data analysis and do little actual counseling. This also may be given over to a specialist in statistics. Other counselors may work primarily with staff members and parents. Others may concentrate solely upon groups of students with similar problems. There is still the pervasive feeling among secondary school guidance people that every counselor must be good at all things, a sort of jack-of-all-trades. Such an approach simply denies the obvious fact that some counselors may be excellent in gathering and using test data and be most effective working with adults. Others may find the counselor-student relationship most challenging and enjoyable. Some counselors find working with teachers and administrators the most unpleasant part of their jobs. Until there can be greater differentiation of work within secondary school guidance departments, further benefits in utilizing guidance services may be minimized.

Guidance Activities in Regimented Schools

Large secondary schools tend to become rigid and impersonal and become preoccupied with rules and formulas. Such dominance of and dependence upon procedures routinizes the school and creates a punitive climate for student and faculty interchange. In such schools the function of guidance as a "cybernetic" or feedback role is extremely difficult.

Regimentation is often a substitute for the development of realistic and valid school goals and the lack of true administrative or school system accountability. Schools without measurable and valid goals cannot be the subjects for rational planning or curriculum development. Regimentation often becomes an end in itself and such schools become impervious to feedback. Furthermore efforts to improve the curriculum based upon the gathering of parent, student or faculty perceptions will be extremely difficult if not impossible.

Guidance and psychological services in the modern secondary school should epitomize more than efforts to simply adjust students to the school or society. Rather they should be a dynamic force to change the school in the direction of the students and the evolving needs and requirements of society in which those students must not only survive but contribute and grow as human beings. If the secondary school is considered a "static" entity, guidance and psychological services will be concerned with one direction adjustment, i.e., pupils to school. Curriculum development will be blind to pupil and parental perceptions. A dynamic secondary school is one which is constantly making adjustments as an institution. In such a school, guidance and psychological services can provide the base for decision-making in maintaining a viable balance among all the parties involved.

CHAPTER REFERENCES

1. Most homerooms in secondary schools are places where the bulletin is read and attendance taken. Few are longer than fifteen minutes. This practice can be compared to earlier times when the homeroom was considered a counseling period. Such topics as personal appearance, smoking, punctuality, how to study, part-time jobs, and a study of occupations were part of the secondary school homeroom program. See J. C. Wright, *Home Room Programs for Four Year High Schools* (Keokuk, Iowa: Extra- Curricular Publishing Co., 1935).

2. See John D. Krumboltz, "Stating the Goals of Counseling," California Counseling and Guidance Association, Monograph No. 1, 1966.

3. See "Revolt against Sex Stereotypes," Chapter 12, in *The Reform of Secondary Education,* A Report of the National Commission on the Reform of Secondary Education (New York: McGraw-Hill, 1973), pp. 146-61.

4. See also Arthur Thomas and Norman Steward. "Counselor Response to Female Clients with Deviate and Conforming Career Goals," *Journal of Counseling Psychology* 18, no. 4 (1971): 353-57.

5. For a review of the schools' sorting functions by race, see "Inside the System: The Character of Urban Schools, 1890-1940," Part IV in *The One Best*

System, David B. Tyack (Cambridge: Harvard University Press, 1974), pp. 177-268.

6. For examples of the way Mexican-American students have suffered discrimination in the schools with recommendations for improving their status, see Norma G. Hernandez, "Variables Affecting Achievement of Middle School Mexican-American Students," Review of Educational Research 43, no. 1 (Winter 1973): 1-40.

7. For an excellent example of a qualitative description of an American secondary school, see "Rome High School and Its Students," Chapter Seven in *Culture against Man,* Jules Henry (New York: Random House, 1963), pp. 182-281.

8. These two terms were extrapolated from Mark Van DeVall, Cheryl Bolas, and Tai S. Kang, "Applied Social Reserach in Industrial Organizations: An Evaluation of Functions, Theory, and Methods," *Journal of Applied Behavioral Science* 12, no. 2 (1976): 158-77.

9. See Alan R. Anderson, "Group Counseling," Part Six, in *The Review of Educational Research* 30, no. 2 (April 1969): 209-26. Special issue on guidance and counseling.

10. James B. Conant, *The American High School Today* (New York: McGraw-Hill, 1959).

11. See Margaret E. Bennett, *Guidance and Counseling in Groups* (New York: McGraw-Hill, 1963).

12. For a critique of the past uses and abuses of the I.Q. test, see Benjamin Fine, *The Stranglehold of the I.Q.* (New York: Doubleday, 1975).

13. For a very controversial and disputed study of the impact of test data on teacher expectation of pupils, see Robert Rosenthal and Lenore Jacobson, *Pygmalion in the Classroom* (New York: Holt, Rinehart and Winston, 1968). For counter arguments against the conclusions of the Rosenthal and Jacobson study, see Janet D. Elashoff and Richard D. Snow, *Pygmalion Reconsidered* (Worthington, Ohio: Charles A. Jones, 1971).

14. See Jack McCurdy and Don Speich, "Drop in Student Skills Unequaled in History," a series of articles in the *Los Angeles Times,* August 15, 1976. These articles received nationwide exposure. See also *Boston Globe,* September 5, 1976, A-3.

15. For a review of the concept of grading by the "curve," see Scarvia B. Anderson, Samuel Ball, Richard T. Murphy et al., *Encyclopedia of Educational Evaluation* (San Francisco: Jossey-Bass, 1974), pp. 184-88.

16. McCurdy and Speich, "Drop in Student Skills."

17. See David J. Mullen, 'A Diagnostic Study of the Human Organization in the Schools," Final Report, Project No. 3-0476, College of Education, University of Geogia, Athens, June 30, 1976.

18. Stuart B. Palonsky, "Hempies and Squeaks, Truckers and Cruisers—A Participant Observer Study in a City High School," *Educational Administration Quarterly* 11, no. 2 (Spring 1975): 86-103.

19. Leon M. Lessinger, *Every Kid a Winner* (Chicago: Science Research Associates, 1970).

FOR FURTHER READING

Arbuckle, Dugald S. "An Existential Humanistic Program of Counselor Education." *Counselor Education and Supervision* 14, (March 1975): 168-74.

Charles, C. M. *Educational Psychology: The Instructional Endeavor,* 2nd ed. Saint Louis: The C. V. Mosby Co.. 1976.

Coop, Richard H., and White, Kinnard, *Psychological Concepts in the Classroom.* New York: Harper and Row, Publishers, 1974.

Gilmore, George E., and Chandy, Jean M. "Teachers' Perceptions of School Psychological Services." *Journal of School Psychology* 11, no. 2 (Summer 1973): 139-47.

Jones, Vernon F. "School Counselors as Facilitators of Healthy Learning Environments." *The School Counselor* 24 (January 1977): 157-64.

Mason, Emanuel J.; Arnold, Daniel S.; and Hyman, Irwin A. "Expectations and Perceptions of the Role of the Guidance Counselor As Described by Students and Parents." *Counselor Education and Supervision* 14 (March 1975): 188-98.

Odell, Louise M. "Secondary School Counseling: Past, Present, and Future." *The Personnel and Guidance Journal* 52 (November 1973): 151-55.

Ohlsen, Merle E. *Group Counseling,* 2nd ed. New York: Holt, Rinehart, and Winston, 1977.

"Social Issues and the School Counselor." *The School Counselor* 22 (May 1975): 309-58. A special series of seven articles on social issues and the school counselor.

Sprinthall, Norman A., and Erickson, V. Lois. "Learning Psychology by Doing Psychology: Guidance through the Curriculum." *The Personnel and Guidance Journal* 52 (February 1974): 396-405.

Telzrow, Cathy Flutz. "The School Psychologist as Director of Career Education." *Psychology in the Schools* 9, no. 12 (April 1975): 197-99.

Waters, Linda G. "School Psychologists as Perceived by School Personnel: Support for a Consultant Model." *Journal of School Psychology* 11 (March 1973): 40-45.

PROLOGUE:
Actions,
Reactions, and
Consequences

IV Decision-
Making:
Today and
Tomorrow

It is appropriate to introduce the concluding chapters of this book with a brief consideration of actions, reactions, and consequences in human affairs. Curriculum development is a dynamic process. It means that those responsible for it will make decisions, rarely alone, but with the considered judgments of many other colleagues at a variety of levels in the secondary school. Decisions require information, definition of the problem, and a knowledge of how to engage in problem-solving.

In human affairs rarely is there one "right" decision. Usually action centered in curriculum development involves hundreds of decisions, none of which singly may make much difference, but when stretched into time together amount to a large impact upon the lives of many teachers and students. Decisions are made within a moving context of reality. There are no static decision-making situations in secondary schools today. All decisions are therefore relative not absolute. Against a moving backdrop of time, energy, and interest, as well as shifting priorities at the national, state, and local levels, curriculum development occurs. By definition it must be a fluid and imprecise activity at best.

Chapter twelve examines the impact of accountability upon education in general and curriculum development in particular. Accountability is more than saying that one should be responsible for his or her actions and their results or consequences. Accountability is an idea about schools, what they should be doing, and how they should be operating. Behind all of the accountability concepts, from performance contracting to the voucher plan, lies a simple model that supports the idea that schools should be able to use results to improve their effectiveness and efficiency. Chapter twelve examines the idea that accountability and all of its ramifications operate around the concept of *suboptimization*. Suboptimization means that the work of an individual or working unit within the total school environment should be able to perform its tasks at the same or decreasing costs, with increasing results. Applied in school situations this simple paradigm becomes enormously complex and controversial. Accountability as suboptimization requires peculiar conditions to be present in the work environment. Some of these do not exist in public schools or school districts today. They must therefore be created. Each of the accountability notions is reviewed in this chapter and its implications for secondary schools assessed.

As a central activity of the secondary school, curriculum development can become a more precise process and assist the staff and school administration to become more accountable to the students for their learning and the general public. To do this will require some changes in the traditional process of developing curriculum. Some of the changes will not require much effort, and others will involve considerable time and energy. It appears that much more time will have to be spent on making clear what is actually being tried in the secondary school when curriculum is being developed than occurred previously.

Sources of resistance to accountability as suboptimization include groups as well as ideas of how curriculum has been perceived in the past. The role of the secondary school principal in curriculum development has been declining. The loss of this generalist function as one of balancing and mediating the interests of teacher and supervisor specialists is apparent with the proliferation of minicourses in secondary schools. Secondary principals must be brought back into the curriculum development picture if the secondary school is to retain a viable balance between the interests of specialists and the knowledge explosion in every subject area.

It seems to the present writers that any concept of accountability must rest upon a foundation of reliable and valid evaluation. Consistency of purposes, findings, and recommendations is fundamental if accountability is to be taken seriously. And beyond factors identified with reliability, such as measurability and consistency, sound evaluation should be broadranging, coherent, and directly focused on the causes and cures for any presumed educational deficiency. Valid evaluation is an inherent obligation to accompany processes of accountability.

Chapter thirteen examines the nature of curriculum evaluation and why efforts in this area are often disappointing. Many educators approach evaluation as a kind of mysterious, highly technical and private affair between a statistician and a computer. The data produced from this match will then yield definitive answers to the school's nagging problems. Evaluation is more than a technical process. It is a human process and its social dimensions often overshadow the technical dimensions. Evaluators must be more than competent technicians, they must be decision-makers who know how to define the evaluation problems in such a way as to enhance the probability that the technical and statistical methods employed can strengthen and improve the quality of decisions which must flow from the data.

Evaluators cannot produce magic. Sloppy definitions of what is being tried in writing curriculum, with little or no thought to sequencing or dealing with intervening or confounding factors, will not provide the "clean" data base for tidy decision-making. Evaluation does not begin with the evaluator and a statistical design. It begins with the curriculum developer and how he or she approaches the definition of curriculum. No highly potent statistical methods can compensate for shoddy design.

Chapter fourteen moves beyond considerations of accountability and evaluation to a consideration of specific procedures to follow to engage in sound curriculum change. Past assumptions did not always produce curriculum capable of being improved in the schools. Such curriculum was impervious to feedback about pupil learning. Having established the fact that results are central to creating a more effective secondary curriculum in the preceding chapters, the final chapter shows how a "curriculumless" process called needs assessment can produce an improvement in curriculum development practices. It also involves the major partners of educational curriculum change: students, community, and the professional staff.

Curriculum change should be an orderly, systematic process, a planned sequence of actions, and not a continuous, defensive reaction either to criticism or to nationally sponsored proposals for curriculum modification. The actions taken on behalf of curriculum improvement and the accompanying reactions and consequences affect the lives of too many people, too directly and too permanently, to be taken casually or treated thoughtlessly.

12   Accountability

Accountability in education is a concept regarding the place of schools within the larger society and the degree to which they are subsequently redefined and assessed by that society. Accountability assumes that schools are means to commonly defined social ends and that they can be shaped to become more effective in reaching those ends. The phrase, "the schools ought to become accountable, or *more* accountable," as echoed in the Gallup Polls (1) implies that the schools are viewed as means to some kinds of ends or outcomes. Even the dissenters of some notions of accountability in retorting, "accountable to whom and for what?" assume the schools are *means* to ends as well.

Within this relationship of means to ends, accountability assumes that the schools are viewed as a channel by which society sets forth its goals and objectives for educating the young. These goals are translated by the schools into a technology or a "how to do it" set of operating procedures and rules. A technology is merely an applied science or repetitious series of procedures (the application of systematic, as opposed to accidental or random means) towards fulfilling broader social goals. The gravamen of the "technical core" of the schools is contained within its curriculum. This is accompanied by teaching methods, scheduling and grouping practices, and a host of other assumptions about what the schools should be doing.

According to James Thompson (2) the technical core or *rationality* of an organization has two aspects. The first has to do with whether a series of actions or directions *actually* achieve the desired results, and the second is an economic question. The latter notion attempts to ascertain if the results obtained from the application of various means represent the *lowest* of possible costs. Thompson notes that for this calculation there are no absolute standards.

Organizations attempt to isolate and "buffer" their core technologies. The purpose of buffering is to add predictability to the organization so that it can be more easily controlled internally. Over a long period of time the control of the procedures within secondary schools and school systems have come to be dominated by educators to the point where they are almost the exclusive proprietors of that core technology. This exclusivity of dominion over the core technology has been further reinforced by collective bargaining agreements which often prohibit and restrict outside influence regarding working conditions in general, and curriculum development in particular.

The Rise of Educational Accountability

The rise of educational accountability was a phenomenon of the late sixties. Escalating school costs followed by taxpayer revolts, rampant student activism, and the failure of the schools within the inner cities to help large masses of the economically disadvantaged to flee a cycle of poverty and powerlessness, were powerful incentives to the accountability movement. (3) Legislators, influential critics, various educational leaders, civil rights groups, taxpayer organizations, apparently joined in a common cry for an examination of the effectiveness of the schools. During this time (and to the present as well) minority groups were charging that the schools were racist and insensitive to the needs of their children, legislators saw sagging test scores as evidence that the schools were being poorly run and were therefore inefficient, and taxpayers charged the schools with overstaffing and concerned with frills rather than basics.

The response by educators, their organizations, the United States Office of Education, and various states took a variety of forms. These will be examined in some detail, but all rested upon the basic assumption that schools as means, and within them the core technology, were malleable and easily manipulated. Accountability assumes the core technology of schools can be arranged and rearranged to discover the most efficient procedures for obtaining the desired results. Obviously a cause-effect relationship must therefore exist between what the schools do and the outcomes they produce. This assumption has been challenged by Christopher Jencks in his national study that indicated that what schools do was largely irrelevant to future societal success of students. (4)

Nonetheless supporters of education and educators themselves can hardly be dissuaded from the idea that schools make a difference (or they ought to) and since this differentiation is contained with the schools' core technology, it is difficult to deny the postulate that it can be made more efficient and effective. The behavior of individuals within schools is therefore purposive rather than accidental or haphazard. As such, schools behave differently from hospitals, prisons, factories, armies, unions, etc., although in certain respects they all have similarities.

If the core technology was not assumed by educators and by the public to be malleable, accountability would have taken a different turn. Even those who propose alternative schools or educational vouchers assume that these approaches are necessary to create the conditions by which the core technology must be changed in order for schools as we know them to survive. Alternative schools and the voucher plan ostensibly create an environment of competition in which the motive of the open market is introduced into the schools to provide an incentive to change the core technology. Such incentives, it is argued, do not exist in large, public monopolies such as schools at the present time.

The concept of altering the core technology of schools in order to find the most effective procedures or approaches to the achievement of the desired results is called *suboptimization*. (5) Almost all of the various facets of accountability in education can be related to creating the conditions within the schools for suboptimization to occur. To illustrate let us examine what conditions must exist in any organization in order for it to attain suboptimization.

Specificity of the organizational outcomes desired. In order for suboptimization to occur in an organization, the outcomes of the working unit or units must be precisely defined. Loose, vague outcomes do not lead to specificity of selcetion of means because almost any combination of means may be shown to "fit." In order to develop clear cause-effect relationships between procedures (means) and outcomes (ends), the outcomes must be assessable in ways in which the means to produce them can be determined to be more or less effective.

Specificity of the most efficient means is possible. Assuming that the desired outcomes can be made specific, the means to attain them become possible to delineate precisely. Procedures, strategies, activities, tasks, must assume a purposive identification which clearly differentiates between alternative procedures, strategies, activities, and tasks. Such specificity is necessary to discriminate effectively between effective ways the desired results may or may not be obtained.

Specificity of the sequence or manner of application is possible. Once the various components, units or activities comprising the means necessary to obtain the outcomes can be designated at the required specificity level, the manner in which they are put together or sequenced must be capable of being identified. What comes first? What follows this result? What sequence of events must follow if preliminary indications show that the results will not be obtained? What adjustments can be made without violating a given sequence totally? Specifying the sequence of the application of various means must also include the latitude or range of variations or combinations permitted.

It is possible to relate data about outcomes to results desired. When the sequence of procedures or activities is completed, data must be capable of being gathered and collated to determine if the desired results were indeed obtained. If the data show that the results were not obtained or only partially obtained, the specificity of sequence employed should clearly indicate what went wrong and what should or can be changed. Maximum effectiveness is always obtained by successive approximation. Sloppy procedures often make this kind of adjustment impossible.

Feedback is utilized to improve the probability of outcome realization. Suboptimization occurs when adjustments from initial efforts are made under specified conditions by which the desired results are realized with the *same* or *decreasing* costs. Since the results are always relative, suboptimization is relative. There is a delicate balance between the results obtained and the means used to reach them in every case. If the results are obtained with *increasing* costs, then suboptimization did not occur, unless the results obtained were greater than specified.

Conditions in the Schools and the Accountability Movement

There is no evidence to indicate that the accountability movement was advanced by a master group of strategists. Rather the impetus appears to have come over an extended period of time from a variety of individuals and groups. However, behind most of the approaches and programs lies the concept of suboptimization. Some accountability thrusts are attempts to create all of the conditions of suboptimization while others merely establish one or more of them and must therefore be seen as sequential within a larger context. Table 12-1 attempts to summarize the major facets or programs of the accountability movement.

Performance Objectives

The development of behavioral or performance objectives has been explored in detail in chapter three. Performance objectives have enabled educators to develop a more precise language which can describe the outcomes of the instructional process and the outcomes of the educational system. The acquisition of a more technical language describing the outcomes desired from the schools is an important key to suboptimization and hence accountability. (6)

Needs Assessment

Needs assessment is the process of developing performance objectives for use as educational outcomes for the schools. It enables the school and/or school district to establish precise outcomes of the schooling process and provides a method for the comparison of results to desired results (a gap or need). The vehicle for such analyses is essential to the feedback function for suboptimization to occur. (7)

Systems Analysis

There are a variety of approaches and models to systems analysis. Most analytic models are centered around specificity of means and involve detailed descriptive statements often in schematic form such as flowcharts. This, too, represents the development of a more precise symbolic language by which cause-effect relationships may be discerned and noted. Through the application of such language the various sequences and applications of a variety of means utilized (and selected) may be retraced and improvements made on the basis of greater economy or greater benefit towards realization of the outcomes specified. (8)

PPBS (Planning, Programming, Budgeting System)

PPBS represents a direct cost method or approach of the accountability movement. It is an attempt to develop precise program descriptions within the school budget and relate them to specific program (sometimes pupil) objectives. PPBS is a descriptive accounting system. If a PPBS model is accompanied by a validated set of pupil performance objectives, it can show the dollar costs of attaining or not attaining such objectives.

Rarely, however, are PPBS models accompanied by a precise set of descriptors about the means used to attain the ends in an instructional sense. PPBS represents an attempt to apply sophisticated financial descriptors to educational programs and instructional outcomes. It, however, provides only a medium of language expression in economic terms. Its utility is quite limited if it is not accompanied by a variety of other accountability tools. (9)

Performance Contracting

Performance contracting represents the epitome of the accountability movement. To be able to contract for the attainment of instructional objectives it is necessary that they be stated precisely. Instructional sequences assume major importance, especially if the contracting involves programmed instruction. Some contracts have involved the specification of detailed means, often involving teaching machines and other types of equipment or audiovisual machines. Data are collected upon testing and fedback to see if the results were obtained and to make adjustments in the programs (means).

Table 12-1

A SUMMARY OF THE MAJOR FACETS OF
EDUCATIONAL ACCOUNTABILITY AS A VEHICLE
FOR SUBOPTIMIZATION OF SCHOOLS

Accountability Program	Conditions of Suboptimization Realized
1. Behavioral (performance) objectives	-specificity of ends (outcomes)
2. Needs assessment	-specificity of ends -collection of data (gap analysis) -feedback and adjustments from actual to desired outcomes
3. Systems analysis	-specificity of means -specificity of sequence
4. PPBS (Program budgeting)	-specificity of ends -specificity of means (programs) -relation of data to outcomes in dollar form
5. Performance contracting	-specificity of ends -specificity of means (with programmed instruction) -specificity of sequence (with programmed instruction) -collection of data about results -feedback and adjustment
6. Voucher plan	-creation of conditions to produce suboptimization (utilize other facets of accountability)
7. Differentiated staffing	-specificity of means
8. Management by Objectives (MBO)	-specificity of ends -specificity of means -collection of data regarding results -feedback and adjustments
9. CBE (Competency Based Education)	-specificity of means
10. National Assessment of Education	-specificity of ends -feedback and adjustment

Performance contracting has been disappointing, however, because instead of developing specific types of instructional objectives which must be met, the early contractors merely specified gains to be made on national standardized achievement tests. (10) When the results were examined spectacular gains were not evident, though there were acceptable gains. In a major study of the results of contracting in five cities in five separate states, Rand Corporation evaluators indicated that performance contracting pushed the educational "state of the art" to the limits. They recommended that more effort be made in the area of developing criterion-referenced tests before the concept (performance contracting) could really be adequately assessed. (11) The over-reliance upon standardized tests may have prematurely doomed performance contracting as an acceptable alternative in the accountability repertoire for some time to come.

The Voucher Plan

The voucher plan had its genesis in the ideas of Nobel Prize-winning economist Milton Friedman at the University of Chicago. In his provocative book *Capitalism and Freedom* (12) Friedman argued that the problems with public education in this country were that there was too little return for the dollars invested, and that the political process was too cumbersome for parents to indicate how educational monies should be spent. He emphasized that uniform teacher salary schedules both overpaid and underpaid teachers, and prohibited any kind of competition developing for wages based upon performance within school systems. This led to an unhealthy monopoly in which teachers and their unions came to exercise primary control of the schools, rather than parents and their elected boards of education.

Friedman discussed the idea of providing each family with funds from the government and giving them the responsibility and latitude to select private or public schools for their children's education. Friedman insisted that the option of parental choice would stimulate competition among schools and school districts for clientele, force teacher salaries to become responsive to market conditions, and promote a better adjustment between changes in the schools and the supply and demand conditions of the free market.

The Office of Economic Opportunity (OEO) funded the voucher plan, but had trouble finding school systems and or states which would be willing to try it. It was implemented in Alum Rock, California, with mixed results. While many positive features of the plan were recounted by its director, such as promoting greater teacher involvement in program planning, choice by parents and students about program components within the schools, better reporting systems, etc., (13) a Rand Corporation evaluation study termed the hard core achievement data "inconclusive." One researcher noted a definite downward trend in achievement scores on standardized tests. Others were not so sure. (14) While the mixed results were not encouraging for OEO from an achievement standpoint, it is not known the degree to which the plan stimulated parental choice, and what the impact upon teachers' salaries was.

Friedman was correct in assessing internal organizational conditions of the schools. An organization demands competition to survive. Otherwise, it will drift in the opposite direction, towards bureaucratic solidification with no economic incentive to correct inefficient practices or streamline wasteful personnel procedures. It is doubtful that the Alum Rock experiment will really test Friedman's voucher plan concept because it is simply not of sufficient magnitude to create a counter impact upon even regional educational market conditions. Charges by the American Federation of Teachers that vouchers would promote racism in the schools and would financially starve the public schools (15) have been answered as false by such advocates as Christopher Jencks. (16) The National Education Association objected to vouchers on the grounds that it felt public education had never been adequately funded, and the concept was a threat to the teaching profession. (17)

The voucher plan concept is perhaps the most sweeping and radical approach toward creating the conditions for suboptimization to occur in the schools. It flies in the face of such time worn approaches as the ESEA Title I program and efforts to increase aid at the state level to the schools. Lurking behind the debate about the voucher plan are unanswered questions about the control of the public schools, the role of teacher unions, the diminishing powers of school boards, and the methods of financing public education which discriminate against poor school districts via the continued employment of the property tax as the major method to support the schools.

Critics of the current educational scene such as Samuel Bowles and Herbert Gintis aver that the schools are now reinforcing a capitalistic society which promotes perpetual inequalities. (18) The educational reforms of the past which attempted to raise the standard of living for those of the bottom rungs of the socioeconomic ladder have all failed because the norms of a capitalistic economy were not changed but reinforced in the schools. As Bowles and Gintis see it, the schools suboptimize a capitalistic economy which retains a system of privilege and exploitation by maintaining large labor pools of skilled persons, thus depressing wages to the lowest point possible. They also legitimate the idea that inequalities in our society are based upon objective training received in the schools, and fragment workers into stratified groups (thus destroying their solidarity) which reflect the cleavages within a bureaucratic and capitalistic economy. Finally, the schools accustom students to accept a way of life of subordinancy and dominance by others.

Whether one approaches the faults of the schools from the eyes of a Milton Friedman who believes that inserting free market pressures within a public monopoly will force them to become more responsive, or from a Marxist notion that the schools promote inequality because they reflect and reinforce a system of capitalistic exploitation, both points of view agree on the inability of the current schools to deal with fundamental inequalities in current U.S. society. Both would agree that more money is not the solution, and that the schools cannot or will not change unless larger societal forces are brought into play.

Differentiated Staffing

Differentiated staffing is an attempt to introduce specialization into the ranks of classroom teachers beyond those which already exist. The following is a preliminary list of differentiated roles in secondary schools:

> department chairperson
> assistant principal
> guidance counselor
> psychologist
> principal
> dean of students
> coordinator of instruction
> director of pupil services

Differentiated staffing has both an economic and instructional motive. Sociologists who have studied teaching as an occupation note that it is lacking several characteristics of a fully professionalized group. Some of these gaps are:

1. The lack of a functional division of labor based upon advanced professional expertise;
2. The lack of a right to privileged communication which reflects a strong occupational culture;
3. Less autonomy from supervision and societal control than is the case with such professions as law and medicine.

Dan C. Lortie notes that within teaching there is a very slow-changing technology as well as great equalitarian pressures. This serves to blunt the ability of school systems to reward competence in any financial manner. Lortie notes that strong pressures to maintain equality within the teaching ranks is apparently a device to blunt administrative control. However, the determination to maintain that equality prohibits the emergence of senior colleagues with advanced expertise, the hallmark of more established professions. (19)

Differentiated staffing proposes to break apart the rigidly equalitarian structure of the classroom teaching cadre by creating a career ladder or staff hierarchy. Each rung of the ladder carries with it different responsibilities and varying salary. This contrasts with Friedman's version of the voucher plan where the result would lead to merit pay. Under a differentiated staffing plan, functional roles would promote increased teacher specialization, allow the emergence of senior colleagues, and move away from the single salary schedule. The rationale was not ignored by the teacher unions/associations which accepted some ideas of differentiated staffing such as the use of aides and greater teacher autonomy, but rejected "verticalism," i.e., the career ladder concept. (20)

Management by Objectives (MBO)

Management By Objectives (MBO) has had some impact upon educational administration of secondary schools. It is a system of precisely identifying work targets in ways which are tangible and measurable, establishing priorities among the objectives, and developing concrete strategies for reaching them. This contrasts with managerial practices in which work targets are not accurately identified, and hence there is a lot of slippage in directing energy and time towards accomplishing what the school most needs.

MBO is an attempt to introduce greater detail into educational management, and to create the indices by which suboptimization can be defined and attained. (21) However, MBO's greatest weakness is that it is a technology, like writing performance or behavioral objectives, and can lead to specificity without necessarily attaining greater validity. Work targets can be precisely defined, but how is it decided that the ones selected are the proper ones? In a superior-subordinate system, it is the superior who helps the subordinate define his or her work objectives. This practice in a highly authoritarian work setting has been facetiously called by some "*my boss'* objectives." MBO has become extremely popular in the field of educational administration. It may be one of the most lasting features of the accountability movement.

Competency Based Education

CBE or CBI, competency based instruction or education represents an approach which tries to identify the exact types of competencies necessary to perform a certain skill or act. It is argued that the more precise definition of these skills can lead to better training and preparation of practitioners. Various CBTE programs have developed at the state level as a response (*Competency Based Teacher Education*). Some states such as New York have required their teacher training centers to identify the exact competencies developed by various courses in teacher education.

National Assessment

The efforts towards National Assessment of Educational Progress (NAEP) sponsored by the Education Commission of the States are aimed at creating common yardsticks of educational outcomes in ten subject matter areas for four age groups. National testing on these items in different regions of the nation has led to greater statewide efforts to develop specific items in reading, writing, mathematics, art and other areas. (22) The results of each cycle of assessment have been widely reported. The assessment program is an effort with the suboptimization concept to reach agreement regarding the outcomes of the educational process. Maximizing the use of resources is dependent upon the specification of the ends desired. National assessment is therefore a key to the accountability movement on a large scale.

Educational accountability is really a complex undertaking on a national level organized around a relatively simple concept. Perhaps the movement as a whole, and from the viewpoint of a specific curricular discipline, can best be summarized in the following excerpt.

Who Are the Arts Real Friends? (23)

Perhaps the time of the arts in the schools has come, if it is not snuffed out by the overwhelming financial crises in which school systems are becoming increasingly entangled.

A good many school systems in Westchester County are exploring and funding poets in the schools, bringing in community and area artists to interact with children and opening up their instructional environments in general. It must be obvious that there is also a growing counter trend. That counter trend is the cry for "back to the basics." It is a call which will not be ignored. As boards of education find themselves with many restless constituencies and crushing priorities to fund with diminishing resources, most everyone knows what will go.

"Why the arts?" our friends ask. "Are they not basic to life?" "Is it not the arts which remain as testimony to the greatness of a culture?" Surely the question is put to administrators and boards as though they were Philistines rejecting entry into the Promised Land.

The arts are being asked to justify their existence and one feels the necessity to jump on the defensive. But artists are not alone. We are all jumping these days, even math, reading and science. Increasingly schools are being asked to justify the resources the community provides them in terms of results.

Results are simple. Results mean what children will learn after they come in contact with a poet or a sculptor. What does a student do, feel, or know after such an experience that he would not be able to do prior to that experience? And if we can explain that, why should the schools provide this experience over some other experience which might be more valuable in terms of the results we expect?

The time has long since passed when happiness will be enough to justify a program. High level testimonials won't work either. We must be able to say what a program *delivers* in terms of results or when our funding friends depart, so will the programs they initiated and supported. If we are looking for an entree to the schools for the arts we must be able to come in the front door and the arts should not have to come their hat in their hands as they search for a curriculum niche.

Hopefully the arts can learn from what has transpired before. Innovations have come and gone. For the arts to make a difference they must be able to illustrate what specific skills, knowledges and attitudes children acquire from them which are unique and lead to the outcomes which should be produced from our educational system.

The greatest hindrance for the arts to find that place of curriculum priority is the cliche about measurement. The argument is that not everything can be easily measured and the heart of the arts is essentially unmeasurable. As a matter of fact we can measure everything if we can identify it, though certainly not in the same fashion as an achievement test. Measurement is not antithetical to creativity, caring, or anything else. The essence of artistic accomplishment is criticism and feedback. In this sense measurement is the lifeblood of artistic performance and creation.

The arts must therefore begin not with the performer or the performance, but with the audience. When we can identify what happens or should happen to the audience we can be more specific about the arts and what they can deliver for us. It will take as much caring and hard work as the actual performance. It is only through this process that the arts will find out who their friends really are. I don't know any other way to woo and win the only lasting friends it takes— the taxpayers.

Curriculum as a Vehicle for
Educational Suboptimization

The curriculum of the secondary school is obviously only one road towards creating the conditions of suboptimization necessary to most efficiently utilize educational resources. Other components would be teachers, their preparation, utilization and attitudes, the school's schedule, educational materials and facilities, and the cohesiveness and characteristics of the student body and surrounding community.

However, inasmuch as the curriculum represents the symbol of learning, and because it is capable of being abstracted, analyzed and debated, it is an appropriate tool to utilize to create the necessary conditions of suboptimization in the secondary school. If the secondary curriculum developer can create valid and precise objectives, lay out a sequence of development which is logical not only from internal subject matter structure but from that of the learner, and define the specific ranges of teaching methodologies to be employed, the curriculum can more nearly become an optimal tool for accountability.

Traditional curriculum development does not lead to these conditions. Rather, it reinforces a kind of ambiguity and lack of attention to details which prevent suboptimization from occurring. Perhaps a review of some of the possible reasons for this problem may help alleviate it in the future.

Problem 1: The Dependence upon Philosophy as a Source of Origin

The wellspring of philosophy has anchored many a book on curriculum and curriculum development. Philosophical premises have their own set of logic and have not traditionally led to the kind of specificity of outcomes which enable suboptimization to become a reality. Philosophy has led to some lively debates, but often fails to include within expressed viewpoints what schools, teachers and students should be doing to clearly demonstrate whether or not the philosophy is producing the desired results. Some philosophical premises are ends in themselves. Action is derived from a series of assumptions about what is right and good. When one observes the actions it is assumed that the philosophy is being implemented. The philosophy from which the actions are derived does not lead to measurable results. Actions lead back to the philosophy which justifies itself with the actions. Such actions justify themselves and may lead to no practical outcomes.

Curriculum development cannot be isolated from premises and assumptions. These inevitably involve some philosophical speculation.

However, those philosophies which eschew specificity are not tools which lead to greater educational accountability. They are not amenable to economic concepts which assess the values in costs and outcomes. An economic format demands a rigor of its own, the key to which is precision of definition. Too often fuzzy philosophical concepts or notions cannot be accurately translated for use in economic analyses.

Problem 2: Lack of an Adequate Theoretical Base for the Development of Testable Hypotheses

Very rarely has curriculum development involved the creation of a sound and holistic theoretical base in which testable hypotheses can be derived. Instead, curriculum development in the secondary school has been traditionally conceptualized as an activity in which course descriptions, topic outlines, lesson plans, or guidelines for curricular coverage are written by teachers with scant attention to what is really being implemented.

Field educators in the secondary schools have not looked upon theory building as a way of dealing with reality, but as an abstraction without practical value. It is impossible to improve curriculum without developing an adequate theory base. A theory is an explanation of how the parts of a whole relate or should relate to each others, and what could or should be done if they are not working adequately. Predictability is contingent upon having some idea of how something should be working and the results it should be producing. It is with a theory base that information can be applied to improve the whole from feedback about its parts.

If a given curriculum is not producing the desired outcomes, what should be changed? What can be done? What instructions can or should be given to teachers or administrators to change in order to enable the curriculum to become more effective? A theory base forms the place to answer these questions.

Problem 3: Imprecise Implementation Practices

If the curriculum is left entirely to each individual teacher to decide approaches, what to emphasize and what not to emphasize, a degree of variability is introduced which makes feedback from results extremely difficult to utilize. If it is not possible to specify the implementation process, it is not possible to improve that process. Rather than lead to a possible straight jacket in which teachers are forced to slavishly follow some guide to the letter, thus emulating a teaching machine, ranges of variation can be spelled out in which teachers should function. Good teachers already have developed such ranges. If deviations occur, as in some situations, they must for effective learning to take place, the degree to which the variations exceed the ranges specified can be made known.

Too often implementation of the curriculum is never specified. Significant variations in time spent on topics or subjects, procedures, and emphasis are not spelled out. These decisions are considered to be the sole domain of the teacher. As long as this attitude prevails, curriculum improvement will be largely confined to updating the content. Since teachers tend to teach the way they were taught, it is important to develop systematic alternatives in the ranges of methods and procedures possible to see which combination of them produces or maximizes a particular configuration. From this perspective, the specification of procedures and teaching methods is very much part of curriculum development.

Problem 4: The Dominance of Form Over Curricular Structure and Substance

Curriculum development takes place within a school organization. We have seen in chapter two how organizational considerations often preclude considerations of everything else. A curriculum must "fit" the organization. Organizational patterns often stem from philosophical assumptions. Curriculum is tailored to fit into the existing organizational pattern and support its philosophical assumptions.

If secondary curriculum development is consistently forced to fit into and support the traditional five or six period day of forty to fifty minutes alloted for each period, a significant degree of impact upon students may be traded away. A school schedule which allows for little variation in learning ability or interest and which assumes all students are equally well motivated leads to the development of a corresponding curriculum which is inflexible.

With the advent of flexible scheduling in secondary schools, curriculum development can proceed as an activity unto itself and then whatever sequence and procedures which are developed should lead to the type of schedule best suited to implement it. This is certainly not the way secondary curriculum has been traditionally developed.

Problem 5: Overlapping Authority

The most powerful lever for curriculum development and often the curriculum personified has been the basal text. Texts have sketched out the parameters of the content areas and specified the sequence of instruction for teachers. That the textbook was in fact *the curriculum* of the school has been acknowledged by generations of teachers and administrators. In some states such as New York, the Regents Examinations have established the curriculum for the secondary school. In other school systems, standardized tests have assumed this role. Where texts and tests once filled a void for the lack of curriculum, they now provide barriers to the development of locally defined, criterion-referenced school and/or district curriculum.

Problem 6: Teacher Union Resistance

Almost all facets of accountability which would lead to the conditions of suboptimization have been opposed by teacher unions or associations. Very rarely have teacher unions been candid about their own organizational motivations for opposing accountability measures. Robert J. Braun's searing expose of AFT tactics and victories in such cities as New York and Newark, New Jersey, point out that teacher unions are fearful of any strategy in which the public would come to exercise more control over the schools. (24)

Accountability or the idea of suboptimization exposes what the objectives of the schools are and how they are to be accomplished. Along with that is the delineation of "who" is to accomplish them. Many practices in secondary schools today, from salary schedules to school scheduling, lead away from sensitive and intelligent responses to reaching precise curricular objectives. Some union leaders consider these practices the bulwark of union power. This places the objectives of unions *qua* unions opposed to those calling for increased school accountability. Resolution to this problem may come from many directions, from changes in collective bargaining practices as the result of national legislation, to changes in union leadership. On a short term basis, however, some unions have been able to embrace some aspects of accountability such as performance objectives, CBTE, needs assessment, and systems analysis.

Problem 7: Unsophisticated Staff Attitudes about Curriculum Development

Curriculum development in secondary schools is a time honored activity. The recent emphasis on the creation of minicourses has made some aspects of curriculum writing fashionable for a great many teachers. The customary procedures involve delineating the major organizing thoughts of a minicourse and writing units or concentrated centers of class activities around them. If a minicourse were to be written about "war" for example, the teacher may develop units around such topics as "Wars of Conquest," "Wars of Revolution," or "Religious Wars." Wars may be approached chronologically such as the "Revolutionary War," "The War of 1812," and the "Civil War." Units are developed into weekly activities involving films, library research, materials and books. The amount of material to be covered is indicated. The composite product is then wrapped up as a minicourse with a few behavioral objectives thrown in to validate it.

This approach presents many problems for curriculum evaluation as the next chapter will indicate. The question of course validity is avoided. Course validity revolves around such inquiries as, "Why this minicourse organized around these ideas rather than that minicourse organized around those ideas?" Too often the sole source of validation for a minicourse is whether enough students will sign up for it so that a teacher can be assigned to teach it. While student interest is certainly an important factor for all courses of the secondary school, should it be the only one? What responsibility does the staff and administration of the secondary school have to develop and offer clusters of minicourses around designated topics?

We suggest that the development of an array of minicourses presents to the teaching staff a sustained and serious responsibility to examine the scope and depth of the existing secondary school curriculum. Minicourses should not be isolated experiences offered to students as substitutes for a sequenced curriculum. They should represent logical extensions of a unified curriculum, with careful attention paid to the degree to which the content overlaps and is reinforced by minicourses. Minicourses can be conceived of as special interest extensions, thematic analyses, or single concept expansions of the unified, secondary curriculum. The isolated, one-shot course which is not related to anything else in the secondary school should be a rare phenomenon. Scant attention is paid to such matters as curriculum coordination in too many schools. Some secondary school catalogs are nothing more than cook books of isolated curricular dishes, particularly at the upper levels when basic course requirements have been met. In this respect the minicourse movement has done a disservice to the logical development of secondary curriculum.

Secondary school personnel who have a responsibility for developing minicourses or regular electives should pay careful attention to matters of content and coordination. The extent to which electives and/or minicourses overlap certain main line content strands or organizing centers should be known, and the degree to which they extend and/or expand main line concepts anticipated. Teachers and counselors offering advice to students about course selection should be able to articulate the similarities and differences which result from following any particular selection pattern. If this cannot be done, we suspect that not enough attention has been paid to the identification of curricular coordination among and between the courses and levels of the secondary curriculum.

Problem 8: The Decline of the School Principal as a Curriculum Leader

The explosion of information within the various disciplines of the secondary school, the national movement of curriculum development in both theory and the production of new materials have left many secondary school principals' training in curriculum obsolete. As a result they feel inadequate to lead the teaching staff in curriculum development. The principal either pushes the responsibilities upon the department chairpersons or relies upon subject area supervisors from the downtown office to develop curriculum. The *generalist function* of secondary school curriculum develonment is one which has been lacking in recent years. The minicourse movement has accelerated and exacerbated the problem.

Whose responsibility is it in the secondary school to balance and coordinate the various course offerings? Whose responsibility is it to ensure that there is a minimum of overlap and a maximum of extension of the school's curriculum? Often the individual interests of the separate departments prohibit much horizontal integration of the curriculum. There are too many pressures exerted upon the subject area chairpersons from their colleagues to want to engage in extended dialogue about horizontal curricular articulation and coordination, particularly when the threat of the loss of resources may be involved.

This responsibility cannot be performed adequately by central office subject area supervisors who are both external to the secondary school, and who have no authority (or expertise) to be equally competent or unbiased in the generalist function. This responsibility is lodged in the secondary principalship and / or its extensions such as an assistant principal in charge of curriculum and instruction. The pressures of the modern seconday school sometimes prohibit principals from spending much time in curriculum coordination and articulation. This is a trend which must be reversed if the curriculum of an individual secondary school is to maintain a healthy balance between subject area specialists and horizontal integration. The secondary school has a responsibility to provide not only a sequential curriculum within subject areas which is logical and of sufficient scope to challenge its students, but one which makes sense to the student as a consumer as he or she simultaneously takes courses in many disciplines. This is the generalist function of curriculum development. If it is not performed by the principal or designee, there will be a tendency of the curriculum over a period of time to become overdeveloped in some areas and underdeveloped in others. Sometimes this pattern follows strong personalities as exhibited in department chairpersons.

Essential Qualities of Curriculum Required for Suboptimization

The secondary school curriculum can become a tool for the creation of the conditions which will lead to suboptimization if the following qualities are present in the secondary school:

A Set of Measurable and Valid Schoolwide Objectives. Curriculum should not be developed in isolation. Curriculum development must take account of composite sets of learning skills, knowledges and attitudes of the total student as a functioning human being in our society. These should be carefully delineated at the outset and precede curriculum development. (See chapter fourteen on curriculum change.)

The Development of an Adequate Theory Base. The development of a theoretical base for curriculum development should not be an exercise in meaningless abstraction. Rather, it should be the listing of assumptions to be used by the curriculum developer in creating curriculum. It can be as simple as making a series of written statements about the nature of society and life, what is believed to be the nature of learning, the nature of school, etc. Regardless, these statements are often absent in secondary curriculum guides. Without them it is extremely difficult to generate testable hypotheses and to construct a meaningful evaluation design to determine the adequacy of curriculum development.

The Delineation of Scope and Sequence. The teacher and/or the students cannot be the sole determiners of curricular scope or sequence. The responsibility of develoning the parameters of the curriculum should include the development of options and ranges of choice. These should be related to a meaningful whole. The purpose of developing a scope and sequence to curriculum development is to create the general domain of a field or area of study by which decisions can be made about how best to reach the outcomes or objectives desired. Without adequate definition of the parameters contained in scope and sequence decisions, it is difficult and perhaps impossible to improve the curriculum.

The Development of Adequate and Appropriate Measurement Tools. If curricular objectives have been adequately established and validated, the identification of appropriate measuring tools should not be difficult. (25) Measuring or assessing curricular outcomes has been a knotty problem because there has not been careful development of definition of the outcomes desired. Curriculum has been developed too loosely and the variables about scope and sequence lacking or imprecisely indicated.

The Development of Incentives to Improve Performance. There are few incentives currently existing within the secondary school which truly stimulate a drive for suboptimization. Despite the rhetoric about individualization of instruction and attention to the unique needs of various groups of learners, there are few viable ways the secondary curriculum has been as responsive as it should have been. Clearly, more attention must be paid to the creation of incentives to suboptimize the curriculum. Ideas to do this run a gamut of radical to conservative responses. Radical ones involve the creation of an internal voucher model, schools within schools, and offshoots to performance contracting. Less radical responses involve providing additional pay for staff as well as training to develop curriculum. These may become fully differentiated teaching roles with time. Other responses might be the creation of extra staffing units beyond those normally required to allow for staff travel and study as a kind of internal sabbatical without leaving the actual secondary school site. Incentives can be created with financial inducements directed towards individuals or groups, or with improved status, time off, or with role differentiation.

The Institutionalization of Curricular Feedback: Public Reporting. Public reporting of how well the staff and administration reached the desired outcomes is a necessity for the feedback process to work. Public scrutiny provides the external incentive required to ensure that feedback is utilized. In large secondary schools beset with many kinds of problems, unless there is a significant requirement to engage in sustained analysis of how well students have learned, the pressures of other events will submerge the curricular feedback function. Some states such as Florida have required each school to send home an annual report to parents about the year's activities. This report includes test data and other measures to indicate pupil progress. For feedback to be important it must be required as a standard operating procedure. The necessity for public reporting simply builds in or institutionalizes the feedback function.

Accountability in curriculum development within the secondary school can become a reality if it is conceptualized as a model to obtain suboptimization of the school as a whole. Curriculum development is one major piece of the elements necessary to suboptimize the secondary school. While the notion of suboptimization is relatively simple, the reality of implementing it in secondary schools is enormously more complex as some of the discussion in this chapter has indicated. This will become even more evident in the next two chapters as well.

CHAPTER REFERENCES

1. *The Gallup Polls of Attitudes toward Education, 1969-73* (Bloomington, Indiana: Phi Delta Kapapa, 1969-73).

2. James D. Thompson, *Organizations in Action* (New York: McGraw-Hill, 1967), p. 14.

3. See Leon M. Lessinger and Ralph W. Tyler, *Accountability in Education* (Worthington, Ohio: Charles A. Jones, 1971).

4. Christopher Jencks et al., *Inequality: A Reassessment of the Effect of Family and Schooling in America* (New York: Basic Books, 1972).

5. Thompson, *Organizations in Action*, p. 94.

6. See G. Michael Kuhn and Lorraine R. Gay, "Instructional Objectives: A National Compendium," State University System of Florida, Division of Academic Affairs, Department of Education, Tallahassee, Florida, May 1972.

7. Jerry L. Patterson and Theodore J. Czajkowski, "District Needs Assessment: One Avenue to Program Improvement," *Phi Delta Kappan* 58, no. 4 (December 1976): 327-29.

8. For an excellent example of "systems" thinking in education, see Leonard C. Silvern, "Systems Engineering of Education I: The Evolution of Systems Thinking in Education," Education and Training Consultants Company, Los Angeles, California, 1965.

9. See Todd A. Anton, "Planning, Programming, Budgeting System for Hillsborough City School District," in *Emerging Patterns of Administrative Accountability,* ed. Leslie H. Browder, Jr. (Berkeley, California: McCutchan Publishing Corporation, 1971) pp. 260-74.

10. For example, in Gary, Indiana, see George R. Hall and M. L. Rapp, "Case Studies in Educational Performance Contracting," prepared for the Department of Health, Education, and Welfare, R-900/1 (HEW) (Santa Monica, California: The Rand Corporation, December 1971).

11. Polly Carpenter and George R. Hall, "Case Studies in Educational Performance Contracting: Conclusions and Implications," prepared for the Department of Health, Education, and Welfare, R-900/1 (HEW) (Santa Monica, California: The Rand Corporation, December 1971), p. vi.

12. Milton Friedman, "The Role of Government in Education," Chapter 6 in *Capitalism and Freedom* (Chicago: University of Chicago Press, 1962), pp. 86-118.

13. For a report by the project director, see Joel M. Levin, "Alum Rock after Two Years: You, Dear Reader, Have a Choice," *Phi Delta Kappan* 56, no. 3 (November 1974): 201-02.

14. "Rand Researchers Don't Agree on Alum Rock Success in Promoting Student Achievement," *Phi Delta Kappan* 56, no. 3 (November 1974): 203.

15. Larry Sibelman, "The Voucher Vultures," *American Teacher* 55, no. 3 (November 1970): 17.

16. Christopher Jencks, "Education Vouchers," in *Accountability in American Education,* eds. Frank Sciara and Richard Jantz (Boston: Allyn and Bacon, 1972), pp. 284-90.

17. Helen Bain, "Voucher Proposal Raises Larger Issues," *NEA Reporter* 9, no. 9 (27 November 1970): 2.

18. Samuel Bowles and Herbert Gintis, *Schooling in Capitalist America* (New York: Basic Books, 1976), p. 56.

19. Dan C. Lortie, "The Balance of Control and Autonomy in Elementary School Teaching," in *The Semi-Professions and Their Organization,* ed. Amitai Etzioni (New York: The Free Press, 1969), pp. 1-53.

20. Fenwick W. English, "AFT/NEA Reaction to Staff Differentiation," *Educational Forum* 36, no. 2 (January 1971): 193-98.

21. See Stephen J. Knezevich, *Management by Objectives and Results* (Arlington, Virginia: American Association of School Administrators, 1973).

22. See Meg Lundstrom, "The Slow But Sure Growth of Statewide Assessments," *Compact* 10, no. 4 (Autumn 1976): 3-5. This is the magazine of the Education Commission of the States, Denver, Colorado.

23. Fenwick W. English, "Who Are the Arts' Real Friends?" *Schoolarts,* Council for the Arts in Westchester, December 1975. Reprinted with permission.

24. Robert J. Braun, *Teachers and Power* (New York: Simon and Schuster, 1972).

25. For an up-to-date review of testing instruments which may be used in secondary schools, see Louis J. Karmel, *Measurement and Evaluation in the Schools* (London: The Macmillan Company, 1970).

FOR FURTHER READING

Browder, Lesley H., Jr.; Atkins, William A., Jr.; and Kaya, Esin. *Developing an Educationally Accountable Program.* Berkeley, California: McCutchan Publishing Co., 1973.

Conable, Daniel B. "A Position Paper on Accountabiltiy." *The Education Digest* 42, no. 3 (November 1976): 26-29.

Goodlad, John. "A Perspective on Accountability." *Phi Delta Kappan* 57 (October 1975): 108-12.

Huber, Joe. "Accepting Accountability." *The Clearing House* 48 (May 1974): 515-18.

Landers, Jacob. "Accountability and Progress by Nomenclature: Old Ideas in New Bottles." *Phi Delta Kappan* 54 (April 1973): 539-41.

McWilliams, Jettie M., and Thomas, Andrew C. "The Measurement of Students' Learning: An Approach to Accountability." *The Journal of Educational Research* 70, no. 1 (September-October 1976): 50-52.

Miller, Richard I. *Developing Programs for Faculty Evaluation.* San Francisco: Jossey-Bass Publishers, 1974.

Moeller, Gerald H., and Mahan, David J. *The Faculty Team.* Chicago: Science Reserach Associates, 1971.

Nickel, K. N. "Accountability: For What? For Whom?" *The Clearing House* 48 (January 1974): 303-07.

Pratte, Richard. "An Uneasy Inquiry into Accountability." *Intellect* 101 (October 1972): 37-40.

Robinson, Donald W. "Accounting for Accountability." *The High School Journal* 60 (October 1976): 41-52.

Smith, Edward B., and Smith, Sharon Clare. "Accountability in the Classroom." *Contemporary Education* 47, no. 4 (Summer 1976): 189-94.

Unruh, Glenys G., and Alexander, William M. *Innovations in Secondary Education,* 2nd ed. New York: Holt, Rinehart and Winston, 1974. See "Accountability and Staff Evaluation and Development" in Chapter 5.

13 Curriculum
Evaluation

How good is our curriculum? Would some other curriculum be more effective? Evaluative questions about curriculum are commonly asked by parents, students, teachers, administrators and board members. Implicit in the questions are qualitative judgments based upon some measure of comparison with alternatives or standards. The process of comparison is commonly called evaluation. The purpose of evaluation in curriculum development is to make decisions about curriculum so that it can become better, i.e., more effective.

To know how good a curriculum is implies that criteria of "goodness" exist somewhere and can be employed to assess it. If the curriculum is viewed as an end in itself, then curriculum evaluation usually consists of developing criteria to determine if the desired essential characteristics are present or absent. (1) Questions about whether the curriculum is effective fall back upon compilation of lists of these essential characteristics with the assumption made that if all of them are present in the desired mixture, the maximum results will be obtained. Such lists or descriptions do not constitute an acceptable evaluative approach if the curriculum has been conceptualized as a means rather than as an end.

Viewed as a means to an end, curriculum evaluation consists of determining if the ends have been reached by the proper interplay between scope and sequence or organizational pattern, methods which produce the desired inductive or deductive set anticipated, and whether the apparent *logic* of the development of facts, skills, concepts or attitudes has produced the necessary outcomes. (2)

Another problem which appears if the curriculum is an end in itself, is that the curriculum developer can produce performance or behavioral objectives in isolation from any measure of their validity or purpose and they stand by themselves as the outcomes of the curriculum. (3) However, if the performance objectives developed must be evaluated not only on characteristics of performance objectives *qua objectives,* but on whether or not they "fit" some larger design, then curriculum becomes a means to implement them and the problem of validity has been partially resolved. From this perspective the entire curriculum is an "enabling objective," i.e., its utilization *enables* the student to attain the "terminal objective." A terminal objective is the final outcome which the curriculum is designed to achieve. Terminal objectives would constitute what has been called "summative evaluation." Enabling objectives are desired processes or methods used to reach the outcomes. These processes or methods can be evaluated separately and comprise "formative evaluation." (4)

What Is Curriculum?

The first problem confronting the curriculum evaluator is to define what is meant by "curriculum." Some curriculum writers include the teacher and teaching methods, all unanticipated and causal experiences possible within the school, scheduling, staffing, class arrangements, facilities as well as the selection and organization of curricular content as curriculum.

Such broad definitions make concentrating upon a particular effect produced by the composite whole almost impossible to assess. The lack of adequate controls which stem from this definition mean that however the school is defined represents the curriculum. The synonymous equalization of school and the curriculum have led to an over-reliance upon standardized testing as almost the sole avenue for evaluating the effectiveness of the curriculum.

With such an umbrella approach to defining curriculum, the variables are assumed to be interconnected and *causal,* that is, the impact of one leads to an impact upon another. Some of these variables may be the following:

Variable 1	the selection of content
Variable 2	the organization of content (scope and sequence)
Variable 3	type of teaching strategy (ies) employed by the teacher
Variable 4	the unique personality aspects of the teacher such as enthusiasm, warmth, etc.
Variable 5	type of school organization which determines class size, length of instructional period, grouping, class meeting schedules, facilities, etc.
Variable 6	location of school, mixture of student body, community expectations, socio-economic factors, etc. (5)
Variable 7	other

If curriculum as defined is composed of all of the variables and perhaps more, an evaluation of curriculum would depend upon the ability to understand the causal relationships between and among the variables. Predictability is to the largest extent based upon at least a conceptual understanding of the chain of events which produces a desired outcome.

If the variables are symmetrical then they could be arranged as shown in Diagram 13-1. Diagram 13-2 hypothesizes that the relationship between the variables is not symmetrical but asymmetrical. A more complex causal model which would include all six variables cited under an *umbrella* definition of the curriculum is shown in Diagram 13-3.

In the complex model of curriculum in Diagram 13-3, variable 2 or the unique personality aspects of the teacher such as enthusiasm or warmth, is an intervening variable between the curriculum type and teaching methods. Location of the school is not included in a causal chain but does bear upon type of school organizational pattern. It is due to the fact that curriculum definitions have not attempted to specify the causal connections of what constituted the curriculum that has led to producing a dilemma of confounding factors in approaching curriculum evaluation. (6) (7)

One of the results of evaluation is to find those situations in which curriculum maximizes desired learning and to continue to utilize within the secondary school the most optimal conditions of which curriculum is one such purposeful condition. To repeat successful conditions with a school is the essence of the function of schooling. Replication is impossible without some precise definition of terms and conditions which are within the power of the school to control or mediate. The latter should include specification of procedure or approach to be used by teachers.

Umbrella definitions of curriculum which confuse and confound the variables add little to the power of curricular predictability. Such definitions are oblivious to feedback because it is not known how the factors should be rearranged to become more effective in producing the desired results. At the present time there are few theories or empirical studies which can definitively illustrate how all six variables function within any given overall configuration to realize a set or range of desired student outcomes.

A more practical approach may be to define the *curriculum* as the selection and specification of content within some logical order (scope and sequence) with perhaps some additional specification of approach or method. Outside factors such as staffing patterns, grouping practices, class size, teacher personality characteristics, etc. can be controlled by adequate attention to sampling within an evaluation design. The rigor of the evaluation design for curriculum then rests upon the degree to which the sites selected for assessment of curriculum are representative of the larger population.

On the Difference between Evaluation and Research

Some evaluation practitioners maintain there is a difference between evaluation and research. (8) Much of the difference between the two

Diagram 13-1
A CAUSAL AND SYMMETRICAL VIEW
OF CURRICULUM

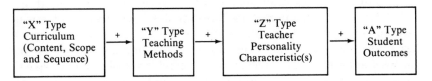

Diagram 13-2
A CAUSAL AND ASYMMETRICAL VIEW
OF CURRICULUM

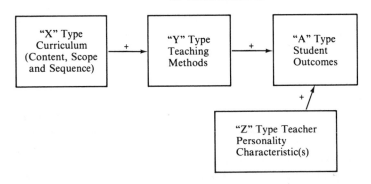

Diagram 13-3
A CAUSAL AND COMPLEX ASYMMETRICAL
VIEW OF CURRICULUM

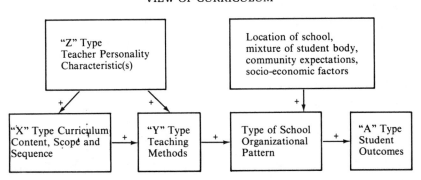

relates to why the educator undertakes an analysis of curriculum. If the educator is interested in making decisions about curriculum within real school situations and limitations, then evaluation is selected. If, however, the educator is more interested in drawing conclusions about aspects of a particular curriculum, a research approach is undertaken. Many evaluation activities utilize the tools and techniques of statistical inference and draw heavily upon research methodology such as the use of experimental design or quasiexperimental design. (9) Educational researchers may have no immediate practical problems or purposes when conducting research. Indeed some research is very difficult to translate immediately into school decision-making contexts. The decision maker in the secondary school is confronted with the reality that, for better or worse, a curriculum now exists there. It is functioning on a day to day basis. It influences what and how something is taught and hopefully that which may be learned. Evaluation activities are undertaken to assess the degree to which the existing curriculum is or is not functioning.

The Role of Sampling in Evaluation Design

If a given curriculum configuration is to be the subject of evaluation, some attention must be given to sampling because it is with sampling that factors influencing the implementation of that configuration can be controlled. The degree to which there is some bias in the selection of subjects receiving a treatment (curriculum configuration) represents the degree to which the results (learner growth) obtained may be suspect. The results may have been artificially skewed or influenced by procedural error in the selection process. This is usually called *biased sampling.* (10)

In the creation of an evaluation approach to curriculum, the decision maker must have some notion of the strength of the design, that is, its *rigor.* Rigorous designs which account for as many factors of bias as possible lead to more confidence in the results and hence in the decision-making process as well. Such designs yield data which are more valid and reliable than designs which cannot account for possible biased results. An evaluation design which provides the proper information about possible sources of bias is called *internally valid* and produces data which are easy to generalize. Confidence in the level of generalization of the data is the criterion of external *validity.* (11) An inference which allows some measure of consistency of the results if repeatedly applied to specified populations refers to *reliability.*

The concept of randomness is basic to procedures of statistical inference. Most evaluators are interested in determining the degree to which a particular curriculum configuration, which when applied to a particular situation or series of situations, produces a desired consequence. They may also be interested in determining what the possible consequences might be with repeated applications. In some cases they may hypothesize that the results will be negative or will be directional (greater or less than no treatment or something else). (12) Once positive results are obtained further specifications of the results can become directional or can be broken into more discriminating hypotheses.

Randomness is merely the idea that if a particular curriculum configuration is applied under similar circumstances to groups of students selected without regard to factors which may not be universal, similar results will be more or less consistently obtained. To do this it is necessary to be able to state that no subject had any more or less opportunity than any other to be included in the sample itself.

Of course, a random school situation is not really random at all. A school, with its organization, roles, materials, facilities, is a man-made artifact. It is established by society so that certain learnings deemed essential by that society are transmitted to the young. School is an institution created by a society to improve upon the odds of chance that these learnings will be acquired in the most economical fashion possible. A school itself is therefore a deliberate configuration of procedures, rules, and activities to improve upon random learnings

Understanding that schools are not random in nature nor in human society, randomness is determined by attempting to include the universe of schools within a sample's parameters or boundaries. To the extent that such parameters exclude some schools or subjects within them represents the degree to which the results obtained may not be universal. If, for example, a curriculum evaluator desired to know what impact a given curriculum configuration in mathematics had upon secondary students when applied according to specifications of scope, sequence and methodology, he or she would attempt to sample secondary schools of the nations of the world. If the sample were limited only to public secondary schools in the United States it has therefore eliminated such schools in Japan, Russia, Britain, Brazil, etc. If the parameters of the sample were further restricted to secondary schools within city systems of not less than 100,000 students the sample is even less universal and not representative of all those found in the United States. If the results of the evaluation were found to be positive the evaluator would be expected to cite possible sources outside of the treatment to explain the results. Each source would have to be systematically studied and possibly eliminated as contributing to the results obtained. (13)

To return to the mathematics curriculum configuration example, the evaluator would have to examine the school systems utilized of district's of 100,000 or more students to ascertain if unique characteristics of those systems might possibly account for positive results. The following aspects may be contributing factors:

1. The greater presence of teacher preparatory and graduate education centers in urban areas;
2. The racial composition of secondary schools and surrounding communities;
3. The organization pattern of the school systems;
4. Factors of wealth such as dollars spent per child and teacher salaries;
5. Family and community characteristics;
6. Others.

Only when these possible variables are dealt with would it be safe to place a great deal of confidence (always relative) in the results obtained.

Evaluating a Given Curriculum Configuration

School curriculum represents a deliberate design or configuration of the elements included within its definition. Curriculum organization usually refers to the manner in which content is selected, developed within some context or relationship to the expected learning environment such as classrooms and teachers, and the boundaries which are drawn to encompass the content selected. *Sequence* refers to the manner in which a curriculum is developed and *scope* refers to the boundaries within which that development occurs. What constitutes sequence and scope rests upon a number of assumptions and viewpoints pertaining to general curriculum development practices.

If the curriculum is viewed as basically an end in itself then arguments about scope and sequence rest upon assumptions about what a specific type of scope and sequence should be doing for students generally as opposed to some other configuration. For example, advancing from the philosophical premise that life is problem-solving and that problems represent holistic entities rather than discrete subject matter areas, some curriculum developers turn to a fused type of curriculum in which subjects are blurred. Learning activities are developed around specified broad themes or problems.

If learning is viewed as the acquisition of certain concepts within broad interdisciplinary areas, then the scope of the curriculum is drawn to include whatever subjects or subject related concepts and skills may be necessary to engage in selected problem-solving. The nature of the problems selected determines the ultimate scope of the curriculum. The development of curriculum is designed around selected student inquiry activities within general problem areas and not around assumptions of complexity or mastery of predetermined, logically developed material. Sequence within this concept of curriculum development is not conceptualized as a staircase of increasing difficulty based upon assumptions of mastery, but a spiderweb of interwoven strands. (14) The learner supplies himself or herself with the "proper" sequence.

To evaluate this type of curriculum configuration in which there are few if any specified outcomes desired, the evaluator would fall back upon determining if the essential ingredients were present within the curriculum as logical extrapolations from a philosophical premise. Such an evaluation would enumerate the philosophical assumptions involved. Some of these might be as follows:

Assumption 1: Effective participation in our society demands problem solving skills;

Assumption 2: The purpose of schooling is to prepare students to respond to the needs placed upon them by their society;

Assumption 3: Schooling should therefore prepare students to be effective problem-solvers;

Assumption 4: Problem-solving cannot be taught outside the experience of the learner; Problem-solving is basically selected self-application to problems;

Assumption 5: A subject-centered, compartmentalized curriculum may impede the development of problem-solving abilities;

Assumption 6: The learner must be actively involved with "real" problems in school or the transfer of problem-solving skills to the "real" world will not occur.

Characteristics of the Curriculum Configuration Demanded by Assumptions 1-6

The assumptions involved in 1-6 lead to a particular curriculum configuration. The curriculum is defined in terms of broad interest areas or thematic concepts. Themes are developed within curriculum units and types of activities which can be a part of those units outlined for students. Learning activity areas may be identified in the school and in the community. These may include library interest centers, resource centers, labs, student display areas, community resource locations, etc. Related instructional materials are used in the classrooms in a broad way to stimulate multisensory learning. No single source could include or be suitable to all of the various kinds of activities selected by students. A variety of outcomes is encouraged and even demanded. No single outcome could represent what the curriculum configuration might accomplish. Specification of the outcomes may be viewed as antithetical to the very purpose of the curriculum configuration. There is essentially no sequence to this configuration. Each learner merely functions as best as he or she can within ranges of instructional options developed by the school. "More is assumed to be better." That is, evidence of an increasingly "effective" configuration is assumed as the range of outcomes achieved by students becomes broader.

An evaluator would approach this curriculum configuration by developing a check list of essential components largely derived from the previously cited assumptions. A single "yes," or "no," checklist might suffice. An example of one derived from the stated assumptions is shown below:

Formative Criteria to Evaluate a Curriculum Configuration

Criterion	Yes	No
1. Has the curriculum configuration been defined in broad interest or thematic areas?	____	____
2. Have multiple learning areas been designated within the school and community?	____	____
3. Are students encouraged to use the multiple learning areas? Do they use them?	____	____
4. Are teachers using a variety of learning materials and audiovisual aids?	____	____
5. Is the range of student response as broad as possible within the themes?	____	____
6. Do the problems selected by students reflect real problems in the real world?	____	____

Perhaps some other criteria could be developed as well but those cited serve to indicate that an affirmative response by the evaluator would indicate that the desired curriculum configuration developed from the philosophical premise was in fact created. The presence of the curriculum configuration closes the evaluation loop since it is assumed that if students are learning self-selected activities which involve problem solving skills they *will* use them when they are encountered in society. No further evidence is really necessary since the assumptions define the ultimate configuration. Such a design is largely impervious to feedback. In fact it is almost impossible to relate data to this curriculum configuration. How would the issues raised by declining SAT (Scholastic Aptitude Test) scores, or declining reading scores on standardized tests be related to the selection of this curriculum configuration? How would student followup study questions be used to reshape the configuration? The lack of a *sequence* within this configuration means that retracing the path selected by teachers to improve the curriculum is impossible. What is possible is a change in the content or themes. But even this is difficult because how would it be known what themes are more potent in developing certain skills than others? On what basis could a unit be rewritten? Despite the fact that it can be demonstrated that curricular sequence is largely arbitrary, some developmental outline is necessary in order to make adjustments in the curriculum by members of the instructional staff. Decision-making to improve the curriculum demands attention to the issue of sequence.

If, however, a given curricular configuration is viewed as a means to an end and the ends are student learning, then the selection of that configuration can continually be tested against whether in fact the outcomes are being attained. Suppose that a group of teachers developed lists of required skills, knowledges, and attitudes which were deemed essential to survive in our society. One group decided to locate the skills within the existing subject-centered curriculum configuration and the other decided to develop their own "problem-centered" and interdisciplinary curriculum configuration. In both cases the delineation of the survival skills as outcome criteria formed an evaluative base for determining the degree of effectiveness of the configuration selected. In the former case, the staff developed a didactic and complexity sequenced curriculum in which the necessary skills, knowledges, and attitudes were systematically taught. In the other the staff developed ranges of problems in which the same skills, knowledges, and attitudes were clustered around themes and emphasis was placed upon inductive or inquiry based approaches. The central question to an evaluation of the selected curriculum configuration is: Have the skills, knowledges, and attitudes selected been attained as desired?

Once again, the curriculum evaluator delineates the assumptions involved.

Assumption 1:   It is possible to develop a valid set of external skills, knowledges, and attitudes upon which a curriculum can be developed;

Assumption 2:   It is possible to teach the desired skills, knowledges, and attitudes in the school in some valid and logical manner;

Assumption 3:   The function of the curriculum is to designate broad ranges within the school in which most students would be expected to learn the desired skills, knowledges, and attitudes;

Assumption 4:   If the desired skills, knowledges, and attitudes are acquired they will later be used in the appropriate "real life" contexts in society;

Assumption 5:   If the learned skills, knowledges, and attitudes are actually used in society they will contribute to the student's survival, happiness, improved welfare and self-actualization as a person.

The identification of discrete external criteria used in this approach means that the determinations of scope and sequence are not general "good things" based upon vague linkages regarding problem-solving. Rather they are very visible and pragmatic ways curriculum development can become more sensitive to "deliver" the intended or desired outcomes.

A curriculum evaluator would approach judging the curriculum configuration by first determining if the external skills, knowledges, and attitudes were valid and represented a genuine consensus on the part of the major partners involved in curriculum development. This is usually accomplished with a needs assessment. (See concluding chapter on curriculum change for the details of a needs assessment). Diagram 13-4 indicates one way the evaluator would determine the effectiveness of either approach selected.

The effectiveness of the scope and sequence of any given curricular configuration should be pragmatically assessed with external criteria. It may become apparent that a logical developmental pattern for one subject is not so logical for another. Various disciplines may have their own peculiar form of logical development or *syntax* (16) Then again certain pupil developmental factors in cognitive ability may preclude forms of logical development from being effectively attained until later schooling in college or life.

Practical Problems of
Curriculum Evaluation

Evaluation of curriculum in actual school settings is beset with practical, procedural, and methodological problems. Too often evaluation efforts are shortsighted, underfinanced or so loosely conceptualized that data produced from them are almost worthless in making future curricular decisions. Beginning from the point of view that the evaluator wants the most rigorous procedures possible in order to engage in decision-making with some confidence, the model of experimental design forms the most desirable standard to follow. It is with procedures of experimental design that questions pertaining to what the treatment was and what effect(s) it produced can be answered most accurately. Also, it is with experimental design that questions about complicating variables can be most rigorously analyzed. (17) However, a true situation for experimental design in practical school settings is most often impossible.

In her penetrating analysis of evaluation problems with ESEA Title 1, Milbrey McLaughlin reports that no realistic results came of several million dollar attempts to answer Congressional questions about the program. Title 1 never defined a range of specific objectives, nor did federal authorities have any control over the 30,000 different "treatments." The famous TEMPO study of Title 1 found difficulty in identifying a Title 1 "program," and in defining and differentiating it from non-Title 1 programs. (18) McLaughlin points out that under these conditions the model of evaluation adopted was basically a PPBS approach and demanded data and controls which were simply not present in Title 1. She notes that if evaluation is considered only as a distinct logic of inquiry unto itself and ignores the political and social context in which it must take place, it may not be successful.

McLaughlin argues that the "decision-making space" of evaluation must be considered. (19) This represents the options and boundaries open to decision-makers who can use the data produced by an evaluation. This means that evaluation efforts should begin by asking, "Given a certain amount of information about X curriculum, what kind of decisions can we really make with it?" If the decision makers are confined to largely methodological or procedural questions, data pertaining to policy development will be useless. A realistic assessment of the position and options of the curriculum decision-maker should precede the development of an evaluation design. Once the context of the evaluation is considered then the curriculum decision-makers can concen-

Diagram 13-4

SUMMATIVE CRITERIA TO EVALUATE TWO CURRICULUM CONFIGURATIONS

	Major Teaching Mode	Scope	Sequence	Results Obtained	Results Not Obtained
Delineation of Survival Skills (Essential knowledges, attitudes and skills) Outcome Criteria Derived from Needs Assessment					
Configuration X Survival Skill A	Deductive	Upper limits defined by full use of skill; Lower limits defined by breaking down skill into subskills and determining factors of pupil maturity to match various skill levels.	Based on order of complexity, simple to complex; structured situations to fully develop subskills and major skill.	_____	_____
Configuration Z Survival Skill A	Inductive	Upper limits defined by ability to solve designated problems using skill; lower limits defined by problems using subskills. Pupil selection of range or problems necessary.	Ranges of types of problems specified by complexity using skills and subskills required to solve problems.	_____	_____

trate upon the design. The steps of formulating a design followed by the evaluation are as follows:

Specification of the Treatment

This step involves the most precise definition of what is being tried. For example, "To implement an inquiry based curriculum approach," is far too general to translate into a design. What constitutes "inquiry?" What is meant by "curriculum?" At this point the evaluators may well have to delve into a variety of theoretical views of curriculum, learning theory, and varying types of analyses of curricular organization. Terms and concepts must be related to some meaningful whole. The development of a sound theoretical base is critical to understanding the data from any type of trial in the field. Sound theory leads to adjustments produced in the feedback process. It is probably only from a theory base that questions pertaining to how specifically a new type or form of curriculum really differs from that which is currently in use can be broached.

It has been said that there are no true "control groups" in the schools. There are instead, "comparison groups." (20) All groups in a school setting are being exposed to teaching. The purpose of teaching is to act as a catalyst for learning. Learning represents a change in behavior. Even comparison groups are being taught with certain goals in mind to change learner behavior. No group is therefore without some sort of treatment. Groups cannot be considered static in any sense of the word. Sometimes the most difficult aspect of establishing a viable curricular design is in defining how the thing which is "new" or "different" specifically differs from what a comparison group may be receiving. Defining what the comparison group is receiving may be as difficult as specifying the treatment.

Developing a Rigorous Testing Design

The next step after specifying the treatment and separating it from what may be occuring in comparison groups is to define the situation in which the treatment is to take place. For example, who is to use the curriculum, under what conditions and with whom? This means that teachers will have to be selected and perhaps trained to use a different curriculum with varying methodologies, and students will have to be selected rather systematically to assess the impact of the treatment in the most representative manner possible.

One of the most vexing problems for in-school curriculum evaluation is the fact that few parents may want to have their children be part of an experiment. This often leads school officials to solicit students in volunteer groups. Volunteer groups reduce rather considerably the rigor of an evaluation design. Not even the practice of matching students with those who don't volunteer can compensate for the inability of the design to control important possible causes of bias which can only really be controlled with random selection.

Curriculum design in secondary schools must also compensate for the inequality of groups which occur as the result of the impact of the elective system. Selecting eleventh grade math classes for the piloting of a new curriculum in math when math is no longer required after the tenth grade means that important factors influencing the formation of random groups are absent. If the result of using the eleventh grade math classes is positive, the designers must account for the fact that the groups were not typical in that a certain spectrum of students were not part of the sample.

Fully defining the treatment situation means giving much thought and time to controlling for possible bias leading to erroneous conclusions about the treatment itself. A school with a high degree of pupil turnover each year may not be the best place to evaluate a new social studies curriculum. Furthermore, schools in which atypical events have occurred such as a serious racial disturbance may become part of a "treatment" response. If only a post test is used to assess learning changes it may be impossible to separate such an event from a curricular treatment in the results.

Almost all curriculum treatments utilize the classroom student group as the basis for comparison simply because classroom instruction constitutes a definable boundary for a "treatment." It is within the context of the classroom that the actions of the teacher can be specified and repeated sampling of what is going on undertaken to control for often unknown effects at work which may influence the results.

The essence of the testing design phase is to develop procedures which can lead to a high level of generalization about the results obtained. If the results are significant the evaluator wants to say something like, "Given situation X, and treatment Y, the results will be effect Z." To be able to make such statements without excessive qualifications requires a strong evaluation design. The function of such designs is to deal with "rival hypotheses" or "explanations" of how the results might have been obtained without the treatment. Rigorous designs will eliminate most rival hypotheses.

Selecting Testing/Observation Instruments

The actual selection of tests and/or observation instruments should follow the construction of the evaluation design in which the sources of rival explanations are dealt with systematically. In too many cases in field experiments, the selection of instruments comes first and the design follows. No nationally normed test accompanied by high powered statistical analyses can compensate for a weak evaluation design that fails to deal with sources of bias to explain away results obtained from a particular treatment.

Furthermore, the selection of testing instruments should be a careful process in which the objectives of the curricular treatment are matched with appropriate sensitivity on the part of an instrument to assess the treatment. The evaluation process should include an analysis of the degree to which the content of any given testing instrument overlaps the content of the curriculum being assessed. This may include an item analysis which matches the objectives of a specific curriculum or curricular sequence to actual test items. Early in the process of developing more student inquiry based curricula, school people loudly complained about the inability of certain standardized tests in use to assess the desired cognitive skills. There had been too little effort to analyze the kinds of skills, knowledges and/or attitudes often contained or left out of standardized tests prior to applying them to assess the new curricula.

Implementation of the Curricular Treatment

Once the treatment or new curriculum is implemented, great care should be taken to follow the design's timetable. Deviations should be noted as well as problems. One of the major problems in using a precise timetable is that if it is found wanting, most teachers will alter a planned approach based upon pupil feedback. This is considered the essence of good teaching. Prearranged implementation timetables may conflict with the obvious fact that there was a blunder in planning and rather than subject pupils to suffer through until the end of the treatment, some modifications may be proposed.

At this juncture the evaluation design may be destroyed because the treatment and its timetable are so significantly altered as to lead to serious questions about both what the treatment was or whether or not under such circumstances the evaluation instruments were still sensitive to pick up the changes even if they were known and specified. If a curriculum experiment involves many teachers, allowing each to "improvise" introduces major complications.

To answer tne dilemma posed in implementation, the curriculum evaluator will have to return to the arena of the practical, the political and the social. If the decisions which can be made with such changes will not be affected by a loss of rigor, the evaluator may decide to make the adjustments, explain them as best he can in qualifying the results, and use the data to make limited changes in the future. If, however, major policy decisions are hinging upon the outcome or may ultimately hinge upon the outcome, the experiment may best be scrapped and begun again rather than run the risk of overgeneralizing upon an imprecise and shaky implementation phase. This is a significant difference between the strategy adopted by an evaluator and one adopted by a researcher. Few research experiments would be scrapped. Failure is regarded as a legitimate outcome in research. Given the overriding importance of decision-making within political jurisdiction of school and school system norms, faculty implementation may doom any repetition in the future and skew decisions for many years thereafter in a negative direction. The curriculum evaluator may well decide under these circumstances not to risk high level decisions on an imprecise data base. However, if there has been adequate planning in the design phase, such situations should be extremely rare. Minor modifications are always part of implementation under normal circumstances. The range of deviations, however, should be known if possible in advance, or specified and recorded as they occur.

Assessment of Results

After the conclusion of the treatment and the post assessment period in which the data are analyzed, the results should be placed into a report which attempts to answer the important questions raised in the design. Such answers should provide curriculum decision-makers with data and suggestions as to ways the curriculum can be made more effective. If the results were not positive or showed no significant difference, the evaluator should have some good notions as to what variables to change to increase the probability that significant differences could occur if specified alterations were made in the future. Lack of adequate attention to specifying the treatment and dealing with design questions may mean that initial inconclusive results one way or another do not help in formulating future curriculum development efforts. If it was not clear what was being tried and how it differed from what would be going on normally, results are meaningless. For this reason adequate attention must be given to descriptions of the comparison groups in a study. Sometimes the beneficial results of curriculum evaluation are not replacing an old curriculum with a new one, but in making adjustments in the old one. Such adjustments are extremely difficult if the old curriculum is not at least as well specified as a potential new one. The degree to which the results of any effort to improve curriculum are meaningful rests largely on adequate specification and design considerations which comprise the initial steps of the curriculum evaluation process.

When Experimental Design
Appears Impossible

The advantages of experimental design should be obvious for the curriculum decision-maker. However, if the developers and evaluators having little leeway in decision-making, are forced to adopt one of a small variation of approaches and possess little control over complicating variables, experimental design may not be a productive way to approach curriculum evaluation.

If, for example, the curriculum design must for all practical purposes be "negotiated" through some central or school curriculum committee comprised of teacher union representatives and administrators who have contractual veto power, there may be little point in trying for design rigor if in trying to control for potential sources of bias the group is alienated. Under these circumstances the evaluator may turn to a nonexperimental approach developed by Malcolm Provus which is based upon precise specification of a school or system intervention with well developed outcomes. (21) The intervention is subdivided into three separate phases called inputs, processes, and outputs. The inputs and processes can be defined in a series of *enabling objectives*. The outputs or outcomes are the desired results of implementing the first two phases. The nonexperimental design is capable of utilizing feedback at all phases to enhance the probability that the desired outcomes will be attained. Also a quasiexperimental design may be possible. In a quasiexperimental design, it is possible to indicate which sources of possible bias may have effected the outcomes. Quasiexperimental design is still rigorous and requires as much time to be spent on definition and procedures as the experimental design.

To return to the example of the school with high pupil turnover, the social studies department may develop a different curriculum which is not only aimed at improving achievement of the transients, but of reducing the level of turnover which may have its origins in school related failure. The Provus model was developed in an actual school situation where it was discovered that the *intra*intervention differences of a treatment (in this case team teaching) were greater than the *inter*differences between schools (those who were not using team teaching) compared.

Any design for curriculum evaluation, whether basically experimental, quasiexperimental, or nonexperimental will depend heavily upon precise statements about the treatment which must include the desired outcomes. While methods may vary and the decision to use various approaches to sampling pragmatically determined by field situations, the essence of rigorous evaluation begins and often ends with definitions of terms and specifications of the possible interaction effects within those interactions. Curriculum evaluation can never be considered a static entity. Evaluation is a relative not an absolute process. It should ideally be conceptualized as a rigorous method of successive approximation by which a more effective school curriculum is eventually derived.

CHAPTER REFERENCES

1. For a good example of means viewed as ends in curriculum design, see J. Cecil Parker and Louis J. Rubin, *Process As Content: Curriculum Design and the Application of Knowledge* (Chicago: Rand McNally, 1966).

2. This approach is best illustrated in Ralph W. Tyler, *Basic Principles of Curriculum and Instruction* (Chicago: University of Chicago Press, 1969).

3. This has been a criticism of the behavioral objective movement. See Arthur W. Combs. *Educational Accountability: Beyond Behavioral Objectives* (Washington, D.C.: Association for Supervision and Curriculum Development, 1972).

4. See Benjamin S. Bloom, J. Thomas Hastings, and George F. Madaus, *Handbook on Formative and Summative Evaluation of Student Learning* (New York: McGraw-Hill, 1971).

5. For a review of these factors, see Norman V. Overly, ed., *The Unstudied Curriculum: Its Impact on Children* (Washington, D.C.: Association for Supervision and Curriculum Development, 1970).

6. For this and other problems in curriculum assessment, see Robert L. Baker, "Curriculum Evaluation," *Review of Educational Research* 39, no. 3 (June 1969): 339-58.

7. The concepts of symmetrical and asymmetrical causal relationships as well as the use of block diagrams to illustrate them have been extrapolated from Hubert M. Blalock, Jr., *Theory Construction* (Englewood Cliffs, New Jersey: Prentice-Hall, 1969), pp. 10-26.

8. Blaine R. Worthen and James R. Sanders, *Educational Evaluation: Theory and Practice* (Worthington, Ohio: Charles A. Jones, 1973), pp 18-39.

9. The classic writing in this area is Donald T. Campbell and Julian C. Stanley, "Experimental and Quasi-Experimental Designs for Research on Teaching," in *Handbook of Research on Teaching,* ed. N. L. Gage (Chicago: Rand McNally, 1963), pp. 171-246.

10. See J. P. Guilford, *Fundamental Statistics in Psychology and Education* (New York: McGraw-Hill, 1956), specifically, "Some Principles of Sampling," pp. 137-142.

11. Worthen and Sanders, *Educational Evaluation,* p. 219.

12. For an excellent review of formulating hypotheses, see Joseph E. Hill and August Kerber, "Problem and Hypothesis," Chapter Three in *Models, Methods, and Analytical Procedures in Education Research* (Detroit: Wayne State University Press, 1967), pp. 23-26.

13. For an example of how sampling can become the source of considerable controversy in research when conclusions may be drawn by one investigator and be challenged by others, see Thomas F. Pettigrew and Robert L. Green, "School Desegregation in Large Cities: A Critique of the Coleman 'White Flight' Thesis," *Harvard Educational Review* 46, no. 1 (February 1976): 1-53.

14. The concept of the curriculum as a spiderweb rather than a staircase is presented in Herbert R. Kohl, *The Open Classroom* (New York: Vintage Books, 1969), p. 54.

15. See Fenwick W. English and Roger A. Kaufman, *Needs Assessment: A Focus for Curriculum Development* (Washington, D.C.: Association for Supervision and Curriculum Development, 1975).

16. The particular word "syntax" was cited in Joseph H. Schwab, "Structure of the Disciplines: Meanings and Significances," in *The Structure of Knowledge and the Curriculum,* eds. G. W. Ford and Lawrence Pugno (Chicago: Rand McNally, 1964), p. 14.

17. See M. L. Rapp, J. G. Root, and G. Sumner, "Some Considerations in the Experimental Design and Evaluation of Educational Innovations," (Santa Monica, California: The Rand Corporation, April 1970).

18. Milbrey W. McLaughlin, *Evaluation and Reform, The Elementary and Secondary Education Act of 1965/*Title 1 (Cambridge, Massachusetts: Ballinger Publishing Co., 1975), pp. 33-41.

19. Ibid., p. 119.

20. The term was taken from Garlie A. Forehand, "Problem Areas in Designing and Implementing Curriculum Evaluation Research," in *Curriculum Evaluation,* ed. D. A. Payne (Lexington, Massachusetts: D. C. Heath Co., 1974), pp. 109-12.

21. See Malcolm Provus, *Discrepancy Evaluation* (Berkeley, California: McCutchan Publishing Corporation, 1971), pp. 183-214.

FOR FURTHER READING

Alkin, Marvin C., and Fitz-Gibbon, Carol T. "Methods and Theories of Evaluating Programs." *Journal of Research and Development in Education* 8, no. 3 (Spring 1975): 2-5. The entire issue is given to articles relating to evaluating educational programs.

Bennis, Warren G. et al., eds. *The Planning of Change,* 3rd ed. New York: Holt, Rinehart and Winston, 1976.

Bushnell, David A., and Rappaport, Donald, eds. *Planned Change in Education: A Systems Approach.* New York: Harcourt Brace Jovanovich, Inc., 1971.

Chaffee, John, Jr., and Clark, James P., eds. *New Dimensions for Educating Youth.* Reston, Virginia: National Association of Secondary School Principals, 1976.

Forbes, Roy H. "Assessing Educational Attainments." *Educational Technology* 16 (June 1976): 27-29.

Iwanicki, Edward F. "Developing a Secondary School Evaluation Program." *NASSP Bulletin* 60 (September 1976): 71-76.

Leles, Sam, and Cruise, Robert J. "Improving Educational Evaluations by Appropriate Use of Knowledge, Product and Performance Learnings." *Educational Technology* 16 (January 1976): 41-43.

Payne, David A., ed. *Curriculum Evaluation.* Lexington, Massachusetts: D. C. Heath and Company, 1974.

Thompson, Ralph. "General Criteria for Curriculum Analysis." *Peabody Journal of Education* 52, no. 4 (July 1975): 247-51.

Zais, Robert S. *Curriculum: Principles and Foundations.* New York: Thomas Y. Crowell Co., 1976. (See Chapter 16, "Evaluation.")

14 Charting the
Course for
Curriculum
Change

There are many ways to change curriculum which stem from various assumptions about what curriculum is or should be. The actual curriculum of the secondary schools is the "what" or "content" of the educational process. That is, after the schooling experience, the sum composite of experiences, skills, knowledges and attitudes which secondary students possess represents the "real" curriculum. On the other hand, the "paper" curriculum, the one that is developed and debated, the one that is planned for and changed, is an abstracted description of those desired composite experiences. In approaching the development of curriculum and the process of changing it, the curriculum developer must be aware of his or her own biases and approaches and must be able to recognize the shape, scope, strengths and weaknesses of the existing secondary school curriculum. (1)

Common Faulty Assumptions about Curriculum Change

Six common assumptions regarding the secondary school curriculum and curriculum change should be dealt with so as to avoid reinforcing unproductive efforts to change the curriculum.

The Secondary Curriculum Can Be Developed Separately from the Student

It is all too common that professionals begin developing curriculum without really considering their own assumptions about what the curriculum is or should be. Sitting down and writing course descriptions or detailed lists of concepts to be introduced which will then be "covered" in some mysterious manner with an unidentified audience runs the risk of producing irrelevant and perhaps even harmful experiences for secondary school students. Too often students are considered as impassive recipients and relegated to a passive place in the planning process at both the conceptual and practical levels of curriculum development. Some subject matter specialists are so enamored of their independent disciplines that they forget that live human beings who come to the secondary learning experience with varying states of motivation, with varying skills, backgrounds and understandings, may not be so enamored. Curriculum which is developed apart from the consideration of the learners runs the risk of building in student failure and discipline problems. This approach risks relegating the teaching-learning process to levels of memorization and superficial exposure to complex understandings in which the learner as a participant and active organizer of knowledge is bypassed.

However, there may be those neoromanticists who feel that any paper curriculum represents an artificial intrusion into the teaching-learning exchange. The dichotomy between the learner and external knowledge was cited by John Dewey as a false separation of reality. Dewey, wrote "Just as two points define a straight line, so the present standpoint of the child and the facts and truths of studies define instruction. It is continuous reconstruction, moving from the child's present experience out into that represented by the organized bodies of truth that we call studies." In fact, Dewey was critical of those who possessed disdain for formal curricula. Again in *The Child and the Curriculum* he noted,

> The child is expected to 'develop' this or that fact or truth out of his own mind . . . Nothing can be developed from nothing; nothing but the crude can be developed out of the crude—and this is what surely happens when we throw the child back upon his achieved self as a finality, and invite him to spin new truths of nature or of conduct out of that. It is certainly as futile to expect a child to evolve a universe out of his own mere mind as it is for a philosopher to attempt that task. (2)

The moment a real teacher in a classroom attempts to implement that curriculum the students and their reactions become the central means to determine its success. Too many secondary curriculum guides, recommended lessons or classroom strategies have died prematurely because the curriculum developers assumed that learners were no more than receivers of information and would respond on cue to attain the goals called for. Millions of dollars have been spent creating curriculum guides that are relegated to closets and shelves in professional libraries and have little or nothing to do with what is really going on in actual secondary school classrooms. Teachers have a way of dealing with irrelevant materials. They are simply ignored. Curriculum which is considered largely as uniform "exposures" of information are usually the ones most often of little assistance to classroom practitioners. There are several approaches to secondary curriculum development which appear to promote the student as a passive and silent partner. Some of these are highlighted below.

The Classical Studies Model of Curriculum

This model of curriculum rests upon the assumption that what was good for the best of the ancient civilizations is appropriate for the education of the young in modern civilizations. The argument is that the studies developed in classical civilizations such as the Greeks and Romans represent the "culled wisdom" of the ancients over thousands of years, and have proven to be the stuff from which intellectual greatness has been produced. (3)(4) Therefore, the curriculum consists largely of gathering together such classical studies and being sure that students are well grounded in them. The rationale for Latin in the school curriculum often was defended in this manner. (5)

The Perfect Man Model of Curriculum

This model of curriculum begins with a portrait of what the "ideal" human being represents. Sketches of homo sapiens' intellectual abilities, sensitivities and differences to other mammals abound. (6) The argument is made that since man is political, politics must be part of his education. The use of verbal expression and symbols are also uniquely human and hence the curriculum must contain reference to these abilities.

The Super Curriculum Model

This approach to curriculum development begins with the advocate analyzing the current secondary school disciplines and attempting to build a more logical and rational curriculum, or a "super" curriculum. Interrelationships between and among the disciplines are carefully explored to obtain maximum "balance" as to what they may consist of if realigned. Once such a curriculum is constructed, it has merely to be organized and implanted in the school in some logical sequence. (7)

All three of these approaches are found in secondary schools today. They often exist in unstated assumptions or overt "philosophies of education" which are preambles to secondary curriculum guides. They all suffer from a number of common weaknesses. These are:

Knowledge Is Considered Static. The most valuable knowledge has been sifted and is therefore inert. It can therefore be set apart from dynamic interchange or questioning from students. Knowledge and reality can be separated. Knowledge can be segregated and compartmentalized.

Learning Is Memorization. If knowledge is inert and compartmentalized, learning can be reduced to memorizing what has become static. The learner is inevitably passive for all modes of instruction. (8)

The Model Cannot Be Improved. The assumptions of the curriculum model are not open to question. The major problems associated with each approach are those involved with implementation not definition.

The model cannot therefore be improved because it is not correctable as it is set apart from the consequences of its implementation. If learners are not learning the cause is either poor teaching, lack of intellience or motivation on the part of learners or faulty materials or environment. Such models do not depend upon feedback. They are impervious to their own results.

None of the above models are morally "wrong," That is, there is nothing inherently incorrect about using them. However, the use of a static curriculum model rests upon assumptions which lead to certain effects upon learners and teachers and in turn helps determine what kinds of places schools will be. If the model is the cause of those consequences and educators are not happy with them, no model should be above reexamination and possible change if necessary. If a model leads to a sterile curriculum which produces failure and boredom in the schools, allows school graduates to acquire skills, knowledges, and attitudes which are of little personal worth or of highly dubious social utility, it should be severely questioned. (9) Furthermore, the effects of using any particular model in the schools by which curriculum is developed should be able to lead to improvement in the set of assumptions which undergird the model itself. But the curriculum cannot be improved if the model upon which it has been developed is above question.

Curriculum in the secondary school which assumes students are passive respondents as a total definition of the role of the student is denying to those learners the acquisition of a given range of inquiry skills and attitudes. These simply cannot be achieved if learners are conceptualized as passive. It is undeniably true that certain curricular skills, knowledges and attitudes require some pupil acquiescence, but others require an active and vigorous dissenting and questioning posture. An approach or model of curriculum development which precludes learners from being prime considerations is simply incapable of producing a full range of skills, knowledges and attitudes which are necessary for students to live successfully in a modern world.

The Secondary Curriculum Can Be Developed Separately from the Teacher

The shock upon the American public of the Russian Sputnik in the late 1950s loosened a barrage of criticism and approbrium upon the schools. The result was the allocation of millions of federal dollars for language labs, and the upgrading of the science and math curricula in the secondary schools. Reexamination of the curriculum by scholars and experts resulted in massive changes in approach and methodology. The secondary curriculum was reshaped, shifted from deductive to inductive, from computational to conceptual emphasis, and done in a series of sweeping reforms by panels of experts and national curriculum writers. New textbooks in math required large scale inservice training.

While some of the curricular reforms did involve teachers as participants, too many reforms considered teachers separate from the central matter of curriculum improvement. To improve the curriculum, the experts put aside the teacher as the principal implementor and attempted to write curricula which were "teacher proof." The role of the teacher as the central translator in the classroom was bypassed. The notion was naive. The teacher remains the central figure in the instructional processes within the schools, then and now. While many organizational schemes have attempted to alter the role of the teacher, and unprecedented numbers of aides and other personnel entered the schools, no plan has as yet been adopted which seriously changes the role of the classroom teachers. The curriculum can be developed solely by outside experts, apart from consideration of teachers, but to do so contradicts what teachers are expected to do in the schools. With the growing power of teachers in curriculum decision-making via collective bargaining the "real" curriculum must involve "real" teachers. While the teacher is not necessarily the only person essential to curriculum development, the curriculum can't be much better than each individual teacher collectively in the secondary school.

Curriculum Development in the Secondary School Is Solely a Professional Concern

There was a time in the development of the secondary schools that citizens more directly controlled the curriculum. Beginning with a curriculum composed of Bible readings, spelling, grammar and rudimentary ciphering which most citizens understood, the curriculum steadily became the domain of college requirements, national panels, aggressive university presidents' recommendations, special lobbying organizations, textbook companies, educators, professional associations, testing companies, ex-admirals, and state legislators.

Stung by developments in collective bargaining which has effectively shut them out of the schools, various parental organizations have sprung up to reinsert their viewpoints into the curriculum decision-making process. Many professionals at the local level have regarded meaningful citizen input on a scale from mild apathy to contemptuous disdain. Occasionally, such professional attitudes have contributed to considerable controversy as in the case of the West Virginia textbook conflict. (10).

The development of the national Gallup Polls of Education (11) have revealed that the public has a great deal of concern about what is happening or not happening in the schools, but that an understanding of what is going on may not be very extensive or detailed. (12) Parents have shown great dismay over declining national test scores in the basic skills and have proposed a variety of remedies. Curriculum development cannot leave out citizen opinion. Given the contemporary structure of decision-making in American schools with mandates from state legislatures to teach about the evils of communism, safe driving skills, ecology, career education, etc., no professional educator can ignore the role of citizens in the curriculum development process. The schools are not the sole domain of professionals and what they do is not above scrutiny or reproach whether it be from elected boards of education who may require certain courses of study or books to be used or abandoned, to the United States Congress which passes laws forbidding the use of materials, courses or programs which are sexist in outlook. Unless citizens are brought into the curriculum development process more directly in partnership with professionals, the continued trend of hostile groups of parental antagonists may further splinter public support of the schools. For professionals to function properly within the schools, a new consensus of the role of the school and what should be going on in them must be fashioned. Professionals in the secondary schools who continue to maintain an elitist perspective will create barriers to the creation of that consensus.

Curriculum Development Is an End unto Itself

Another faulty assumption regarding curriculum development in the secondary school has been that it has been visualized as an activity in itself rather than as an activity aimed at accomplishing specific objectives. Curriculum development has not been conceptualized as creating configurations of time, space, materials and human interaction. Instead, curriculum has been "forced" to fit into the existing time frame, and teacher pupil roles in departmentalized schools. Once the curriculum was developed it was deemed adequate and often it was very hard if not impossible to ascertain how good it really was. Imagine an administrative or teaching staff trying to discover whether mathematics curriculum package A or curriculum package B was better? What would serve as the criteria of adequacy? One method might be to develop a check list of desired characteristics such as the one used below:

Checklist for Comparing Math Curricula

Criteria	Mathematics Curricula A		Mathematics Curricula B	
	Yes	No	Yes	No
1. The curriculum was pilot tested prior to full-scale development.	___	___	___	___
2. The package helps the teacher identify specific math skills to be learned in a logical sequence of instruction.	___	___	___	___
3. The package provides for alternative procedures for students who have failed to understand critical concepts or skills.	___	___	___	___
4. Pre and post tests are provided for all skills and concepts.	___	___	___	___
5. The package includes some sample lesson plans and lesson strategies.	___	___	___	___
6. Examples are included which indicate how test data can be used to develop an individual pupil math achievement profile for each student.	___	___	___	___
7. Recommended bibliographies indicate where teachers can find additional information.	___	___	___	___
8. The packages are clearly illustrated with examples students can understand.	___	___	___	___
9. The package can easily be adapted to team teaching and flexible scheduling.	___	___	___	___
10. The package is accompanied with a variety of audiovisual materials.	___	___	___	___

While one curriculum package may get a "superior" rating on such criteria, do students learn more or better with the same one? The usual procedure of using some form of standardized test may show that both are *inadequate* or show no significant difference. The only way a curriculum package may be shown to be "better" in terms of results is to have a list of validated and specific pupil performance objectives developed by which any curriculum package may be examined, selected, and evaluated. Curriculum developed without such objectives is considered an end activity in itself. Any curriculum should be perceived as a means to an end, and the end (pupil performance) should be specified to the point where relevant decisions can be made regarding the desirability of any type of curriculum package available. In none are available the beginnings have been set for writing a locally adapted one, or developing one from scratch. Pupil performance objectives provide the base for determining the adequacy of a locally developed curriculum or an adapted one from a national curriculum publisher.

Curricular Reliability Is the Same as Curricular Validity

The advent and wide scale utilization of behavioral objectives in curriculum development has brought with it some confusion regarding the difference between measurability and validity. As teachers and curriculum developers began shaping instructional objectives into behavioral terms, the exercise was deemed one in which curricular indices became validated. Experience has shown that almost any kind of experience can be made "behavioral," and that the validity of an objective is not determined by whether it is measurable, but by the match between the desired outcome for students and the degree to which the curriculum is able to produce those outcomes.

Matters of curricular reliability are concerned with consistency, continuity, scope, sequence and balance. Questions such as, does the stated curriculum appear to possess characteristics of some logical sequence of presentation? pertain to issues of reliability. Questions which pertain to whether or not the "content" of the curriculum is adequate or whether some other content would better deliver the expected outcomes involve the question of curricular validity.

Gathering some teachers and administrators together to write behavioral objectives for social studies once every afternoon for a semester is an exercise in reliability at best and may have nothing to do with improving the validity of the social studies curriculum. Trivia and nonsense can be made "measurable." Questions as to the selection of learning experiences and which ones are better than others revolve around issues of curricular validity. Too often curriculum developers have been solely concerned with measurability and have erroneously assumed that what was being made "behavioral" was valid. In the development of curriculum both reliability and validity are important considerations.

The Integrity of the Existing Curricular Disciplines Is Valid

Curriculum in the schools has been influenced by mandates of state legislatures, federal funding, the local movement towards minicourses, scholars working within established disciplines, research sponsored by private foundations, etc. In this process the integrity and validity of the separate curricular disciplines has too often been held inviolate. The secondary school is consistently adding such disciplines to the curriculum. Whereas once social studies appeared adequate as a curricular umbrella, one finds today in the secondary curriculum courses on ecology, consumerism, psychology and economics. Rarely are disciplines which are "added on" attacked or old ones questioned, or alternative schemes of curricular consolidation proposed. The splitting of the school curriculum into compartments has added to the isolation of teaching staff and made curricular reform immensely more difficult. As specialization and compartmentalization proliferate within the secondary school curriculum, problems of balance are often obliterated with requirements and electives in the newly added disciplines. Lost is the somewhat common sense notion that life and reality fail to possess such clean delineations. Confining inquiry within such disciplines may produce a false sense of security on the part of secondary school students. Real problems in the real world have a proclivity to cut across such disciplines. Specialization may look good in course catalogs or as public relations gimmicks, but may be unnecessary if compared to external criteria which required the identification of the *actual* skills, knowledge and attitudes required by students to survive and contribute to our ciety.

The faulty assumptions or fallacies discussed in this section have been that:

The secondary curriculum can be developed separately from the student.

The secondary curriculum can be developed separately from the teacher.

Curriculum development in the secondary school is solely a professional concern.

Curriculum development is an end unto itself.

Curricular reliability is the same as curricular validity.

The integrity of the existing curricular disciplines is valid.

Teachers and curriculum workers who attempt to bring about curriculum change on the basis of such assumptions can only reinforce present unproductive efforts to match curriculum content with the needs of students in a changing society.

An Approach to Curriculum Development

An approach to curriculum development and change appears to be required which does not support any of the previous strategies cited in order to avoid their limitations. Such an approach must not only recognize that reality is fluid and moving, that society is in a state of evolution and change, but also that assumptions of a permanent base of knowledge cannot produce a curriculum which effectively bridges the gap between the school and the society in which it functions. Every discipline, fact, theory, concept and/or attitude embraced by the school and embodied in its curriculum should be periodically and systematically examined.

A second criterion for an approach to curriculum development is peculiarly a problem of management. Curriculum not only encompasses the content of learning but also relates to the ability of the secondary school or school system to assemble its resources to maximize the impact of a chosen curriculum configuration. The shaping of curriculum is therefore a central aspect of the administration of the secondary school. As such, administration or management is concerned with resource acquisition and resource allocation. Allocation criteria relate to the idea that resources are limited. Therefore, priorities regarding allocation must be established. (13)

Educational institutions have been troubled with resource allocation inasmuch as concrete organizational objectives have rarely existed for schools. The lack of specific objectives for the schools has also resulted in poor supervision of personnel and the development of insulation between administration and teaching staffs. (14)

Some approaches to curriculum development bypass these dilemmas by ignoring them. The development of behavioral objectives within the separate disciplines is encouraged as an exercise for teachers to posit specific instructional objectives for the classroom. This process was outlined in some detail in chapter three. Curriculum development must also be envisioned as a method for shaping the activities of an entire secondary school. Until and unless curricular objectives are melded together with management requirements there can be little effective planning for the allocation of the resources of the school. Recently a very promising model has been tried in a number of locations in the country which establishes curricular objectives as institutional objectives. They are stated as performance objectives but function differently. The process has been called *needs assessment.* (15) The idea is to develop a validated set of pupil performance objectives which will serve as a set of specifications to examine and change the curriculum. Any specific curricular configuration can be assessed against such objectives as a measure of its effectiveness in reaching them. Curriculum is clearly a means to an end with this approach. Classroom performance objectives may then be derived from the statements about desired pupil outcomes on an institutional level. Pupil performance objectives then serve several useful functions. Stated as institutional outcomes they form the base for an evaluation of the current curriculum configuration (see chapter thirteen on evaluation). They also serve as a focal point in the derivation of classroom instructional objectives.

Needs assessment is a student centered, social survival approach to curriculum development. It assumes that the production of a written curriculum is a constant process of successive approximation of integrating the student and his or her individual needs with the demands placed upon the schools for general social improvement. These are ultimately translated into specific subject matter.

The process does not assume a "model" human being to exist nor assume the priority of classical studies or some other "ultimate" curricular theory or construct. It is based upon the assumption that the students as secondary school consumers or clients, the community, and the professional staff are equal partners in the development of institutional pupil performance objectives by which curriculum is then assessed, developed, or changed.

Preliminary Steps of a Needs Assessment

Needs assessment per se is *curriculumless,* that is, it is a generic procedure outside of any specific curricular discipline or curriculum which will develop external criteria for determining curricular validity. The first step is the development of educational goals.

Educational Goals

Educational goals are abstract statements of pupil behaviors stated in nonperformance terms. These are examples of educational goals:

The student will learn to become a responsible citizen in a democratic society;
The student will acquire the values of inquiry and curiosity;
The student will learn to appreciate and respect the rights of others;

One of the problems in stating educational goals is that means and ends are often confused. *Means* are ways schools or teachers reach the desired educational outcomes. The following are examples of means:

individualized instruction
bilingual education
discussion and debate
modular scheduling
accreditation
counseling and guidance
curriculum development
differentiated staffing
audiovisual materials
educational television (ETV)
minicourses
personalized education
open classrooms
federal projects

Contrary to some professional opinion, *individualized instruction* is not an outcome of the educational program, but a means to achieve specified ends or objectives. The following statement is a fairly typical example of the confusion of means and ends at a secondary school. The confusion occurs in a "philosophy of education" of West High School. It appears in a mythical student handbook. Examine the statement closely. Note where means and ends (outcomes) have been confused.

The Philosophy of Education at West High School

We at West High School believe in the individual dignity of each and every student. We believe that the schools should provide for the individual differences of each student so that each may become a functioning and contributing citizen to our democratic nation.

We believe students should leave West High School embued with a spirit of curiosity and be skilled in methods of inquiry in the natural and social sciences. We believe that students must become dispassionate observers of our society in order to form objective judgments of our society's needs.

We know that students must practice democracy and therefore student government is more than a name. Students are encouraged to practice dissent and to express their opinions in oral and written form in the student newspaper and in debate.

West High School is a humanistic and humane place. We encourage pupil diversity and artistic expression. We believe in the disciplined and orderly process of learning and of mutual respect between teachers and students. We practice individualized instruction via independent learning and study within the advanced placement programs. Students must earn a living so our occupational and vocational educational programs are active and vital, an integral part of student life at West.

West High School is more than a name. It is the embodiment of our highest ideals, our release of the growing human spirit, and the development of those essential human characteristics that have epitomized the march of civilization.

Now compare the following facts gleaned from West High School:

The dropout rate has been at least 50 percent between grades nine and twelve;

The vocational and occupational education classes have at least 60-70 percent minority enrollments; several protests have been received about this "involuntary" tracking from NAACP and CORE as well as neighborhood associations during the last two years;

A state mandated reading test shows that 48 percent of the tenth grade is below average in reading skills compared to the rest of the state;

There is no student newspaper because of a lack of faculty support and student interest; students are apathetic about participating in student government;

Faculty turnover has been between 15-20 percent over the last three years;

A followup study of West graduates indicates that at least 42 percent felt they were unprepared for the world of work and had little knowledge about contemporary social issues such as welfare and abortion;

A study of students suspended from West due to truancy, fighting, and smoking in school indicated that twice as many black students were expelled as white students for the same infractions.

West is apparently failing to meet its own philosophy, or is it? The philosophy is not the sounding board for curricular revision or school reform. From the philosophy how would one know if enough individualized instruction had occurred, or if the amount or type was related to being a humane place? How would the school, its staff or community know if students had left the school "imbued with a spirit of curiosity?" What evidence will indicate that those same students are "skilled in methods of inquiry in the natural and social sciences?"

The confusion of means and ends, the ambiguity and lack of specific indices for determining the goals of the school make most statements like West's philosophy an irrelevant piece of educational prose. Another school tried shaping objectives this way: To help each student discover that he or she is a worthwhile person in his or her own right. However, if the school wanted to know if it had attained the goal, what would it assess, the help or the acquisition of "being a worthwhile person?" Typically curricular goals are stated either as *exposures* or *processes*. An educational goal stated as exposure would be as follows:

> The student will take three semesters of French;
> The student will be exposed to the beauty of various literary genres;
> The student will come to see that race and place have had a significant impact upon school desegregation patterns.

Educational goals stated as processes would say something like:

> The student will engage in a debate of significant issues;
> The student will interact with ecological principles in a natural setting at the lake;
> The student will experience the joys of constructing a Civil War diorama;
> The student will discover that certain language patterns have come to be preferred in various social situations.

Very rarely are educational goals stated as *outcomes*. Educational goals stated as *outcomes* would look something like:

> The student will be able to list the five ways physical health can be maintained;
> The student will be able to fill out a job application with no errors in spelling or punctuation;
> The student will be able to read the editorial page and indicate which statements are opinion and which are fact with at least 80 percent accuracy.

Those who argue that the process or exposure is the product should think through again what that process will enable the learner to do that he or she might not have been able to do, think, or feel prior to engaging in the process. It is that outcome that is desired.

Objectives can be written within curricular disciplines for a needs assessment within a particular subject area. For example, a needs assessment can be conducted within the field of mathematics, social studies, physical education or science. However, if this is done, the creation of external criteria by which to ascertain if those independent disciplines should be changed or merged is lost. A needs assessment within mathematics assumes that math as a discipline should be maintained, and within social studies, that subject area should be preserved. Possible reorganization of the secondary school curriculum can become a reality if those conducting a needs assessment will think outside of the traditional subject area disciplines. One of the best ways to do this is to conceptualize the educational goals as statement of survival, minimum competencies or essentials that each student should acquire before she or he graduates from high school. In this way the goals function as a kind of educational "floor." Such goals should not attempt to act as a ceiling or lid upon educational achievement. Such goals as "To educate each student to achieve her or his potential," are blatantly unrealistic and assume that it is within the power of educational officials to somehow *know* what the potential of another human being might actually be. Attempts by schools to deal with issues related to determining human potential have been the source of criticism that schools are racist and sexist social sorting institutions. (16)

Secondary curriculum developers should begin framing statements of educational goals outside of the disciplines of the school. After such statements are reaffirmed by the three basic constituencies to be involved, i.e., professionals, community, and students, they can be translated into performance statements and located within the school's disciplines if the decision is made to maintain the existing curricular disciplines of the secondary school.

Goals can be created any number of ways by brainstorming or by going to existing sources. (17) One way of starting is to ask, "What are the things a student must possess upon leaving school to survive and contribute to our society?" Some typical responses might be:

> He or she should have at least one saleable skill in order to earn a living and avoid welfare;
>
> She or he should be able to communicate effectively, orally and in writing;
>
> She or he should have a working knowledge of how to participate as an effective citizen at the local, state, and national levels;
>
> She or he should be able to engage in a variety of recreational and cultural activities which are self-fulfilling and maintain emotional and physical health;
>
> He or she should be prepared to engage in learning as a life long process and understand the dynamics of formal and informal learning.

It can be seen that such broad goals are not couched within any specific curricular area but represent composite learnings which are clusters of skills, knowledges, concepts and attitudes which may be acquired and reinforced in many disciplines in the secondary school. Once a list of educational goals which are statements of *outcomes* of the secondary schooling process are framed, the curricular developers are ready for the next step.

Goal Validation

Validating educational goals refers merely to seeking consensus that they are acceptable at some agreed upon level with the three basic referent groups: professionals, community, and students. This can be accomplished at the same time step three is performed.

Goal Ranking

The educational goals should be sorted into some ordinal relationship or priority. While all of the goals may be important, they are all not equally important given a fixed level of resources provided the school for secondary education. For adequate planning and utilization of resources to occur, it is necessary to establish the level of priorities or the expected outcomes of any human enterprise. While the public may be surprised or feel uncomfortable about ranking outcomes, it should be explained to them that administrators and teachers are continually forced by the boundaries of the school system to make such choices. Involving parents, citizens, and students in the process merely establishes from the beginning the public priorities of all three groups so that a working level of administrative consensus can be established. At the time the three groups are involved in goal validation, they can rank the goals as well. In one school district a third step was added, that of validating the *goal indicators* along with the goals. A sample format for performing all three operations is shown on pages 336-40 (18) It is important that equal weighting be given to the ranking of each group so as not to skew the results in favor of the opinions of any one group. The results of one such community survey are shown in Diagram 14-1.

Translation of Goals into Performance or Operational Objectives

The educational goals must eventually be translated into performance or operational terms and conditions. This can be accomplished in a variety of ways, by farming out the work to individuals, or having teachers and/ or administrators work in teams. Parents, students, and other interested citizens could be involved, but many may find the terminology and underlying educational concepts formidable barriers to full-fledged participation at this point.

In translating a goal into a performance objective, a middle step has been developed. This step is illustrated below in the community goal survey. Goal indicators are merely benchmarks of what conditions would prevail if the goal were to be attained. Another way of stating it is, "What would be the prevailing conditions for learners if this goal were attained by them?" Examples are shown in the educational goal ranking

---

Community Survey of Educational Goals

Part I: Goal Ranking

Directions: Read each educational goal and then indicate by marking how important you think it should be in *one* of the three rankings possible for each educational goal.

YOUR RANKING OF GOAL IMPORTANCE			EDUCATIONAL GOAL
High	Medium	Low	*By the time a student graduates from our high school he or she should have learned:*
			1. How to get a job and/or how to go on to complete college.
			2. To appreciate and participate in a rich and varied varied cultural life.
			3. That he or she is a worthwhile person in his or her own right.
			4. The basic ideas and ways of thinking within the sciences and social sciences.
			5. The basic skills of communication and reasoning necessary to live a full and productive life.
			6. How to participate as an effective citizen and consumer in our society.
			7. To develop competence in the process of developing values in order to appreciate and respect the rights of others.
			8. The ability to maintain mental, physical and emotional health.
			9. How to engage in learning as a life long process.
			10. (Write in your choice if not shown above and then enter its rank)_____

Part II: Measurement Indicators
(What We Will Test)

Directions: After ranking the goals in Part I, now indicate which (one or more) of the many ways the goal could be measured as learned by students would be acceptable to you.

Your Opinion				GOAL 1: How to get a job and/or how to go on to complete college by being able to:
Agree			Disagree	
High	Medium	Low		
				A. Know a variety of work opportunities available.
				B. Have the necessary employable skills to get a job and the work habits to keep a job.
				C. Apply and be accepted to college of his or her choice.
				D. Enroll and complete further occupational training.
				E. Understand the dignity of all forms of human labor.
Agree			Disagree	GOAL 2: To appreciate and participate in a rich and varied cultural life by being able to:
High	Medium	Low		
				A. Understand and value a variety of artistic, musical, literary and dramatic forms as methods of human expression.
				B. Locate and use cultural resources such as libraries, museums and historical sites.
				C. Engage in a variety of cultural activities to express himself or herself.
Agree			Disagree	GOAL 3: That he or she is a worthwhile person in his or her own right by being able to:
High	Medium	Low		
				A. Feel confident about going into new fields.
				B. See himself or herself positively.
				C. Cope with criticism and accept it if valid.
				D. Use both successes and failures as learning experiences.
				E. Set realistic personal goals.

Your Opinion				GOAL 4: *The basic ideas and ways of*
Agree			Disagree	*thinking within the sciences*
High	Medium	Low		*and social sciences by being able to:*
				A. Show knowledge of the basic methods of inquiry in each field.
				B. Develop skill in handling the basic ideas and terms within each subject and understand how they developed historically.
				C. Understand the scientific method and the impact of scientific advances.
				D. Show knowledge of the family as a basic unit of our society.
Agree			Disagree	GOAL 5: *The basic skills of communication and reasoning necessary to live a full and productive life by being able to:*
High	Medium	Low		A. Read with comprehension, speak and write clearly.
				B. Understand and be able to perform basic mathematical operations.
				C. Think creatively and critically in order to analyze problems.
Agree			Disagree	GOAL 6: *How to participate as an effective citizen and consumer in our society by being able to:*
High	Medium	Low		A Show an understanding of our legal, economic and political processes.
				B. Explain our historical heritage as a democratic people.
				C. Participate actively in the life of the community and nation.
				D. Show an understanding of national and international problems.

Agree			Disagree	GOAL 7: *To develop the competence in the process of developing values in order to appreciate and respect the rights of others by being able to:*
High	Medium	Low		
				A. Understand and compare his or her values with others.
				B. Understand and relate to other social, racial, religious groups.
				C. Live peaceably in a community with groups possessing many values.
				D. Avoid imposing his or her own values upon others.
				E. Appreciate and use the common standards of social courtesy.

Your Opinion				GOAL 8: *The ability to maintain mental, physical and emotional health by being able to:*
Agree			Disagree	
High	Medium	Low		
				A. Show knowledge of good health habits to maintain physical/mental health.
				B. Show knowledge of problems caused by drug addiction and other harmful activities upon physical and emotional well-being.
				C. Show knowledge of public health standards and practices.
				D. Participate cooperatively in team sport activities.
				E. Understand when competition or cooperation are called for.
				F. Show knowledge of general safety principles and practices.

Agree			Disagree	GOAL 9: *How to engage in learning as a life long process by being able To:*
High	Medium	Low		
				A. Know where to obtain information on most problems.
				B. Participate and seek a variety of learning activities.

Part III: Open Response

Directions: Feel free in your own words to indicate how you think the schools may be improved and in what areas the schools are doing a good job. Please use the space below.

What is your overall opinion of the schools? _____ _____
High   Medium

_____ _____
Low   Undecided

survey instrument for each goal. Of course, goal indicators are not performance objectives. For a goal to become a performance objective it must possess certain features. These characteristics are: 1. the goal must be translated to indicate what overt behaviors (acts) the student is to exhibit to show she or he has learned or mastered the intended or stated outcome; 2. the criterion of judgment should be indicated by which the student performance is to be assessed; and 3. each objective should include a standard or acceptable level of performance indicated. An example of the translation process is shown below.

The Translation of an Educational Goal into an Institutionalized, Operational Objective

Goal: Upon graduation the student will be able to obtain a job and/or go on to college.

Goal Indicator: The student should be able to know a variety of work opportunities available.

Performance Objectives: 1. The student should be able to list five standard sources of information about job opportunities without help, e.g. employment agencies, want-ads, government publications; 2. The student should be able to locate one job in each of five given occupation categories on a want-ad page of a local newspaper. (Four of the five must be located within five minutes each). 3. The student should be able to sort fifty jobs on a given list into ten correct job categories according to basic skills required with 60 percent accuracy, or 4. The student, when given five different jobs,

Diagram 14-1

SAMPLE GOAL RANKING RESULTS BY STAFF, COMMUNITY AND STUDENTS

Total Rank	Total Mean	Education Goal	Community Response					Staff Response					Student Response				
			Rank	Mean	% high	% med	% low	Rank	Mean	% high	% med	% low	Rank	Mean	% high	% med	% low
1	2.81	The basic skills of communication and reasoning necessary to live a full and productive life.	1	2.88	88	11	—	1	2.82	83	16	1	2	2.55	60	35	5
2	2.70	How to get a job and/or how to go on to complete college.	2	2.69	75	20	5	6	2.64	69	27	4	1	2.77	78	21	1
3	2.61	That he or she is a worthwhile person in his or her own right.	3	2.59	68	22	10	2	2.81	83	14	3	3	2.54	58	39	3
4	2.57	To develop competence in the process of developing values in order to appreciate and respect the rights of others.	4	2.58	67	24	9	4	2.66	69	27	4	5	2.47	53	42	5
5	2.52	The ability to maintain mental, physical, and emotional health.	6	2.50	60	30	10	3	2.68	69	30	1	4	2.48	58	33	9
6	2.49	How to engage in learning as a life long process.	5	2.55	64	26	10	9	2.53	59	36	5	6	2.21	34	53	13
7	2.44	How to participate as an effective citizen and consumer in our society.	8	2.46	55	37	8	5	2.65	69	26	5	7	2.20	62	31	7
8	2.43	The basic ideas and ways of thinking within the sciences and social sciences.	7	2.47	58	38	4	7	2.55	60	34	6	8	2.19	31	58	11
9	2.29	To appreciate and participate in a rich and varied cultural life.	9	2.27	41	45	14	8	2.53	55	44	1	9	2.13	28	57	15

including two selected by the student and their requirements as listed in *The Occupational Outlook Handbook,* will be able to compare her or his skills with those required by each job, and express the comparison in a written paragraph for each. Using these paragraphs he or she should be able to rank his or her probability of success in each job on an ordinal scale. Criterion: internal logic and consistency of three of the five paragraphs. (19)

Beginning with a set of ten educational goals, the scope of expansion of the goals would be approximately forty to fifty goal indicators which might ultimately become 150 or 200 performance objectives. Once such objectives are developed, refined and validated, the secondary school possesses the external criteria to judge the adequacy of its curriculum, ascertain curricular balance, and assess the power of the various disciplines, singly or in combinations, to produce the desired outcomes.

A needs assessment is nothing more than the comparison of future desired learner behaviors to the present level of learner behaviors. The difference is a *need* or *gap*. Most secondary schools do not possess adequate definitions of future desired pupil performance in assessable terms. The usual procedure is to develop a philosophy of education which attempts to fulfill this purpose. It has already been shown how such statements do not serve as a sufficient focus to develop or assess the curriculum of the secondary school.

The secondary school, particularly the high school, sets the exit standard for a school system. These are translated into performance terms at grade twelve and then throughout the rest of the system. Usually, the organizational breakpoints are the final grades (or years) in each of the major buildings within a school system. A K-6-3-3 system would have exit objectives for grade twelve, nine and six. A K-5-3-4 pattern would have exit objectives for twelve, eight and five. These breakpoints serve as periods in which a school system formally assesses learner gaps (needs) and organizes and reorganizes its curriculum, staffing, and allocation of materials to close identified gaps (or meet the needs).

Comparison of Exit Standards to Actual
Pupil Performance

Once the exit standards have been established and validated (by consensus), the actual process of comparing them to present pupil performance is initiated. This means that the curriculum development process involves the acquisition of and use of test data, anecdotal information at the school level which is pertinent to assess student and school performance. Such anecdotal data may be in the form of truancy rates, dropout statistics, referral figures for disciplinary reasons, percentages of certain books and materials checked out from the school library, analysis of grades, etc. (20) The actual comparison and the discrepancy are then constructed into a list of gaps.

Development of the Gap List

The development of the initial gap or needs list completes the needs assessment cycle. A sample gap list and how it is derived is illustrated as follows:

Institutional Performance Objective: At least 75 percent of the graduates of the high school should be able to sort numbered statements in a newspaper editorial into two categories, statements of opinion or interpretation with statements of fact with 80 percent accuracy.

Current (Assessed) Performance: When presented with an editorial from the New York Times 63 percent of the graduates were able to sort such statements with 80 percent accuracy.

Documented Gap: 12 percent discrepancy of graduates.

Institutional Performance Objective: At least 90 percent of the high school graduates should be able to list the following information from an electric bill, a telephone bill, and one other standard credit invoice (e.g. gasoline company)

the last payment made;

the payment now due;

the rate of interest charged;

the amount of interest charged;

the services being charged with 65 percent accuracy.

Current Performance: When given several such samples in math classes, only 78 percent were able to list the required information with at least 65 percent accuracy.

Documented Gap: 18 percent discrepancy of graduates.

Each objective is merely compared to indicators of current pupil performance. The sources may be extrapolated from existing standardized test data and the more detailed item analyses, or special criterion-referenced assessment items may have to be especially constructed. (21)

The needs assessment process is now completed, but there are several post assessment steps to be taken. The needs assessment process indicates what the actual gaps in pupil performance are, but it does not indicate why the gaps exist. The determination of the reasons or causes for the gaps requires professional diagnosis and interpretation.

Post Assessment Activities

The secondary school curriculum developer does a needs assessment primarily to ascertain the following:

1. The degree to which. curricular offerings are meeting identified and validated pupil performance objectives;
2. The degree to which current organizational groupings of curriculum, i.e., identification of departmentalization or grade level or staffing patterns, appear to be facilitating the attainment of required pupil performance objectives;
3. The degree to which the current secondary testing program adequately assesses the desired pupil performance objectives (an indicator of the program's overall validity);
4. The degree to which the existing secondary school curriculum is really balanced, i.e., meets the stated external criteria in a variety of forms (courses) and or classes within various curricular groupings.

The needs assessment process establishes validated, external criteria for answering all four of the questions above. Once the gaps are listed in a fashion shown they can be located within their respective curricular disciplines and grade levels, or whatever other type of delineation may be used in the particular secondary school. Assume for the moment that 38 percent of the gaps cited fall in the math-science areas of the school and can be located within specific courses. The professionals using such data should begin asking questions about the adequacy of the curriculum for these courses. Other questions may pertain to introducing more advanced or shorter minicourses, changing pupil grouping procedures, changing or adding texts or testing, teacher inservice training, etc. Still other solutions may be to alter the scheduling of the secondary school to reorganize its departments to more adequately take into account teacher interest and specialization. The *power* of any curricular discipline is simply its ability to comply with at least the minimum expectancies for the students as indicated from the needs assessment. A strong department should be able to deliver many of the desired outcomes if they are properly located within the discipline of that faculty. Once the secondary school staff begins to locate gaps within the curriculum, a rational and public base exists for proposing a variety of reforms.

Suppose a secondary school has just conducted its needs assessment. This school is also faced with declining enrollment. a changing student body, highly tenured staff and a shrinking budget. These conditions portend cutbacks in services, staff and other resources for the instructional program. The needs assessment shows that the school must expand its course offerings to include more enrichment on the one hand, and more shorter skills based minicourses on the other. By locating the objectives and gaps within the existing school curriculum, it is possible to expand the curriculum, even with staff reductions made necessary by falling enrollments are reduced revenues. The quality of the program can be enhanced despite a punitive financial climate. By moving to a reorganization of the curriculum and organization of the school, incorporating flexible scheduling and team teaching, the educational program is able to be changed, made more pertinent and expanded. Perhaps the reorganization might look like the example shown below:

Curricular/Organizational Adjustments

Old Curricular/Organizational Pattern	New Curricular/Organizational Pattern
Social Studies (Chairperson/6 teachers)	*HUMANITIES* (Chairperson)
English (Chairperson/6 teachers)	Social Studies, 5 teachers
Foreign Language (Chairperson, 3 teachers)	English, 5 teachers
Art (Chairperson, 2 teachers)	Foreign Language, 2 teachers
Music (Chairperson, 3 teachers)	*ARTS* (Chairperson)
Physical Education (Chairperson, 4 teachers)	Art, 2 teachers
Home Economics (Chairperson, 2 teachers)	Music, 2 teachers
Industrial Arts (Chairperson, 2 teachers)	Home Economics, 1 teacher
Business Education (Chairperson, 3 teachers)	Industrial Arts, 2 teachers

Driver Education (one teacher)   Business Education, 2 teachers
Mathematics (Chairperson,   *SCIENCES* (Chairperson)
5 teachers)
Science (Chairperson, 4 teachers)   Mathematics, 4 teachers
                                        Science, 4 teachers

The example is only one of many types of curricular and organizational adjustments which might be made. Even in a period of retrenchment the secondary school can be moving towards a more effective instructional program.

The Process in Retrospect

When compared to older more traditional methods for developing curriculum cited much earlier in the chapter, the needs assessment process has decided advantages. It is a public and open process for establishing educational goals and priorities. It involves the major partners in determining curricular goals and curricular priorities. It is able to use public input and feedback to improve the secondary curriculum. It is open to criticism and the results can be used to challenge the model.

Those favoring the concept of discovering a stable base of facts and concepts which have proven to be "true" over hundreds of years may point out that the process is largely perceptual and must be grounded in the realities of the present. One interesting approach to dealing with this issue has been developed with the Delphi Technique (22), a process for developing clearer pictures of the future. One major school system has used it as a base for developing its educational goals, i.e., by using the Delphi Technique as a method for creating future desired standards to be compared to present performance. (23)

Any base used for curriculum development must ultimately be translated into performance terms in order to determine its adequacy. Adequacy is, after all, the degree to which any procedure, content, method or model attains the desired level of performance. There is plenty of evidence that the traditional secondary school lacks appeal, power and rationality, and can hardly be defended from the point of view of logical development or organization.

The fact that the needs assessment model to curriculum development in the secondary school makes no pretensions about "ultimate" wisdom and is capable of being improved is its strongest point. Models or approaches which are not capable of being questioned cannot be improved. They must either be continued or abandoned. The needs assessment process is an evolutionary approach to attaining a more realistic and efficient secondary school curriculum. Its commitment to greater involvement of the public and students in the process of deciding upon whether and how the secondary school curriculum ought to be changed has made it a powerful tool for achieving greater community consensus about the mission of the secondary school in our society.

CHAPTER REFERENCES

1. For an excellent overview of various approaches to curriculum development, see Ralph W. Tyler, *Basic Principles of Curriculum and Instruction* (Chicago: University of Chicago Press, 1969), pp. 3-43.

2. John Dewey, *The Child and the Curriculum* (Chicago: University of Chicago Press, 1962), p. 18.

3. See Mortimer J. Adler, "In Defense of the Philosophy of Education," National Society for the Study of Education, Part 1 (Chicago: University of Chicago Press, 1942), pp. 197-246.

4. Robert M. Hutchins, *The Conflict in Education* (New York: Harper and Row, 1953).

5. See also Jacques Maritain, *Education at the Crossroads* (New Haven: Yale University Press, 1943).

6. For a model of curriculum built upon human characteristics, see Arthur R. King, Jr., and John A. Brownell, *The Curriculum and the Disciplines of Knowledge* (New York: John Wiley, 1966).

7. See Philip H. Phenix, *Realms of Meaning* (New York: McGraw-Hill, 1964).

8. For an eloquent statement of what happens when knowledge is considered "static," see Alfred N. Whitehead, *The Aims of Education and Other Essays* (New York: Macmillan, 1959).

9. See Roger A. Kaufman, Robert E. Corrigan, and Donald W. Johnson, "Towards Educational Responsiveness to Society's Needs, A Tentative Utility Model," *Journal of Socio-Economic Planning Science* 3 (August 1969): 151-57.

10. In writing about the West Virginia situation, former New Jersey Commissioner of Education Carl Marburger noted, "It seems to me that if parent participation had continued in Kanawha, it is unlikely that the situation would ever have become so aggravated," from "The West Virginia Textbooks," *New York Times,* October 24, 1974, Part C, p. 41.

11. *The Gallup Polls of Attitudes toward Education, 1969-1973* (Bloomington, Indiana: Phi Delta Kappa1 1969-1973).

12. See Dale Mann, "Public Understanding and Education Decision-Making," *Educational Administration Quarterly* 10, no. 2 (Spring 1974): 1-18.

13. See Roger A. Kaufman and Fenwick W. English, *Needs Assessment: A Guide to Improve School District Management* (Arlington, Virginia: American Association of School Administrators, 1976).

14. Robert Dreeben, "The School as a Workplace," in *The Second Handbook of Research on Teaching,* ed. Robert M. Travers (Chicago: Rand McNally, 1973), pp. 450-73.

15. Fenwick W. English and Roger A. Kaufman, *Needs Assessment: A Focus for Curriculum Development* (Washington, D.C.: Association for Supervision and Curriculum Development, 1975).

16. Colin Greer, *The Great School Legend* (New York: Basic Books, 1972).

17. See Will French, *Behavioral Goals of General Education in High School* (New York: Russell Sage Foundation, 1957).

18. Fenwick W. English, "Preliminary Analysis of the Results of the Educational Goal Ranking Survey," Hastings Public Schools, Hastings-on-Hudson, New York, 1976. (Xeroxed.)

19. Extrapolated from M. Lieneck et al., "Report of the Task Force on Minimum Learner Competencies," Hastings Public Schools, Hastings-on-Hudson, New York, Fall 1976. (Mimeographed.)

20. For other types of data such as these, see Eugene J. Webb et al., *Unobtrusive Measures* (Chicago: Rand McNally, 1973).

21. See W. James Popham, ed., *Criterion-Referenced Measurement* (Englewood Cliffs, New Jersey: Prentice-Hall, 1971).

22. Olaf Helmer, *Analysis of the Future: The Delphi Method* (Santa Monica, California: The Rand Corporation, March 1967), P3558, 11 pages. (Xeroxed.)

23. Atlanta, Georgia, Public Schools.

Author Index

Subject Index